TRAVELLING AND TOURISM

TRAVELLING AND TOURISM

By

Mahadev Kertwal

2008

CYBER TECH PUBLICATIONS
4264/3, Ansari Road, Daryaganj, New Delhi-110002 (India)
Ph.: 011-23244078. Fax: 011-23280028
E-Mail: cyberpublicationsdelhi@yahoo.com

TRAVELLING AND TOURISM

Mahadev Kertwal

First Edition 2008

Published by :

G.S. Rawat for **Cyber Tech Publications**
4264/3, Ansari Road, Daryaganj, New Delhi-110002 (India)
Ph.: 011-23244078. Fax: 011-23280028
E-Mail: cyberpublicationsdelhi@yahoo.com

Printed at : **Amit Enterprises**, Maujpur, Delhi, (9810878184)

Preface

It is the human nature to wander here and there for amusement and to get knowledge about the place, culture and tradition or sometimes to migrate. Moving here and there for long periods comes under the category of tourism. Now a days travel agencies arrange for the tickets lodging etc. for the Atourist on their fixed service charges. However there is no dearth of books on the subject but every book has its own area of focus and style of presenting the fact.

Travel Agency and Tourism is the first book of its kind which touches upon at length all typical travel agency and tour operator management issues, challenges, and gray areas such as, concept of agency and tour operation, changing dimensions of tour operators, itinerary planning, tour package management, Tour costing and Pricing, Travel agency marketing, Travel agency HRD, Cruise industry, Hotel industry, Financing tourism ventures and projects, Airline ticketing, Case studies, etc. The salient features of the book are that it incorporates academic and industrial topics to meet present as well as future requirements. Cases, examples, thumbs, tabs and illustrations are given for easy understanding and referencing.

It focuses on students as supervisor, tour planner, tour manager, trainer and tour executive and prepare them for new assignments, duties, and responsibilities.

I hope that a long felt gap of the any specific book focusing on the area of travel agency and tourism and their functioning, problems and laws are all discussed in this book will be filled.

— *Author*

Contents

1

INTRODUCTION

TRAVEL AGENCY

A travel agency is a business that sells travel related products and services, particularly package tours, to end-user customers on behalf of third party travel suppliers, such as airlines, hotels, tour companies, and cruise lines. In addition to dealing with ordinary tourists, most travel agents have a special department devoted to travel arrangements for business travellers, while some agencies specialise in commercial and business travellers. Some agencies also serve as general service agents for foreign travel companies in different countries.

ORIGINS

The British company, Cox & Kings is sometimes said to be the oldest travel agent in the world, but this rests upon services that the original bank (established in 1758) supplied to its wealthy clients. However, the modern travel agent first appeared in the second half of the nineteenth century. Thomas Cook, in addition to developing the package tour, established a chain of agencies in the last quarter of the nineteenth century, in association with the Midland Railway. These not only sold their own tours to the public, but represented other tour companies. Other British pioneer agencies were Dean and Dawson, the Polytechnic Touring Association, and the Co-operative Wholesale Society.

Travel agencies became more commonplace with the development of commercial aviation starting in the 1920s. Originally, the agencies largely catered to middle-class customers, but the post-war boom in mass-market package holidays resulted in travel agencies on the main streets of most British towns, catering to a working class clientèle looking for a cheap overseas beach holiday.

OPERATIONS

As the name implies, their main function is to act as an agent, that is to say selling travel products and services on behalf of a supplier. Consequently, unlike other retail businesses, they do not keep a stock in hand. A package holiday or a ticket is not purchased from a supplier unless a customer requests that purchase. The holiday or ticket is supplied to them at a discount. Thus, the agent's profit is the difference between the supplier's price and the price at which the product is advertised or sold to the customer. This profit is called the agency commission, and varies a great deal. In Britain, 12% would be considered a good commission. Other commercial operations are undertaken, especially by the larger chains. These can include the sale of in-house insurance, travel guides and timetables, car rental, and the services of an on-site bureau de change dealing in the most popular holiday currencies.

The majority of travel agents have felt the need to protect themselves and their clients against the possibilities of commercial failure, either their own or a supplier. They will advertise the fact that they are bonded (posting a financial bond with an organisation). In the case of a failure, the customers are guaranteed either an equivalent holiday to that which they have lost, or (if they prefer) a refund. Many British agencies (and tour companies too) are bonded with IATA for those who issue their own tickets, ATOL for those who order tickets in, or ABTA for those who sell package holidays on behalf of a tour company.

Of course, a travel agent is supposed to offer impartial travel advice to the customer. This function almost disappeared with the mass-market package holiday, and some agency chains seemed to develop a 'holiday supermarket' concept, in which customers chose their holiday from brochures on racks and then booked it from a counter. However, a variety of social and economic changes have now contrived to bring this aspect to the fore once more, particularly the advent of multiple no-frills airlines.

TYPES OF TRAVEL AGENCY

There are three different types of agencies: these are Multiples, Miniples and Independent Agencies. The former comprise a number of national chains, often owned by international conglomerates (Thomson Holidays is now a subsidiary of TUI, the German multinational). It is now quite common for the large mass-market tour companies to purchase a controlling interest in a chain of travel agencies, in order to control the distribution of their product. (This is an example of vertical integration.)

The smaller chains are often based in particular regions or districts. Independent Agencies usually cater for a special or niche market. Some cater to the needs of residents in an upmarket commuter town or suburb, or concentrate upon a particular area or group (catering to the travel needs of Polish expatriates, perhaps), or an activity such as sports(servicing the needs of football supporters).

CRITICISMS

Travel agencies have been accused of employing a number of restrictive practices, the chief of which is known as 'racking'. This is the practice of only displaying the brochures of those travel companies whose holidays they wish to sell, the ones that pay them the most commission. Of course, the average customer tends to think that these are the only holidays on offer, and are unaware of possible alternatives.

Generally speaking, small or specialist tour companies do not sell their product through travel agents, since they could not afford to pay the rates of commission that would be demanded. There are a few exceptions to this rule. Independent agents might sell or take bookings for local tour companies (such as coach companies) or tour companies offering specialist holidays that fit into their target market.

Consequently, even before the advent of the internet, small niche tour companies ignored travel agents and sold direct to their customers.

THE INTERNET THREAT

With the advent of general public access to the internet, many airlines and other travel companies began to sell directly to passengers. As a consequence, airlines no longer needed to pay the commissions to travel agents on each ticket sold. Since 1997, travel agencies gradually became victims of disintermediation, the reduction in costs caused by removing layers from the package holiday distribution network.

Many travel agencies have developed an internet presence by posting a website, with detailed travel information. Full travel booking sites are often complex, and require the assistance of outside travel technology solutions providers such as Travelocity, Patheo and Open Fares. These companies use travel service distribution companies who operate Global Distribution Systems (GDS), such as Sabre Holdings, Amadeus, Abaccus, Galileo and Worldspan, to provide up to the minute, detailed data on tens of thousands of flight, hotel, and car rental vacancies.

Some on-line travel sites allow visitors to compare hotel and flight rates with multiple companies for free. They often allow visitors to sort the travel packages by amenities, price, and or proximity to a city or landmark.

Travel agents have applied dynamic packaging tools to provide fully bonded (full financial protection) travel at prices equal to or lower than a member of the public can book on-line. As such, the agencies' financial assets are protected in addition to professional travel agency advice. All travel sites that sell hotels on-line work together with numerous outside travel agents. Once the travel site sells a hotel, one of the supplying travel agents is contacted and will try to get a confirmation for this hotel. Once confirmed or not, the customer is contacted with the result. This means, that booking a hotel on a travel website will not get you an instant answer. Only some of the hotels on a travel website can be confirmed instantly (which is normally marked as such on each site). As different travel websites work with different suppliers together, each site has different hotels that it can confirm instantly. Some examples of such on-line travel websites that sell hotel rooms are Expedia, Travelocity, Tripadvisor, Excelloz, Travel Tickets Plus and Venere.

Careers

With the many people switching to self service internet websites, the number of available jobs as travel agents is decreasing.

Most jobs that become available are from older travel agents retiring. Counteracting the decrease in jobs due to internet services is the increase in the number of people travelling. Since 1995, many travel agents have exi ed the industry, and relatively few young people have entered the field due to less competitive salaries. However, others have abandoned the "brick and mortar" agency for a home-based business to reduce overheads, and those who remain have managed to survive by promoting other travel products such as cruise lines and train excursions, or by promoting their ability to aggressively research and assemble complex travel packages on a moment's notice (essentially acting as a very advanced concierge).

CARGO

A small number of companies work with cargo airlines and ships which are connected to cargo business.

FLIGHT ATTENDANT

In aviation flight attendants-also known as sky girls, air hostesses, stewardesses or stewards-are members of a flight crew employed by airlines to ensure the safety and comfort of the passengers aboard commercial flights.

Overview

The primary and overriding responsibility of flight attendants is passenger safety. However, they are often tasked with the secondary function of seeing to the care and comfort of the passengers, insofar as this does not interfere with their safety responsibilities. They are often perceived by the flying public as waitresses or servants because only this latter function is normally seen outside the extremely rare event of in-flight emergency; and historically this perception has been portrayed by airlines in ads and commercials.

The role of a flight attendant ultimately derives from that of similar positions on passenger ships or passenger trains, but it has more direct involvement with passengers because of the confined quarters and often shorter travel times on aircraft. Additionally, the job of a flight attendant revolves around safety to a much greater extent than those of similar staff on other forms of transportation. Flight attendants on board a flight collectively form a cabin crew, as distinguished from pilots and engineers on the flight deck.

Outside the exceptional case of an in-flight emergency, flight attendants usually provide courtesy services for passengers, such as preparation distribution of in-flight meals and drinks, management of in-flight entertainment systems, sale of duty-free and other merchandise, and the like. As the most visible representatives of their airlines, their importance to customer relations and the image of their airlines is considerable. Many jurisdictions mandate the presence of flight attendants on commercial aircraft, based on the passenger capacity of the aircraft and other factors. This mandate generally relates only to their function as safety technicians.

Qualifications

Training

Flight attendants are normally trained in the hub or headquarters city of an airline over a period that may run from six weeks to six months, depending on the country. The main focus of training is safety. One flight attendant is required for every 50 passenger seats on board in the United States, but many airlines have chosen to increase that number. One of the most elaborate training facilities was Breech Academy which TWA opened in 1969 in Overland Park, Kansas, United States. Other airlines were to also send their attendants to the school. However, during the fare wars the school's viability declined and it closed around 1990.Safety training includes, but is not limited to: emergency passenger evacuation management, use of evacuation slides / life rafts, in-flight fire fighting, survival in the jungle / sea / desert / ice, first aid, CPR, defibrillation, ditching / emergency landing procedures, decompression emergencies, crew resource management and security.

Language

Multilingual flight attendants are often in demand to accommodate international travellers. The languages most in demand, other than English, are Mandarin, Cantonese, Japanese, French, German, Spanish, and Portugese.

Height and Weight

Some airlines, such as EVA Air, have height requirements for purely aesthetic purposes. Horizon Air and other regional carriers have height restrictions because their aircraft have low ceilings. A typical acceptable range is from 5'2" (1.57 m) to 6'0" (1.83 m). Flight attendants are also subject to weight requirements as well. Weight must usually be in proportion to height; persons outside the normal range may not be qualified to act as flight attendants.

History

The first flight attendant, a steward, was reportedly a man on the German Zeppelin LZ10 Schwaben in 1911. Imperial Airways of the United Kingdom had "cabin boys" or "stewards" in the 1920s. In the USA, Stout Airways was the first to employ stewards in 1926, working on Ford Tri-Motor planes between Detroit and Grand Rapids, Michigan. Western Air Express (1928) and Pan Am (1929) were the first US carriers to employ stewards to serve food. Ten-passenger Fokker Aircraft used in the Caribbean had stewards in the era of gambling trips to Havana, Cuba from Key West, Florida. The first female flight attendant was a 25-year-old registered nurse named Ellen Church: Hired by United Airlines in 1930, she also first envisioned nurses on aircraft.

Other airlines followed suit, hiring nurses to serve as stewardesses on most of their flights. The requirement to be a registered nurse was relaxed at the start of World War II, as so many nurses enlisted into the armed forces.

Uniforms

The first stewardess uniforms were designed to be durable, practical, and inspire confidence in passengers. The first stewardesses for United Airlines wore green berets, green capes and nurse's shoes. Other airlines, such as Eastern Airlines, actually dressed stewardesses in nurses' uniforms.

Perhaps reflecting the military aviation background of many commercial aviation pioneers, many early uniforms had a strongly military appearance; hats, jackets, and skirts showed simple straight lines and military details like epaulets and brass buttons. Many uniforms had a summer and winter version, differentiated by colours and fabrics appropriate to the season: navy blue for winter, for example, khaki for summer. But as the role of women in the air grew, and airline companies began to realize the publicity value of their stewardesses, more feminine lines and colours began to appear in the late 1930s and early 1940s. Some airlines began to commission designs from high-end department stores and still others called in noted designers or even milliners to create distinctive and attractive apparel.

Unions

Flight attendant unions were formed, beginning at United Airlines in the 1940s, to negotiate improvements in pay, benefits and working conditions. Those unions would later challenge what they perceived as sexist stereotypes and unfair work practices such as age limits, size limits, limitations on marriage, and prohibition of pregnancy. Many of these limitations have been lifted by judicial mandates.

The largest flight attendants union is the Association of Flight Attendants, representing over 50,000 flight attendants at 22 airlines within the United States.

In the United Kingdom, cabin crew can be represented by either Cabin Crew '89, or the much larger and more powerful Transport and General Workers Union.

Discrimination

Airline managers commonly subjected flight attendants to various forms of discrimination from the early days of the profession until the 1990s. Flight attendants at US-based airlines, and others as well, were forced to resign or were fired if they got married, if they were overweight, wore eyeglasses, if they turned 30 years of age (or 32 at some airlines). These discriminatory policies came under attack in the United States after passage of Title VII of the Civil Rights Act of 1964. Flight attendant unions like the Association of Flight Attendants used Title VII, in the courts and at the bargaining table, to bring an end to such practices and recognize the professionalism of the flight attendant career.

The no-marriage rule was eliminated throughout the US airline industry by the 1980s. The last such broad categorical discrimination, the weight restrictions, were eliminated in the

1990s through litigation and negotiations. By the end of the 1970s, the term stewardess had generally been replaced by the gender-neutral, and more wordy, alternative flight attendant. More recently the term cabin crew has begun to replace 'flight attendants,' because of the term's recognition of their role as members of the crew.

After September 11, 2001

The role of flight attendants received heightened prominence after the September 11, 2001 attacks when flight attendants (such as Sandra W. Bradshaw, Robert Fangman, CeeCee Lyles, Renee May, Betty Ong and Madeline Amy Sweeney) actively attempted to protect passengers from assault, and also provided vital information to air traffic controllers on the hijackings.

In the wake of the terror attacks of September 11, 2001, many flight attendants at major airlines were laid off on account of decreased passenger loads.

Roles in an Emergency

Actions of flight attendants in emergencies have long been credited in saving lives; in the United States, the NTSB and other aviation authorities view flight attendants as essential for safety, and are thus required on Part 121 aircraft operations. Studies, some done in light of the Manchester air disaster, have concluded that assertive cabin crew are essential for the rapid evacuation of airplanes. Notable examples of cabin crew actions include:

- Scandinavian Airlines Flight 751, when cabin crew recognized an emergency landing was imminent and commanded the passengers to "bend down...hold your knees" to adopt the brace position.
- A Delta Connection (Atlantic Southeast Airlines) flight attendant who provided emergency briefings, brace and evacuation commands to the passengers when a EMB-120 Brasilia aircraft sustained serious damage to one of its engine and crash landed. She was the only flight attendant on board. The NTSB acccident report commended "the exemplary manner in which the flight attendant briefed the passengers and handled the emergency".

- British Airways Flight 5390, in which a flight attendant was able to prevent a pilot from being lost through a cockpit window that had failed.
- Southern Airways Flight 242, on which the cabin crew provided safety briefings to their passengers, and on their own initiative, warned passengers of the impending crash by commanding passengers to adopt the brace position. At least one flight attendant is known to have assisted in rescuing trapped passengers.
- Air Florida Flight 90, in which the lone surviving flight attendant passed the only lifevest she could find to another passenger. She is recognized in the NTSB report for this "unselfish act."
- TWA flight attendant Uli Derickson who protected passengers during the TWA Flight 847 hijacking by assisting with negotiation efforts.
- TWA Flight 843, when a TWA L-1011 aircraft crashed after an aborted takeoff in 1992. The aircraft was destroyed by fire. Nine flight attendants, along with five off-duty flight attendants, evacuated all 292 persons on board without loss of life. The NTSB in their after accident reported noted, "The performance of the flight attendants during the emergency was exceptional and probably contributed to the success of the emergency evacuation."
- On British Airways Flight 2069, cabin crew stopped the plane from being crashed by a mentally ill passenger. It was a highly mediatized episode of air rage.
- Crew on American Airlines Flight 63 prevented a shoe bomber from blowing up the plane.
- Flight attendants on Qantas flight 1737 prevented their plane from being hijacked by a passenger with mental health issues. Two of them were taken to hospital with stab wounds.
- Aloha Airlines Flight 243 suffered a decompression which tore an 18-foot section of fuselage away from the plane. Despite her injuries, flight attendant Michelle Honda crawled up and down the aisle reassuring passengers.

- Senior Purser Neerja Bhanot saved the lives of passengers and crew when Pan Am Flight 73 was hijacked. She was killed while protecting children from the terrorists. After her death she received the Special Courage Award from the United States Department of Justice.
- Flight Attendants on Air Canada Flight 797 used procedures which were not specifically taught in training such as instruction passengers to open over wing window exits to allow passengers to evacuate quicker, moving passengers to the front of the aircraft to move them away from the fire and smoke, and passing out towels for passengers to cover their nose and mouths with while the cabin was filling with smoke.

2

THE TECHNOLOGY OF TRAVELLING

INTRODUCTION

Travel technology is a term used to describe applications of Information Technology (IT), or Information and Communications Technology (ICT), in travel, tourism and hospitality industry. Travel technology may also be referred to as tourism technology or even hospitality automation. Web 2.0 is a current buzzword in the travel technology community, used to describe various social software applications. XML is an increasingly important aspect of travel technology for handling metadata toward the semantic web. Immigration technology, known as tecurity, such as the biometric passport may also be included as travel technology in the broad sense.

DEFINITION

Since travel implies locomotion, travel technology was originally associated with the computer reservations system (CRS) of the airlines industry, but now is used more inclusively, incorporating the broader tourism sector as well as its subset the hospitality industry. While travel technology includes the computer reservations system, it also represents a much broader range of applications, in fact increasingly so. Travel technology may also be referred to as e-travel / etravel or e-tourism / etourism (eTourism), in reference to "electronic travel" or "electronic tourism".

In other contexts, the term "travel technology" can refer to technology intended for use by travellers, such as light-weight laptop computers with universal power supplies or satellite

Internet connections. That is not the sense in which it is used here.

THE APPLICATIONS

Travel technology includes many processes such as dynamic packaging which provide useful new options for consumers. Today the tour guide can be a GPS tour guide, and the guidebook could be an audioguide, podguide or I-Tours, such as City audio guides.

HISTORY

Certainly travel technology was born on the coattails of the airline industry's use of automation and their need to extend this out to the travel agency partners. It should be kept in mind that there was an on-line world before the advent of the world wide web in the form of private and commercial on-line services, via packet switched network using X.25. Travel technology played a significant role in the so-called dot-com boom and bust, circa 1997-2001.

IN-FLIGHT ENTERTAINMENT

In-flight entertainment (IFE) refers to the entertainment available to aircraft passengers during a flight. After World War II commercial aviation flights became a daily event in which entertainment was requested by passengers to help the time pass. This was delivered in the form of food and drink services, along with an occasional projector movie during lengthy flights. The concept of IFE took on a new meaning starting in the 1980s. In 1985 the first personal audio player was offered to passengers, along with noise cancelling headphones in 1989. During the 1990s the demand for better IFE was a major factor in the way airlines designed and retrofitted their cabins. Before then, the most a passenger could expect was a movie projected on a screen at the front of a cabin, which could be heard via a headphone socket at their seat.

Major manufacturers of IFE systems include Panasonic Avionics Corporation, Thales Group, Honeywell Rockwell Collins and LiveTV. Most of the difficulties these producers encounter are traditional to those of avionic electronic systems. Such issues are system safety, cost efficiency, software reliability, hardware maintenance, and user compatibility.

History

The first in-flight entertainment began to first appear in the 1960s on Boeing 707 and Douglas DC-8 aircraft. These early in-flight entertainment systems consisted of in-seat audio that can be heard with hollow tube headphones. When widebody aircraft (such as the Boeing 747 and McDonnell Douglas DC-10) began to enter service, the first video systems began to appear, featuring a film projected onto a screen. In the late 1970s and early 1980s, CRT-based projectors began to appear on newer widebody aircraft, such as the Boeing 767. Some airlines upgraded the old film IFE systems to the CRT-based systems in the late 1980s and early 1990s on some of their older widebodies. Around the same time, CRT-based displays began to appear over the aisles of narrowbody and widebody aircraft. In the mid 1990s, the first in-seat video systems began to appear, and LCD technology started to replace CRT technology as the display technology of choice for overhead video. In the late 1990s and early 2000s, the first in-seat audio/video on-demand systems began to appear.

IFE is offered as an option on almost all wide body aircraft in service today, while some narrow body aircraft are not equipped with any form of IFE at all. This is mainly due to the aircraft storage and weight limits. The Boeing 757 was the first narrow body aircraft to widely feature both audio and video IFE and today it is rare to find a 757 without an IFE system. Most 757s feature ceiling-mounted CRT screens, although some newer 757s may feature drop-down LCDs. Many Airbus A320 series and Boeing 737NG aircraft are also equipped with drop-down LCD screens. Some airlines, such as WestJet and Delta Air Lines, have equipped some narrow body aircraft with personal video screens at every seat. Others, such as Air Canada, have even equipped some regional jets with audio-video on demand (AVOD).

System Safety and Regulation

One major obstacle of creating an IFE system is the system's safety. With the sometimes miles of wiring involved, voltage leaks and arcing become a problem. To contain any possible issues, the IFE system is typically isolated from the aircraft's main systems. In the US, in order for a company's product to be considered safe and reliable, it must be certified by the FAA and pass all of the applicable requirements found in the Federal Aviation Regulations. The concerning section, or title, dealing with the aviation industry and the electronic systems embedded in the aircraft, is CFR title 14 part 25. Contained inside part 25 are many specific rules, each relating to a specific portion of the aircraft's electronic system. There are two major codes that regulate IFE systems and their safety: code 1301 which approves the electronic equipment for installation and use, by assuring that the system in question is properly labeled, and that its design is appropriate to its intended function. Code 1309 states that the electrical equipment must not alter the safety or functionality of the aircraft upon the result of a failure. In order for the intended IFE system to pass this code, it must be independent from that of the aircraft's main power source and processor. By separating the power supplies and data links from that of the aircraft's performance processor, in the event of a failure the system is self sustained, and can not alter the functionality of the aircraft. Upon the completion of all applicable codes the IFE system is up to standards for use in the United States, however the rules and regulations may be different when applying for use in other countries.

Cost Efficiency

Further complicating issues when creating a safe IFE system is the concept of cost efficiency. The large companies currently involved, along with those future prospects, are in a constant battle to cut costs of production, without cutting the systems quality and compatibility. Cutting production cost consists of anything from altering the housing for personal televisions, to reducing the amount of embedded software in the IFE processor. Difficulties with cost are also present with the customers, or airlines, looking to purchase IFE systems. Most IFE systems are purchased by existing airlines as an upgrade package to an existing fleet of aircraft. This cost can be anywhere from $2 Million-$5 Million for seat back LCD monitors, with an embedded IFE system. Some of the IFE systems are being purchased already installed in a new aircraft, such as the Airbus A320, which eliminates the possibility of having upgrade difficulties.

Each airline is finding interesting ways to pass on this additional cost to their customers. Some airlines are passing the cost directly into the customers ticket price, while some are charging a user fee based on an individual customers use. Some are also attempting to get a majority of the cost paid for by advertisements on, around, and in their IFE.

Software Reliability

Software for IFE systems must be aesthetically pleasing, dependent, reliable, compatible, and also must be user friendly. These restrictions account for expensive engineering of individually specific software. In addition to the regular software reliability issues, comes the issue of the software being touch screen sensitive, allowing interaction between each seat in the aircraft and the flight attendants, which is wireless in some systems. Along with a complete aircraft intranet to deal with, the software of the IFE system must be reliable when communicating to and from the main IFE processor. These additional requirements not only place an additional strain on the software engineers, but also on the price. Boundary value errors can slip through the testing phases of the software and, once installed, truly cause problems.

Varieties of in-flight Entertainment

Cabin Music

Soft music is often piped through the PA system and is heard in the cabin upon boarding, disembarkation, taxiing and take-off of the aircraft. The music is often chosen to be pleasant and soothing, and exhibits characteristics similar to elevator music. In accord with the cabin music, some airlines are now installing music in the restrooms. This is done to ease some of those who become sick and uncomfortable while in the air.

Cabin Lighting

A recent addition to commercial aircraft with IFE systems, cabin lighting allows the IFE system to adjust the cabins LED overhead lighting system when appropriate. Implemented through software, the lighting in the cabin can be adjusted through an array of colors, from a deep purple to a refreshing neon green. The lighting is also beginning to be implemented as to follow the cabin music currently playing. The first major implementation of cabin lighting is present in the new Virgin America Airbus A-320's.

Audio Entertainment

Audio entertainment is provided in the form of several selected channels a passenger may choose covering various genres of music, as well as news, information and comedy. Much like radio shows, most music channels are pre-recorded and feature their own DJs to provide chatter, song introductions and interviews with featured artists.

In audio-video on demand (AVOD) systems, software such as MusicMatch is used to select music off the music server. Phillips Music Server is one of the most widely used servers running under Windows Media Center used to control AVOD systems.

This form of in-flight entertainment is experienced through headphones that are distributed to the passengers after take-off.

The headphone plugs are usually only compatible with the audio socket on the passenger's armrest (and vice-versa), and some airlines may charge a small fee in order to obtain a pair. The headphones provided can also be used for the viewing of personal televisions, if any.

Recent IFE systems have been made compatible with XM Satellite Radio, and also with I-Pod's, allowing for passengers to access their own accounts, or bring their own music, along with offering extensive libraries of full audio CD's from an assortment of artists.

Video Entertainment

Traditionally, video entertainment is provided via a large video screen at the front of a cabin section, as well as smaller monitors situated every few rows above the aisles. Sound is supplied via the same headphones distributed for audio entertainment.

However in recent times, personal televisions (PTVs) for every passenger have become more popular, providing passengers with a selection of channels broadcasting new and classic films, as well as comedies, documentaries, children's shows and drama series.

Some airlines also present news and current affairs programming, which are often pre-recorded and delivered in the early morning before flights commence.

PTVs are operated via an In flight Management System which stores pre-recorded channels on a central server, and streams them to PTV equipped seats during flight. AVOD systems store individual programs separately, allowing a passenger to have a specific program streamed to them privately, and be able to control the playback. Some airlines also provide video games as part of the video entertainment system.

For example, Singapore Airlines passengers have access to a number of Super Nintendo games as part of its KrisWorld entertainment system. Also Virgin America's new RED Entertainment System offers passengers a wide variety of internet gaming over a Linux-based operating system. RED also provides an open source gaming link, so passengers who are experienced in writing games can upload certain created games to the server.

In-flight Movies

The first motion picture to be played on an airline, was a silent film shown on a Deutsch Lufthansa flight over Germany in 1925. Regularly scheduled in flight movies began to premiere in 1961 on flights from New York to Los Angeles.Today there are various types of in flight movies that are offered.

There are those personal on demand videos which are stored in an aircraft main IFE computer system. From there they can be viewed on demand by the user as they choose. Along with the on demand concept comes the ability for the user to pause, rewind, fast forward, or jump to any point in the movie. There are also the movies that are commonly shown throughout the aircraft at one time usually on a screen in the front of the cabin.

Personal Televisions

Most major airlines have now installed personal televisions (otherwise known as PTVs) for every passenger on most long-haul routes. These televisions are usually located in the seat-backs or tucked away in the armrests for front row seats and first class. Many different systems are used and vary from different airlines.

There are those that utilize a few channels, or direct broadcast satellite television which enable passengers to view live TV broadcasts. Some airlines also offer video games using PTV equipment.

In accordance with increasing amenities being provided on board flights, audio-video on demand (AVOD) entertainment has also been introduced. This enables passengers to pause, rewind, fast-forward or stop a program that they have been watching.

This is in contrast to older entertainment systems where no interactivity is provided for. AVOD also allows the passengers to choose between an assortment of movies stored in the aircraft computer system.

With the introduction of new aircraft and the rapid advances in aviation technology, it is rare to find new long-haul planes being delivered without PTVs. Lufthansa is the only airline in the world to order new long haul aircraft like the Boeing 747 without fitting PTVs in Economy Class.

Moving-map Systems

A moving-map system is a real-time flight information video channel broadcast through PTVs and cabin video screens. In addition to displaying a map that illustrates the current position and direction of the plane, the system also reveals details concerning the flight to passengers such as the altitude, airspeed, distance to destination, distance from origination and local time.

Moving-map system information is derived from the aircraft's flight computer systems. It is often generically referred to as Airshow, one of the first moving-map systems now owned by Rockwell Collins. Panasonic Avionics Corporation now offers a similar product known as iXPLOR on their latest IFE systems. Honeywell also offers a similar product known as JetMap.

Data Communication

IFE producers have begun to introduce intranet type systems into their designs. Virgin America's RED Entertainment System allows for passengers to chat amongst one another, compete against each other in the provided games, talk to the flight attendants and request, and pay for in advance, food or drinks, and have full access to the internet and email.

In an upcoming Airbus A380 aircraft, data communication via satellite system will allow passengers to connect to live Internet from the individual IFE units or their laptops via the in-flight Wi-Fi access..

Next-generation Systems

Currently there are only a few complete IFE systems incorporating live data/TV and on-demand capabilities. Jet Blue's personal television with limited audio and video files on demand, including XM radio and DirectTV is an example of one of the more advanced IFE systems deployed today. Air Canada also provides their passengers with PTV's accompanied by a pre-arranged selection of movies and video games that are rescheduled monthly.

Currently there are three IFE Systems in the aviation industry that are billed as "next-generation", Singapore Airlines' KrisWorld, Emirates Airlines' ICE Entertainment, and the soon-to-be-released RED entertainment system from Virgin America.

KrisWorld

Audio, Video, and Games on Demand

Installed in Singapore Airlines' new Boeing 777-300ER aircraft, KrisWorld is an example of a next-generation IFE System. Currently boasting the highest resolution of any IFE at 1280 x 768 pixels, these personal LCD displays are located in the seat back in front of the passenger.

KriWorld contains 80 on-demand movies for passenger viewing, a predetermined assortment of television shows, 12 music channels and 180 CD titles on demand. KrisWorld has also contracted with Nintendo to provide 91 Nintendo game titles for passenger use on demand.

KrisWorld Interactive

KrisWorld also includes Flight Path, an improvement on the existing moving map system present in most IFEs. KrisWorld also includes a feature dubbed Destination Info, an interactive guidebook for each of Singapore Airlines destination cities. Destination Info gives passengers access to street directions, restaurant guides, and local event listings for a particular day.

Live Text News is KrisWorld's in-flight news service. It updates via satellite once every hour, and includes content on the stock market, local news,sports, and weather.

Language Tutorials

KrisWorld is also the first IFE system to introduce Berlitz World Traveler as a feature of their IFE. Berlitz World Traveler is a program that assists passengers in learning any one of 22, providing access to tutorials and quizzes.

ICE

Information

Operated by Emirates Airline, ICE is another example of a next-generation in-flight entertainment system. ICE (Information Communication Entertainment) is currently operating in all of Emirates Airline's Airbus A340-500, and all of Emirates Airline's Boeing 777-300ER and Boeing 777-200 fleet. ICE provides passengers with a direct data link to BBC News. ICE is the first IFE system to be connected directly to automatic news updates.

This is complemented by ICE's Airshow moving-map software from Rockwell Collins. Along with this software comes ICE's unique system of exterior cameras located on the aircraft. These cameras can be viewed by any passenger through the IFE system during takeoff and landing.

Communication

ICE also contains a link to an in-flight email server which allows passengers to access, send or receive emails for US $1 per message. Similar to KrisWorld, ICE also contains a seat-to-seat chat server.

Entertainment

Similar to KrisWorld, the entertainment system from Singapore Airlines, ICE allows passengers to choose from a library of movies, audio CDs, and video games. ICE offers over 130 on-demand movie titles and 15 video-on-demand channels, 60 prerecorded television channels, 350 audio channels, and around 50 video-game titles. ICE can also be accessed in 10 different languages are English, French, Spanish, Arabic, Korean, and Japanese.

Virgin America's RED

Audio, Video, and Gaming

Set to premiere in summer of 2007, Virgin America's RED IFE system will be installed in all of Virgin America's Airbus A320's. RED allows similar functions to KrisWorld's and ICE's IFE system.

RED allows passengers to watch live TV, including 18 live TV channels provided by Dish Network. RED also provides 25 on-demand pay-per-view movies, over 2000 MP3 audio tracks, and more than 20 audio channels. Access is provided through a 9", 1024x768-pixel LCD touch screen monitor located in the seat back in front of each passenger. One of RED's unique characteristics is passengers' ability to create play lists of movies and MP3s. RED is built upon a Linux platform, and Virgin America plans to use Linux' open source nature to port games for in-flight use.

RED Interactive

RED's controller is the first to provide a QWERTY keyboard. Another interactive feature of RED is the ability passengers have to bring along their own keyboard, or mouse and use the provided USB port to use their own devices with the IFE system. Passengers can also directly order food and drinks from the flight attendants from the menu section of the IFE. All paid-for services such as movies and food can be paid for by the credit card reader located at the bottom of the IFE screen. RED also offers passengers full broadband access to chat, and instant message amongst passengers, along with having unrestricted access to the internet, and email.

3

Economic Impacts of the Tourism

The tourism industry generates substantial economic benefits to both host countries and tourists' home countries. Especially in developing countries, one of the primary motivations for a region to promote itself as a tourism destination is the expected economic improvement.

As with other impacts, this massive economic development brings along both positive and negative consequences.

According to the World Tourism Organization, 698 million people traveled to a foreign country in 2000, spending more US$ 478 billion. International tourism receipts combined with passenger transport currently total more than US$ 575 billion-making tourism the world's number one export earner, ahead of automotive products, chemicals, petroleum and food.

***Source:* WTTC**

NEGATIVE ECONOMIC IMPACTS OF TOURISM

There are many hidden costs to tourism, which can have unfavorable economic effects on the host community. Often rich countries are better able to profit from tourism than poor ones. Whereas the least developed countries have the most urgent need for income, employment and general rise of the standard of living by means of tourism, they are least able to realize these benefits.

Among the reasons for this are large-scale transfer of tourism revenues out of the host country and exclusion of local businesses and products.

Leakage

The direct income for an area is the amount of tourist expenditure that remains locally after taxes, profits, and wages are paid outside the area and after imports are purchased; these subtracted amounts are called leakage. In most all-inclusive package tours, about 80% of travelers' expenditures go to the airlines, hotels and other international companies (who often have their headquarters in the travelers' home countries), and not to local businesses or workers. In addition, significant amounts of income actually retained at destination level can leave again through leakage.

A study of tourism 'leakage' in Thailand estimated that 70% of all money spent by tourists ended up leaving Thailand (via foreign-owned tour operators, airlines, hotels, imported drinks and food, etc.). Estimates for other Third World countries range from 80% in the Caribbean to 40% in India.

Source: *Sustainable Living*

Of each US$ 100 spent on a vacation tour by a tourist from a developed country, only around US$ 5 actually stays in a developing-country destination's economy. The figure below shows how the leakage happens.

There are two main ways that leakage occurs:

Import Leakage: This commonly occurs when tourists demand standards of equipment, food, and other products that the host country cannot supply. Especially in less-developed countries, food and drinks must often be imported, since local products are not up to the hotel's (i.e. tourist's) standards or the country simply doesn't have a supplying industry. Much of the income from tourism expenditures leaves the country again to pay for these imports.

The average import-related leakage for most developing countries today is between 40% and 50% of gross tourism earnings for small economies and between 10% and 20% for most advanced and diversified economies, according to UNCTAD.

Even in developed regions, local producers are often unable to supply the tourism industry appropriately even if good will is present: the 64-room hotel "Kaiser im Tirol" in Austria, an award-winning leader in sustainable practices, cannot find organic food suppliers in the local farming networks in the appropriate quantity, quality and reliability, as production cycles and processes are not compatible with its needs.

Source: *Austrian Preparatory Conference for the International Year of Ecotourism, September 2001*

Export leakage Multinational corporations and large foreign businesses have a substantial share in the import leakage. Often, especially in poor developing destinations, they are the only ones that possess the necessary capital to invest in the construction of tourism infrastructure and facilities. As a consequence of this, an export leakage arises when overseas investors who finance the resorts and hotels take their profits back to their country of origin.

A 1996 UN report evaluating the contribution of tourism to national income, gross levels of incomes or gross foreign exchange, found that net earnings of tourism, after deductions were made for all necessary foreign exchange expenditures, were much more significant for the industry. This report found significant leakage associated with: (a) imports of materials and equipment for construction; (b) imports of consumer goods, particularly food and drinks; (c) repatriation of profits earned by foreign investors; (d) overseas promotional expenditures and (e) amortization of external debt incurred in the development of hotels and resorts. The impact of the leakage varied greatly across countries, depending on the structure of the economy and the tourism industry. From the data presented in this study on the Caribbean, St. Lucia had a foreign exchange leakage rate of 56% from its gross tourism receipts, Aruba had 41%, Antigua and Barbuda 25% and Jamaica 40%.

Source: *Caribbean Voice*

Enclave Tourism: Local businesses often see their chances to earn income from tourists severely reduced by the creation of "all-inclusive" vacation packages. When tourists remain for their entire stay at the same cruise ship or resort, which provides everything they need and where they will make all their expenditures, not much opportunity is left for local people to profit from tourism.

The Organization of American States (OAS) carried out a survey of Jamaica's tourist industry that looked at the role of the all-inclusives compared to other types of accommodation. It found that 'All-inclusive hotels generate the largest amount of revenue but their impact on the economy is smaller per dollar of revenue than other accommodation subsectors.'

It also concluded that all-inclusives imported more, and employed fewer people per dollar of revenue than other hotels. This information confirms the concern of those who have argued that all-inclusives have a smaller trickle-down effect on local economies.

The cruise ship industry provides another example of economic enclave tourism. Non-river cruises carried some 8.7 million international passengers in 1999. On many ships, especially in the Caribbean (the world's most popular cruise destination with 44.5% of cruise passengers), guests are encouraged to spend most of their time and money on board, and opportunities to spend in some ports are closely managed and restricted.

OTHER NEGATIVE IMPACTS

Infrastructure Cost

Tourism development can cost the local government and local taxpayers a great deal of money. Developers may want the government to improve the airport, roads and other infrastructure, and possibly to provide tax breaks and other financial advantages, which are costly activities for the government. Public resources spent on subsidized infrastructure or tax breaks may reduce government investment in other critical areas such as education and health.

Increase in Prices

Increasing demand for basic services and goods from tourists will often cause price hikes that negatively affect local residents whose income does not increase proportionately. A San Francisco State University study of Belize found that, as a consequence of tourism development, the prices for locals increased by 8%.

Tourism development and the related rise in real estate demand may dramatically increase building costs and land values. Not only does this make it more difficult for local people, especially in developing countries, to meet their basic daily needs, it can also result in a dominance by outsiders in land markets and in-migration that erodes economic opportunities for the locals, eventually disempowering residents.

In Costa Rica, close to 65% of the hotels belong to foreigners. Long-term tourists living in second homes, and the so-called amenity migrants (wealthy or retired people and liberal professionals moving to attractive destinations in order to enjoy the atmosphere and peaceful rhythms of life) cause price hikes in their new homes if their numbers attain a certain critical mass.

Economic Dependence of the Local Community

Diversification in an economy is a sign of health, however if a country or region becomes dependent for its economic survival upon one industry, it can put major stress upon this industry as well as the people involved to perform well. Many countries, especially developing countries with little ability to explore other resources, have embraced tourism as a way to boost the economy. In The Gambia, for instance, 30% of the workforce depends directly or indirectly on tourism.

In small island developing states, percentages can range from 83% in the Maldives to 21% in the Seychelles and 34% in Jamaica, according to the WTO. Over-reliance on tourism, especially mass tourism, carries significant risks to tourism-dependent economies. Economic recession and the impacts of natural disasters such as tropical storms and cyclones as well as changing tourism patterns can have a devastating effect on the local tourism sector.

> *Malta has only 380,000 residents, but received 1.2 million tourists in **1999**. As 25% of GDP (and indirectly 40%), tourism generated more than **$650** million in foreign exchange earnings. Malta's high dependence on tourism and a limited number of export products makes its trade performance vulnerable to shifts in international demand.*
>
> **Source:** *Washington Times*

Seasonal Character of Jobs

The seasonal character of the tourism industry creates economic problems for destinations that are heavily dependent on it. Problems that seasonal workers face include job (and therefore income) insecurity, usually with no guarantee of employment from one season to the next, difficulties in getting training, employment-related medical benefits, and recognition of their experience, and unsatisfactory housing and working conditions.

Other Industry Impacts Affecting Tourism

Economic crises, like the Asian crisis that hit Thailand, Malaysia and Indonesia a few years ago, can be devastating to inbound tourism flows. The financial turmoil triggered a sharp fall in tourism flows to affected countries during 1997 and 1998. In the Philippines, the crisis and the temporary closure of Philippine Airlines affected inbound arrivals significantly as there was a decline of almost 3.3% in 1998.

***Source:** Hotel-online*

TOURISM CONTRIBUTION TO ECONOMIC CONSERVATION

The main positive economic impacts of tourism relate to foreign exchange earnings, contributions to government revenues, and generation of employment and business opportunities. These are discussed briefly here; further information on economic contributions from tourism can be found at the World Travel & Tourism Council's home page.

Foreign Exchange Earnings

Tourism expenditures and the export and import of related goods and services generate income to the host economy and can stimulate the investment necessary to finance growth in other economic sectors. Some countries seek to accelerate this growth by requiring visitors to bring in a certain amount of foreign currency for each day of their stay and do not allow them to take it out of the country again at the end of the trip.

An important indicator of the role of international tourism is its generation of foreign exchange earnings. Tourism is one of the top five export categories for as many as 83% of countries and is a main source of foreign exchange earnings for at least 38% of countries.

***Source:** World Tourism Organization*

Contribution to Government Revenues

Government revenues from the tourism sector can be categorized as direct and indirect contributions. Direct contributions are generated by taxes on incomes from tourism employment and tourism businesses, and by direct levies on tourists such as departure taxes. Indirect contributions are those originated from taxes and duties levied on goods and services supplied to tourists.

The United States National Park Service estimates that the 273 million visits to American national parks in 1993 generated direct and indirect expenditures of US$ 10 billion and 200,000 jobs.

When visits to land managed by other agencies, and to state, local, and privately-managed parks, are added, parks were estimated to bring around US$ 22 billion annually to the US economy. These expenditures also generate significant tax revenues for the government.

The World Travel and Tourism Council estimates that travel and tourism's direct, indirect, and personal tax contribution worldwide was over US$ 800 billion in 1998-a figure it expects to double by 2010. (Source: WTTC/Michigan State University Tax Policy Center)

Employment Generation

The rapid expansion of international tourism has led to significant employment creation. For example, the hotel accommodation sector alone provided around 11.3 million jobs worldwide in 1995. Tourism can generate jobs directly through hotels, restaurants, nightclubs, taxis, and souvenir sales, and indirectly through the supply of goods and services needed by tourism-related businesses. According to the WTO, tourism supports some 7% of the world's workers.

Stimulation of Infrastructure Investment

Tourism can induce the local government to make infrastructure improvements such as better water and sewage systems, roads, electricity, telephone and public transport networks, all of which can improve the quality of life for residents as well as facilitate tourism.

Contribution to Local Economies

Tourism can be a significant, even essential, part of the local economy. As the environment is a basic component of the tourism industry's assets, tourism revenues are often used to measure the economic value of protected areas. For example, Dorrigo National Park in New South Wales, Australia, has been estimated to contribute 7% of gross regional output and 8.4% of regional employment. The importance of tourism to local economies can also be illustrated by the impacts when it is disrupted: the catastrophic 1997 floods that closed Yosemite National Park in California cause locally severe economic losses to the areas around the park. In the most heavily impacted county, Mariposa County, 1997 personal income was reduced by an estimated US$1,159 per capita (US$18 million for the entire county)-a 6.6% decline. The county was also estimated to have lost US$1.67 million in county occupancy and sales tax revenues, and 956 jobs, a significant number in a county of fewer than 16,000 residents.

There are other local revenues that are not easily quantified, as not all tourist expenditures are formally registered in the macro-economic statistics. Money is earned from tourism through informal employment such as street vendors, informal guides, rickshaw drivers, etc. The positive side of informal or unreported employment is that the money is returned to the local economy, and has a great multiplier effect as it is spent over and over again. The World Travel and Tourism Council estimates that tourism generates an indirect contribution equal to 100% of direct tourism expenditures.

4

Purposes and Types of Tourism

ADVENTURE TOURISM

Adventure tourism is a type of niche tourism involving exploration or travel to remote areas, where the traveler should expect the unexpected. Adventure tourism is rapidly growing in popularity as tourists seek unusual holidays, different from the typical beach vacation.

Adventure tourism typically involves traveling into remote, inaccessible and possibly hostile areas. It may include the performance of acts that require significant effort and grit and may also involve some degree of risk.

According to the (U.S.-based) global Adventure Travel Trade Association, "adventure travel" may be any tourist activity including two of the following three components: a physical activity, a cultural exchange or interaction, and engagement with nature.

Mountaineering expeditions, trekking, bungee jumping, rafting and rock climbing are frequently cited as an examples of adventure tourism.

MOUNTAINEERING

Mountaineering is the sport, hobby or profession of walking, hiking, trekking and climbing up mountains. It is also sometimes known as alpinism, particularly in Europe. It may be said to consist of three aspects: rock-craft, snow-craft and skiing, depending on whether the route chosen is over rock, snow or ice. All require great athletic and technical ability, and experience is also a very important part of the matter.

Technique

Snow

Snowshoes can be used to walk through deep snow approaching the mountain or on lesser slopes up the mountain. Skis can be used when conditions allow, and can be a form of the sport by itself, called Ski Mountaineering. Crampons can be used on hard snow (neve) and ice.

Glaciers

When traveling over glaciers, crevasses pose a grave danger. These giant cracks in the ice are not always visible as snow can be blown and freeze over the top to make a snowbridge. At times snowbridges can be as thin as a few inches. Climbers use a system of ropes to protect themselves from such hazards. Basic gear for glacier travel includes crampons and ice axes. Teams of two to five climbers tie into a rope equally spaced. If a climber begins to fall the other members of the team perform a self-arrest to stop the fall. The other members of the team enact a crevasse rescue to pull the fallen climber from the crevasse.

Ice

Multiple methods are used to safely travel over ice. If the terrain is steep but not vertical protection in the form of pickets or ice screws can be driven into the snow or ice and attached to the rope by the lead climber. Each climber on the team must clip past the anchor, and the last climber picks up the picket. This allows for safety should the entire team be taken off their feet. This technique is known as Simul-climbing. If the terrain becomes vertical then standard ice climbing techniques are used.

Shelter

Climbers use a few different forms of shelter depending on the situation and conditions. Shelter is a very important aspect of safety for the climber as the weather in the mountains is very unpredictable. Tall mountains require many days of camping on the mountain.

Hut

Particularly the European alpine regions have a tight network of mountain huts, in most cases managed by full time, seasonal employees. These huts offer shelter, warm and cold meals, rooms or sleeping dormitories and sanitary facilities. In terms of luxury and comfort they vary by a great deal. Most huts are only open during the spring, summer and fall months to serve recreational mountaineers but also offer a self-service section to provide shelter and a cooking place for winter mountaineers. Using the hut system enables the mountaineer to travel without heavy tent, sleeping bag and cooking supplies.

Bivy

A bivy or bivouac is simply getting a sleeping bag and Bivouac sack and laying down to sleep. Many times small half sheltered areas like cracks in rocks or simply a trench dug in the snow are used to provide a basic means of shelter as well. This technique is performed by most people only in cases of emergency, however in good weather this can be pleasant. Some climbers steadfastly committed to Alpine Style climbing plan on bivying in order to save the weight of a tent when snow conditions are not suitable for a snow cave.

Tent

Tents are the most common form of shelter used on the mountain. A four season tent is required for any camp high in the mountains. Many climbers do not use tents at high altitudes unless the snow conditions do not allow for snow caving. One of the downsides to tenting is that storm winds can be very unnerving and can cause the tent to collapse, however modern mountaineering tents are usually tested for wind speeds up to 125mph. Even so, very intense flapping of the tent fabric can hinder sleep and raise doubts about the security of the shelter in windy conditions.

Snow cave

Snow caves are the preferred way for many climbers to shelter high on the mountain. Unlike tents snow caves are silent and are actually much warmer than a tent. A correctly made snow cave will hover around freezing, which relative to outside temperatures can be very warm. Igloos are used by some climbers, but are deceptively difficult to build and require specific snow conditions.

Hazards

The craft of climbing has been developed to avoid three main types of danger: the danger of things falling on the climber (objective danger), the danger of the climber falling and inclement weather. The things that may fall include rocks, ice, snow, other climbers or their gear; the mountaineer may fall from rocks, ice or snow, or into a crevasse. In all, there are eight chief dangers: falling rocks, falling ice, snow-avalanches, falls,the climber falling, falls from ice slopes, falls down snow slopes, falls into crevasses and dangers from weather. To select and follow a route using one's skills and experience to mitigate these dangers is to exercise the climber's craft.

Falling Rocks

Every rock mountain is slowly disintegrating due to erosion, the process being especially rapid above the snow-line. Rock faces are constantly swept by falling stones, which are generally possible to dodge. Falling rocks tend to form furrows in a mountain face, and these furrows (couloirs) have to be ascended with caution, their sides often being safe when the middle is stoneswept. Rocks fall more frequently on some days than on others, according to the recent weather. Ice formed during the night may temporarily bind rocks to the face but warmth of the day or direct sun exposure may easily dislodge these rocks. Local experience is a valuable help on determining typical rockfall on such routes.

The direction of the dip of rock strata often determines the degree of danger on a particular face; the character of the rock must also be considered. Where stones fall frequently debris will be found below, whilst on snow slopes falling stones cut furrows visible from a great distance. In planning an ascent of a new peak mountaineers must look for such traces. When falling stones get mixed in considerable quantity with slushy snow or water a mud avalanche is formed (common in the Himalaya). It is vital to avoid camping in their possible line of fall.

Falling Ice

The places where ice may fall can always be determined beforehand. It falls in the broken parts of glaciers (seracs) and from overhanging cornices formed on the crests of narrow ridges.

Large icicles are often formed on steep rock faces, and these fall frequently in fine weather following cold and stormy days. They have to be avoided like falling stones. Seracs are slow in formation, and slow in arriving (by glacier motion) at a condition of unstable equilibrium.

They generally fall in or just after the hottest part of the day, and their debris seldom goes far. A skillful and experienced ice-man will usually devise a safe route through a most intricate ice-fall, but such places should be avoided in the afternoon of a hot day. Hanging glaciers (i.e. glaciers perched on steep slopes) often discharge themselves over steep rock-faces, the snout breaking off at intervals. They can always be detected by their debris below. Their track should be avoided.

Avalanches

The avalanche is the most underestimated danger in the mountains. People generally think that they will be able to recognize the hazards and survive being caught. The truth is a somewhat different story. Every year, 120-150 people die in small avalanches in the Alps alone. The vast majority are reasonably experienced male skiers aged 20-35 but also include ski instructors and guides.

There is always a lot of pressure to risk a snow crossing. Turning back takes a lot of extra time and effort, supreme leadership, and most importantly there seldom is an avalanche to prove the right decision was made. Making the decision to turn around is especially hard if others are crossing the slope, but any next person could become the trigger.

There are two types of avalanche:

1. *The Slab Avalanche:* This type of avalanche occurs when a plate of snow breaks loose and starts sliding down; these are the largest and most dangerous.
    1. Hard Slab Avalanche-formed by hard-packed snow in a cohesive slab. The slab will not break up easily as it slides down the hill, resulting in large blocks tumbling down the mountain.
    2. Soft Slab Avalanche-formed again by a cohesive layer of snow bonded together, the slab tends to break up more easily.

2. *The Loose Snow Avalanche:* This type of avalanche is triggered by a small amount of moving snow that accumulates into a big slide. Also known as a "wet slide or point release" avalanche. This type of avalanche is deceptively dangerous as it can still knock a climber or skier off their feet and bury them, or sweep them over a cliff into a terrain trap.

Dangerous slides are most likely to occur on the same slopes preferred by many skiers: long and wide open, few trees or large rocks, 30 to 45 degrees of angle, large load of fresh snow, soon after a big storm, on a slope 'lee to the storm'. Solar radiation can trigger slides as well. These will typically be a point release or wet slough type of avalanche. The added weight of the wet slide can trigger a slab avalanche. Ninety percent of reported victims are caught in avalanches triggered by themselves or others in their group.

When going off-piste or traveling in alpine terrain, parties have a moral responsibility to always carry:

1. avalanche beacon
2. probe
3. shovel (retrieving victims with a shovel instead of your hands is five times faster)

and to have had avalanche training! Paradoxically, expert skiers who have avalanche training make up a large percentage of avalanche fatalities; perhaps because they are the ones more likely to ski in areas prone to avalanches.

Even with proper rescue equipment and training, there is a one-in-five chance of dying if caught in a significant avalanche, and only a 50/50 chance of being found alive if buried more than a few minutes. The best solution is to learn how to avoid risky conditions.

Falls from Rocks

The skill of a rock climber is shown by one's choice of handhold and foothold, and his adhesion to those one has chosen. Much depends on a correct estimate of the firmness of the rock where weight is to be thrown upon it. Many loose rocks are quite firm enough to bear a person's weight, but experience is needed to know which can be trusted, and skill is required in transferring the weight to them without jerking. On rotten rocks the rope must be handled with special care, lest it should start loose stones on to the heads of those below. Similar care must be given to handholds and footholds, for the same reason. When a horizontal traverse has to be made across very difficult rocks, a dangerous situation may arise unless at both ends of the traverse there be firm positions. Mutual assistance on hard rocks takes all manner of forms: two, or even three, people climbing on one another's shoulders, or using an ice axe propped up by others for a foothold. The great principle is that of co-operation, all the members of the party climbing with reference to the others, and not as independent units; each when moving must know what the climber in front and the one behind are doing. After bad weather steep rocks are often found covered with a veneer of ice (verglas), which may even render them inaccessible. Crampons are useful on such occasions.

Ice Slopes

For travel on slopes consisting of ice or hard snow, crampons are a standard part of a mountaineer's equipment. While step-cutting can sometimes be used on snow slopes of moderate angle, this can be a slow and tiring process, which does not provide the higher security of crampons. However, in soft snow or powder, crampons are easily hampered by balling of snow which reduce their effectiveness. In either case, an ice axe not only assists with balance but provides the climber with the possibility of self-arrest in case of a slip or fall. On a true ice slope however, an ice axe is rarely able to effect a self-arrest. As an additional safety precaution on steep ice slopes, the climbing rope is attached to ice screws buried into the ice.

True ice slopes are rare in Europe, though common in mountains located in the tropics, where newly-fallen snow quickly thaws on the surface and becomes sodden below, so that the next night's frost turns the whole mass into a sheet of semi-solid ice.

Snow Slopes

Snow slopes are very common, and usually easy to ascend. At the foot of a snow or ice slope is generally a big crevasse, called a bergschrund, where the final slope of the mountain rises from a snow-field or glacier. Such bergschrunds are generally too wide to be stepped across, and must be crossed by a snow bridge, which needs careful testing and a painstaking use of the rope. A steep snow slope in bad condition may be dangerous, as the whole body of snow may start as an avalanche. Such slopes are less dangerous if ascended directly than obliquely, for an oblique or horizontal track cuts them across and facilitates movement of the mass.

New snow lying on ice is especially dangerous. Experience is needed for deciding on the advisability of advancing over snow in doubtful condition. Snow on rocks is usually rotten unless it is thick; snow on snow is likely to be sound. A day or two of fine weather will usually bring new snow into sound condition. Snow cannot lie at a very steep angle, though it often deceives the eye as to its slope. Snow slopes seldom exceed 40°. Ice slopes may be much steeper. Snow slopes in early morning are usually hard and safe, but the same in the afternoon are quite soft and possibly dangerous; hence the advantage of an early start.

Crevasses

Crevasses are the slits or deep chasms formed in the substance of a glacier as it passes over an uneven bed. They may be open or hidden. In the lower part of a glacier the crevasses are open. Above the snow-line they are frequently hidden by arched-over accumulations of winter snow. The detection of hidden crevasses requires care and experience.

After a fresh fall of snow they can only be detected by sounding with the pole of the ice axe, or by looking to right and left where the open extension of a partially hidden crevasse may be obvious. The safeguard against accident is the rope, and no one should ever cross a snow-covered glacier unless roped to one, or even better to two companions. Anyone venturing onto crevasses should be trained in crevasse rescue.

Weather

The primary dangers caused by bad weather centre around the changes it causes in snow and rock conditions, making movement suddenly much more arduous and hazardous than under normal circumstances.

Whiteouts make it difficult to retrace a route while rain may prevent taking the easiest line only determined as such under dry conditions. In a storm the mountaineer who uses a compass for guidance has a great advantage over a merely empirical observer. In large snow-fields it is, of course, easier to go wrong than on rocks, but intelligence and experience are the best guides in safely navigating objective hazards.

Summer thunderstorms may produce intense lightning. If a climber happens to be standing on or near the summit, they risk being struck. There are many cases where people have been struck by lightning while climbing mountains. In most mountainous regions, local storms develop by late morning and early afternoon. Many climbers will get an "alpine start"; that is before or by first light so as to be on the way down when storms are intensifying in activity and lightning and other weather hazards are a distinct threat to safety.

Altitude

Rapid ascent can lead to altitude sickness. The best treatment is to descend immediately. The climber's motto at high altitude is "climb high, sleep low", referring to the regimen of climbing higher to acclimatize but returning to lower elevation to sleep. In the South American Andes, the chewing of coca leaves has been traditionally used to treat altitude sickness symptoms.

Common symptoms of altitude sickness include severe headache, sleep problems, nausea, lack of appetite, lethargy and body ache. Mountain sickness may progress to HACE (High Altitude Cerebral Edema) and HAPE (High Altitude Pulmonary Edema), both of which can be fatal within 24 hours.

In high mountains, atmospheric pressure is lower and this means that less oxygen is available to breathe. This is the underlying cause of altitude sickness. Everyone needs to acclimatize, even exceptional mountaineers that have been to high altitude before. Generally speaking, mountaineers start using bottled oxygen when they climb above 7,000 m. Exceptional mountaineers have climbed 8000-metre peaks (including Everest) without oxygen, almost always with a carefully planned program of acclimatization. In 2005, researcher and mountaineer John Semple established that above-average ozone concentrations on the Tibetan plateau may pose an additional risk to climbers.

Locations

Mountaineering has become a popular sport throughout the world. In Europe the sport largely originated in the Alps, and is still immensely popular there. Other notable mountain ranges frequented by climbers include the Caucasus, the Pyrenees and the Tatra mountains. In North America climbers frequent the Rockies and Sierra Nevada of California, the Cascades of Washington and the high peaks of Alaska. There has been a long tradition of climbers going on expeditions to the Greater Ranges, a term generally used for the Andes and the high peaks of Asia including the Himalaya, Pamirs and Tien Shan. In the past this was often on exploratory trips or to make first ascents. With the advent of cheaper long-haul air travel mountaineering holidays in the Greater Ranges are now undertaken much more frequently and ascents of even Everest and Vinson Massif (the highest mountain in Antarctica) are offered as a "package holiday". Other popular mountaineering areas of more local interest include the Southern Alps of New Zealand, the Japanese Alps the Scottish Highlands and the mountains of Scandinavia.

History

- Though it is unknown whether his intention was to reach a summit, Ötzi ascended at least 3,000 m in the Alps about 5,300 years ago. His remains were found at that altitude, preserved in a glacier.
- The first recorded mountain ascent in the Common Era is Roman Emperor Hadrian's ascent of Etna (3,350 m) to see the sun rise in 121.
- Peter III of Aragon climbed Canigou in the Pyrenees in the last quarter of the 13th century.
- The first ascent of the Popocatépetl (5,426 m in Mexico) was reported in 1289 by members of a local tribe (Tecanuapas)
- Jean Buridan climbed Mont Ventoux around 1316.
- The Italian poet Petrarch wrote that on April 26, 1336 he, together with his brother and two servants, climbed to the top of Mont Ventoux (1,909 m). His account of the trip was composed later as a letter to his friend Francesco Dionigi. Subsequently, April 26, 1336 came to be regarded

as the "birth of alpinism", and Petrarch (Petrarca alpinista) as the "father of alpinism".

- The Rochemelon (3,538 m) in the Italian Alps was climbed in 1358.
- In the late 1400s and early 1500s ascents were made of numerous high peaks in the Andes, for religious purposes by the citizens of the Inca Empire and their subjects. They constructed platforms, houses and altars on many summits and carried out sacrifices, including human sacrifices. The highest peak they are known for certain to have climbed is Llullaillaco (6,739 m). They may also have ascended the highest peak in the Andes, Aconcagua (6,962 m) as a sacrifice victim has been found at over 5,000 m on this peak.
- In 1492 the ascent of Mont Aiguille was made by order of Charles VIII of France. The Humanists of the 16th century adopted a new attitude towards mountains, but the disturbed state of Europe nipped in the bud the nascent mountaineering of the Zurich school.
- Leonardo da Vinci climbed to a snow-field in the neighborhood of the Val Sesia and made scientific observations.
- In 1642 Darby Field made the first recorded ascent of Mount Washington, then known as Agiocochook, in New Hampshire.
- Konrad Gesner and Josias Simler of Zurich visited and described mountains, and made regular ascents. The use of ice axe and rope were locally invented at this time. No mountain expeditions of note are recorded in the 17th century.
- Richard Pococke and William Windham's historic visit to Chamonix was made in 1741, and set the trend for visiting glaciers.
- In 1744 the Titus was climbed, the first true ascent of a snow-mountain.
- The first attempt to ascend Mont Blanc was made in 1775 by a party of natives. In 1786 Dr Michel Paccard and Jacques Balmat gained the summit for the first time.

Horace-Bénédict de Saussure, the initiator of the first ascent followed next year.

- The Norwegian mountain climber, Jens Esmark was the first person to ascend Snøhetta in 1798, part of the Dovrefjell range in Southern Norway. The same year he lead the first expedition to Bitihorn, a small mountain in the southernmost outskirts of Jotunheimen, Norway. In 1810 he was the first person to ascend Mount Gaustatoppen in Telemark, Norway.
- The Jungfrau was climbed in 1811, the Finsteraarhorn in 1812, and the Breithorn in 1813. Thereafter, tourists showed a tendency to climb, and the body of Alpine guides began to come into existence as a consequence.
- Citlaltépetl (5720 m in Mexico) was first climbed in 1848 by F. Maynard & G. Reynolds.
- Systematic mountaineering, as a sport, is usually dated from Sir Alfred Wills's ascent of the Wetterhorn in 1854. The first ascent of Monte Rosa was made in 1855.
- The Alpine Club was founded in London in 1857, and was soon imitated in most European countries. Edward Whymper's ascent of the Matterhorn in 1865 marked the close of the main period of Alpine conquest-the Golden age of alpinism-during which the craft of climbing was invented and 'perfected', the body of professional guides formed and their traditions fixed.
- Passing to other ranges, the exploration of the Pyrenees was concurrent with that of the Alps. The Caucasus followed, mainly owing to the initiative of D. W. Freshfield; it was first visited by exploring climbers in 1868, and most of its great peaks were climbed by 1888.
- The Edelweiss Club Salzburg was founded in Salzburg in 1881, and had 3 members make the First Ascent on 2 Eight-thousanders, Broad Peak (1957) and Dhaulagiri (1960).
- Trained climbers turned their attention to the mountains of North America in 1888, when the Rev. W. S. Green made an expedition to the Selkirk Mountains. From that time exploration has gone on apace, and many English and American climbing parties have surveyed most of

the highest peaks; Pikes Peak (14,115 ft.) having been climbed by Mr. E. James and party in 1820, and Mt. Saint Elias (18,008 ft.) by the Duke of the Abruzzi and party in 1897. The exploration of the highest Andes was begun in 1879-1880, when Whymper climbed Chimborazo and explored the mountains of Ecuador. The Cordillera between Chile and Argentina was visited by Dr. Gussfeldt in 1883, who ascended Maipo (17,270 ft.) and attempted Aconcagua (22,841 ft.). That peak was first climbed by the Fitzgerald expedition in 1897.

- The Andes of Bolivia were first explored by Sir William Martin Conway in 1898. Chilean and Argentine expeditions revealed the structure of the southern Cordillera in the years 1885-1898. Conway visited the mountains of Tierra del Fuego.
- New Zealand's Southern Alps were first visited in 1882 by the Rev. W. S. Green, and shortly afterwards a New Zealand Alpine Club was founded, and by their activities the exploration of the range was pushed forward. In 1895, Major Edward Arthur Fitzgerald, made an important journey in this range. Tom Fyfe and party climbed Aoraki/ Mount Cook on Christmas Day 1894, denying Fitzgerald the first ascent. Fitzgerald was en route from Britain with Swiss guide Matthias Zurbriggen to claim the peak. So piqued at being beaten to the top of Mount Cook, he refused to climb it and concentrated on other peaks in the area. Later in the trip Zubriggen soloed Mount Cook up a ridge that now bears his name.
- The first mountains of the arctic region explored were those of Spitzbergen by Sir W. M. Conway's expeditions in 1896 and 1897.
- Of the high African peaks, Kilimanjaro was climbed in 1889 by Dr. Hans Meyer, Mt. Kenya in 1899 by Halford John Mackinder, and a peak of Ruwenzori by H. J. Moore in 1900.
- The Asiatic mountains were initially surveyed on orders of the British Empire. In 1892 Sir William Martin Conway explored the Karakoram Himalaya, and climbed a peak of 23,000 ft. In 1895 Albert F. Mummery died while

attempting Nanga Parbat, while in 1899 D. W. Freshfield took an expedition to the snowy regions of Sikkim. In 1899, 1903, 1906 and 1908 Mrs Fannie Bullock Workman made ascents in the Himalayas, including one of the Nun Kun peaks (23,300 ft.). A number of Gurkha sepoys were trained as expert mountaineers by Major the Hon. C. G. Bruce, and a good deal of exploration was accomplished by them.

- The Rucksack Club was founded in Manchester, England in 1902.
- The American Alpine Club was founded in 1902.
- In 1902, the Eckenstein-Crowley Expedition, lead by mountaineer Oscar Eckenstein and occultist Aleister Crowley, was the first to attempt to scale Chogo Ri (now known as K2 in the west). They reached 22,000 feet before turning back due to weather and other mishaps.
- In 1905, Aleister Crowley led the first expedition to Kanchenjunga, the third highest mountain in the world. Four members of that party were killed in an avalanche. Some claims say they reached around 21,300 feet before turning back, however Crowley's autobiography claims they reached about 25,000 feet.
- The 1950s saw the first ascents of all the eight-thousanders but two, starting with Annapurna in 1950 by Maurice Herzog and Louis Lachenal. The world's highest mountain (above mean sea level), Mount Everest (8,848 m) was first climbed on May 29, 1953 by Sir Edmund Hillary and Tenzing Norgay from the south side in Nepal. Just a few months later, Hermann Buhl made the first ascent of Nanga Parbat (8,125 m), a remarkable solo climb, the only eight-thousander to be solo'd on the first ascent. K2 (8,611 m), the second highest peak in the world was first scaled in 1954. In 1964, the final eight-thousander to be climbed was Shishapangma (8,013 m), the lowest of all the 8,000 metre peaks.

TOURISM AND EDUCATION

Outdoor education usually refers to organized learning that takes place in the outdoors. Outdoor education programs often involve residential or journey-based experiences in which students participate in a variety of adventurous challenges such as hiking, climbing, canoeing, ropes courses, and group games. Outdoor education draws upon the philosophy and theory of experiential education and on environmental education.

Terminology

Outdoor education is closely related to terms such as adventure education, challenge education, experiential education, and environmental education. These terms, however, all represent slightly different emphases in philosophy and method. Adventure education, for example, focuses on participating in activities with perceived risks and does not necessarily occur outdoors. Consensus about the meaning of these terms is somewhat loose and varies between cultures.

Aims

Some typical aims of outdoor education are:

- to learn how to overcome adversity
- to learn alongside others
- to develop a deeper relationship with nature.

Outdoor education spans the three domains of self, others, and the natural world. The relative emphasis of these three domains varies from one program to another. An outdoor education program can, for example, emphasize one (or more) of these aims:

- to reduce recidivism
- to enhance teamwork
- to teach outdoor survival skills
- to promote spirituality
- to understand natural environments
- to develop leadership skills
- to improve problem solving skills

HISTORY

Modern outdoor education owes its beginnings to a number of separate initiatives. Organized camping was in evidence in the late nineteenth century and early twentieth century in

Europe, the UK, the USA, Australia and New Zealand. The Scouting movement, established in 1907 by Robert Baden-Powell, employs non-formal education with an emphasis on practical outdoor activities. The first Outward Bound centre at Aberdovey in Wales was established during the second world war. The Forest Schools of Denmark are examples of programs with similar aims and objectives. A key outdoor education pioneer was Kurt Hahn, a German educator who founded schools such as the Schule Schloss Salem in Germany, Gordonstoun School in Scotland, and Atlantic College in Wales, the United World Colleges movement, the Duke of Edinburgh Award scheme (which emphasizes community service, craftsmanship skills, physical skill, and outdoor expeditions) and the Outward Bound movement.

The second half of the twentieth century saw rapid growth of outdoor education in all sectors (state, voluntary and commercial) with an ever-widening range of client groups and applications. In this period Outward Bound spread to over 40 countries around the world, including the USA in the 1960s. This, in turn, spawned many offshoot programs, including Project Adventure and the National Outdoor Leadership School. (Further 'North America' developments are described in the 'Around the World' section below.) Other fields that are related to (or part of) 'outdoor education' include: adventure therapy, adventure recreation, adventure tourism, and ropes courses. A history of outdoor education in the UK has been documented by Lynn Cook (1999) and a history of outdoor education in New Zealand has been published in Pip Lynch's 'Camping in the Curriculum' (2007).

Philosophy

People are at their rawest level when outdoors. We remember that we are part of a greater ecosystem and are not as bound by social customs and norms. In essence we are more true to ourselves and it is easier to see people as people regardless of race, class, religion etc. Outdoor education also helps instill the basic elements of teamwork because we are forced to work together and rely on others. For many people a high ropes course or an outdoor activity may stretch their comfort zone and cause them to challenge themselves physically which in turn can lead to challenging oneself mentally.

Theory

A wide range of social science and specific outdoor education theories and models have been applied in an effort to better understand outdoor education. Amongst the key theoretical models or concepts are:

- Group development theories
- the Outward Bound Process Model
- Stress, optimal arousal, and psychological flow theories
- Psychoevolutionary theory and the Biophilia hypothesis

AROUND THE WORLD

Outdoor education occurs, in one form or another, in most if not all countries of the world. However, it can be implemented very differently, depending on the cultural context. Some countries, for example, view outdoor education as synonymous with environmental education, whilst other countries treat outdoor education and environmental education as distinct. Modern forms of outdoor education are most prevalent in UK, USA, Australia, New Zealand, Europe and to some extent Asia and Africa. A map is available of locations of outdoor education organisations, facilities, and people.

United Kingdom

After the second world war many local authorities in the UK emulated the Outward Bound principles and set up their own outdoor education centres for school children. Visits to these outdoor centres were often subsidised, allowing many children from the towns and cities their first real experience of the outdoor world.

By the late 1980s most UK local education authorities had an outdoor education centre, and there was a growing private sector offering similar experiences. Government moves to offer more autonomy to schools have badly affected this provision. Under regulations for the local management of schools that took effect in England and Wales from 1992 onwards, the majority of the money spent on education in the UK now goes direct to the school, and local authorities often find it difficult to subsidise their outdoor education centres. As a result many have closed.

One of the most significant changes in outdoor education in Great Britain came as a result of the Lyme Bay kayaking tragedy in March, 1993. This tragedy accelerated governmental discussions until, in January 1995, the Activity Centres (Young Persons' Safety) Act 1995 was passed through Parliament in January 1995 and an independent licensing authority, the Adventure Activities Licensing Authority (AALA) was formed.

Overall, the AALA appears to have succeeded in its mission, but it has also created debate regarding whether it is possible for young people to experience adventure in an 'educational way' within tight regulations. Some people view AALA regulations as tight and thus, restricting their opportunity to provide what they believe to be meaningful outdoor education.

One further area worthy of note is the Campaign for Adventure (Campaign for Adventure, 2000a). This campaign started in 2000 following a one day conference titled "A Question of Balance." Since then the campaign has concentrated on lobbying political individuals and parties to support risk taking and to acknowledge and work against the increasing trends indicated by a "culture of fear." This phrase is the title of Furedi's (1997) book, which is heavily cited in recent UK outdoor education literature. As with most political campaigns it is difficult to assess progress but the work of those involved in the campaign can be followed on line (Campaign for Adventure, 2000a). Consistent with this position, a recent report from the Office of Standards in Education, which covers England and Wales, concluded that outdoor education is uniquely placed to offer structured opportunities for students to identify hazards, calculate the related risks and decide the significance of a risk in order to determine and implement the precautions necessary to eliminate and minimise risk. Students' involvement in risk management makes them aware of potential harm and contributes towards their being able to take greater responsibility for their own and others' safety. (Ofsted, 2004, p. 13)

While on the surface Ofsted may appear to be consistent with the Campaign for Adventure there are some significant inconsistencies here worthy of brief explanation. It appears that Ofsted is suggesting that the very idea of risk taking is to be avoided and the role of outdoor education could be to enable students to assess risk and then 'eliminate or minimise' it. A contrary position is taken by the Campaign for Adventure based on adventure and risk as, at least an educational value, and perhaps even as central to life and a way of being, which is threatened by a culture of fear. The Campaign for Adventure believe that life is best approached with a spirit of adventure and that absolute safety is unachievable.

Recently there has been concern expressed about the decline in the number and quality of school trips in the UK. In 2005 the Parliamentary select committee on Education published a report on 'Education outside the classroom' which called on the UK government to do more to protect and promote outdoor education. In response the government promised to issue a manifesto for outdoor education, setting out what schools ought to offer their pupils.

North America

The origin of outdoor education in the USA is difficult to pinpoint. North American culture, particularly since European colonization in the 17th century, has embraced a pioneering spirit. This contributed to the extensive development of organized camping programs during the 20th century, Outward Bound programs since the 1960s, as well as many related off-shoot programs including Project Adventure, the National Outdoor Leadership School, the ropes course industry, and many other applications including wilderness orientation programs within colleges and universities and adventure therapy. In the 1970's, the Association for Experiential Education was also formed, along with the Journal of Experiential Education which continues to have a strong focus on adventure education scholarship and practice.

India

Outdoor Education in India

Outdoor education is relatively new to schools in India, though it is quite well established abroad. Acceptance is slowly increasing with a few schools advocating outbound adventure based programmes among students, to enhance personal growth through experiential learning and increase awareness about various subjects like the environment, ecology, wildlife, history, archaeology, geography and adventure sports. Some organisations that currently offer such programmes for schools are OETS and Wide Aware in Mumbai.Youreka& Ozonewho offer open summer programs based out of Delhi in north and Bangalore in South.

Germany

The term 'outdoor education' doesn't seem to have an exact equivalent in the German language although Kurt Hahn, one of key figures in the development of outdoor education in the twentieth century was German. In general, outdoor or adventure education is not as widespread in Germany as in other developed regions, such as North America, Australia, and the UK. However, a closely related educational approach called experiential education (In German: "Erlebnispädagogik") is commonly applied.

Most organisations and companies offering programs and activities based on experiential education for children and youth also offer similar programs for adults and especially corporate teams which are then mostly referred to as 'outdoor trainings'.

Judging from the kind of outdoor training programs available in an internet search, the main clientele of German outdoor training providers seem to be corporate teams and organisations seeking team building and personal development. There is also a wide range of organisations offering outdoor programs based on experiential education for children, adolescents, families and school classes with or without disabilities. German schools have seemingly started to make increased use of outdoor and experiential possibilities when planning their school trips but the experiential approach is rarely implemented in the normal school system and it is by no means as common for school students to experience outdoor education trips as it is other countries.

A more detailed summary of German outdoor education and experiential educational providers and networks is available.

Critical Views

Loynes (1998) has suggested that outdoor education is increasingly an entertainment park consumption experience.

In a controversial paper critiquing the algorithmic paradigm Loynes (2002) has also called for an increase in "creativity, spontaneity and vitality" (p. 124). These dialogues indicate a need for those working in outdoor education to examine assumptions to ensure that their work is educational (Hovelynck & Peeters, 2003).

Effects

There is much anecdotal evidence about benefits of outdoor education experiences; teachers, for example, often speak of the improvement they have in relationships with students following a trip. However, hard evidence showing that outdoor education has a demonstrable long-term effect on behaviour or educational achievement is harder to identify; this may be in part because of the difficulty involved in conducting studies which separate out the effects of outdoor education on meaningful outcomes.

A major meta-analysis of 97 empirical outcome studies indicated a moderately positive overall effect of adventure education programs on outcomes such as self-concept, leadership, and communication skills. Interestingly, this study also indicated that there appeared to be ongoing positive effects, unless most educational interventions whose effects tend to fade.

RAFTING

Rafting or whitewater rafting is a recreational activity utilizing a raft to navigate a river or other bodies of water. This is usually done on whitewater or different degrees of rough water, in order to thrill and excite the raft passengers. The development of this activity as a leisure sport has become popular since the mid 1970s.

History

Rafting is one of the earliest means of transportation, used as a means for shipping people, hunting, and transferring food.

In 1842, Lieutenant John Fremont of the U.S. Army first journalized his rafting expedition on the Platte River. Horace H. Day designed the equipment he used in rafting. Day's rafts were constructed from four independent rubber cloth tubes and wrap-around floor.

In 1960s, rafting was then recognized and paths like Grand Canyon were routed and whitewater rafting companies were established. In 1970s, rafting marked its major development as a leisure sport when it was then included in the Munich Olympic

Games. In 1980s, as rafting continued to gain its popularity, a lot of rivers were opened for rafting activities. Rivers in South America and Africa were just a few of them.

In 1990s, rafting was included in major game events like the Barcelona Games in 1992, Atlanta Games in 1996, and the whitewater events of the Summer Olympic Games hosted by Ocoee River in Tennessee Valley. In addition, the International Federation of Rafting was instituted in 1997 and in 1999 the first Official International Championship was held. Nowadays, river rafting is still gaining popularity among extreme water sports in order to thrill and excite the raft passengers.

Whitewater Rafts

Rafts were originally the simplest form of man's transportation in water and were then made of several logs, planks or reeds which were fastened together. Nowadays, inflatable boat were used as rafts which were later adopted by the military for beach assaults. It consists of very durable, multi-layered rubberized or vinyl fabrics with several independent air chambers. Its length varies between 3.5 m (11 ft) and 6 m (20 ft), the width between 1.8 m (6 ft) and 2.5 m (8 ft). The exception to this size rule is usually the packraft, which is designed as a portable single-person raft and may be as small as 1.5m long and weigh as little as 4 lbs.

Rafts come in a few different forms. In Europe the most common is the symmetrical raft steered with a paddle at the stern. Other types are the asymmetrical, rudder-controlled raft and the symmetrical raft with central helm (oars). Rafts are usually propelled with ordinary paddles and typically hold 4 to 12 persons. In Russia, rafts are often hand made and are often a catamaran style with two inflatable tubes attached to a frame. Pairs of paddlers navigate these rafts. Catamaran style rafts have become popular in the western United States as well, but are typically rowed instead of paddled.

Classes of Whitewater:

Class 1: Very small rough areas, requires no manuevering. (Skill Level: None)

Class 2: Some rough water, maybe some rocks, might require manuevering.(Skill Level: Basic Paddling Skil)

Class 3: Whitewater, small waves, maybe a small drop, but no considerable danger. May require significant manuevering. (Skill Level: Experienced paddling skills)

Class 4: Whitewater, medium waves, maybe rocks, maybe a considerable drop, sharp manuevers may be needed. (Skill Level: Whitewater Experience)

Class 5: Whitewater, large waves, maybe large rocks and hazards, maybe a large drop, precise maneuvering (Skill Level: Advanced Whitewater Experience)

Class 6: Whitewater, huge waves, huge rocks and hazards, maybe huge drops. Attempting a Class 6 will most likely end in serious injury or death. If someone navigates a 6 without harm, luck can be given most of the credit. (Skill Level: Expert)

Safety

Whitewater rafting can be a dangerous sport, especially if basic safety precautions are not observed. In the past there have been many accidents; both commercial trips and private trips have seen their share of injuries and fatalities, though private travel has stereotypically been associated with greater risk. Depending on the area, legislated safety measures now exist for rafting operators, ranging from certification of outfitters, rafts, and raft leaders, to more stringent regulations about equipment and procedures.

It is generally advisable to discuss safety measures with a rafting operator before signing on for a trip. The equipment used and the qualifications of the company and raft guides are essential information to be considered. Like most outdoor sports, rafting in general has become safer over the years. Expertise in the sport has increased, and equipment has become more specialized and increased in quality. This is no doubt as a result of the difficulty rating of most river runs has changed.

A classic example would be the Colorado River in the Grand Canyon, which has swallowed whole expeditions in the past, leaving only fragments of boats but is now run safely by commercial outfitters hundreds of times each year, with relatively untrained passengers.

Risks in whitewater rafting stem from both environmental dangers and from improper behavior. Certain features on rivers are inherently unsafe and have remained consistently so despite the passage of time. These would include "keeper hydraulics", "strainers" (e.g. fallen trees), dams (especially low-head dams, which tend to produce river-wide keeper hydraulics), undercut rocks, and of course dangerously high waterfalls. Rafting with experienced guides are the safest way to avoid such features. Even in safe areas, however, moving water can always present risks—such as when a swimmer attempts to stand up on a rocky riverbed in strong current, risking foot entrapment. Irresponsible behavior along the lines of rafting while intoxicated has also contributed to many accidents.

To combat the illusion that rafting is akin to an amusement park ride, and to underscore the personal responsibility each rafter faces on a trip, rafting outfitters generally require customers to sign waiver forms indicating understanding and acceptance of the risks. Rafting trips often begin with safety presentations to educate customers about problems that may arise. Having said all this, the overall risk level on a rafting trip with experienced guides using proper precautions is low. Thousands of people safely enjoy raft trips every year.

Issues with Rafting

Like all wilderness sports, rafting has to balance the conflict between nature protection and nature use. Because of frequent problems in the past, some rivers now have regulations restricting or specifying the annual and daily operating times.

Conflicts have also arisen with environmentalists when rafting operators, often in co-operation with municipalities and tourism associations, alter the riverbed by dredging and/or blasting in order to eliminate safety risks or create more interesting whitewater features in the river. Incongruously these measures usually are only temporary, since a riverbed is subject to permanent changes.

On the other hand, rafting contributes to the economy of many alpine regions which in turn may contribute to the protection of rivers from hydroelectric power generation and other development. Additionally, white water rafting trips can promote environmentalism. By experiencing first hand the beauty of a given river, individuals who would otherwise be indifferent to the environmental concerns of an area may gain a strong desire to protect and preserve that area because of a positive outdoors experience.

POPULAR RAFTING LOCATIONS

Africa

- Bujagali Falls on the Nile
- Omo River
- Tana River
- Zambezi River

Asia and Oceania

- Tully River in Queensland, Australia
- Kelani River at Kitulgala in Sri Lanka
- Ganga (Ganges River) and its tributaries in India
- Zanskar River in India
- Yoshino River in Japan
- Bhote Koshi river in Nepal
- Kali Gandaki river in Nepal
- Karnali river in Nepal
- Kawarau River in New Zealand
- Shotover River in New Zealand
- Whataroa River, New Zealand
- Hokitika River, New Zealand
- Chico River, Kalinga, Philippines
- Cagayan de Oro, Philippines
- Jeram Besu, Pahang, Malaysia
- Padas River, Sabah, Malaysia Image:Padasraft c.jpg
- Kiulu River, Sabah, Malaysia

Carribean

- Rio Yaque del Norte near Jarabacoa, Dominican Republic

Europe

- River Findhorn near Aviemore in Scotland, United Kingdom

- Afon Tryweryn near Bala in Wales, United Kingdom
- Tiroler Oberland in the Landeck and Imst Region in Tirol, Austria
- Enns River in Austria
- Tara River (Montenegro), Montenegro
- Una River, Bosnia and Herzegovina
- Neretva River, Bosnia and Herzegovina
- Drina River in Bosnia and Hercegovina
- Soca River in Slovenia
- Sjoa River in Norway
- Lim river in Serbia

Middle East

- Al Assi in North East Lebanon, Northern Bekaa Valley
- Al Litani in East Lebanon, in the Bekaa Valley
- Nahr Al Kalb in West Lebanon

North America

Eastern

- Black River in Watertown, New York
- Chattooga River near Clayton, Georgia in South Carolina
- Cheat River in Albright, West Virginia
- Cheoah River near Robbinsville, North Carolina
- Delaware River, along the border of New Jersey and Pennsylvania
- Deerfield River in northwest Massachusetts
- Nolichucky River flowing into Erwin, Tennessee (northeast Tennessee)
- Gauley River and New River "Grand Canyon of the East" in West Virginia
- Hudson River near Lake George, New York
- James River in Virginia (particularly in Richmond)
- Kennebec River, Dead River, and Penobscot River in Maine
- Lachine Rapids in Montreal, Quebec

- Lehigh River in Pennsylvania
- Moose River near Old Forge, New York
- Nantahala River in Bryson City, North Carolina
- Ocoee River and Appalachian Mountains in the southeastern United States
- Ocoee River flowing into Copperhill, Tennessee (southeast Tennessee)
- Ottawa River at Calumet Island in the Whitewater Region, Ontario
- Pigeon River flowing into Hartford, Tennessee (east Tennessee)
- U.S. National Whitewater Center in Charlotte, North Carolina
- Watauga River flowing into Elizabethton, Tennessee (northeast Tennessee)
- Youghiogheny River in Ohiopyle, Pennsylvania

Western

- American River near Coloma, California in the USA
- Arkansas River near the Royal Gorge in Colorado
- Colorado River, especially through the Grand Canyon starting at Lee's Ferry, Arizona
- Denali National Park and Preserve, starting at the Denali Lodge
- Deschutes River in central Oregon
- Kern River in California
- Kicking Horse River in Golden, British Columbia, Canada
- Lochsa River in Idaho
- Methow River near Methow, Washington
- Rogue River near Grants Pass, Oregon
- Salmon River and its tributaries in Idaho
- Skagit River near Marblemount, Washington
- Skykomish River near Gold Bar, Washington
- Snake River near Jackson Hole, Wyoming
- Tieton River near Naches, Washington

- Truckee River near Lake Tahoe, California starting at Lake Tahoe Dam
- Tuolomne River near Groveland, California
- Wenatchee River near Leavenworth, Washington
- White Salmon River near Husum, Washington

Central America

- Cahabon River in Guatemala
- Nahualate River in Guatemala
- Pacuare River in Costa Rica

South America

- Futaleufu River in Chile, South America

RIVER TREKKING

River trekking or river tracing is a form of hiking or outdoor adventure activity, particularly popular in Hong Kong and Taiwan, and, in some ways, similar to canyoning or canyoneering.

River trekking is a combination of trekking and climbing and sometimes swimming along the river. It involves particular techniques like rock climbing, climbing on wet surfaces, understanding the geographical features of river and valleys, knotting, dealing with sudden bad weather and find out possible exits from the river.

RIVER TREKKING IN DIFFERENT COUNTRIES

Hong Kong

River trekking has developed in Hong Kong since mid-20th century. Currently, there are numerous hiking groups organize regular trekking activities in Hong Kong. However, river trekking is a bit underground. There are no formal schools, formal coaches, formal sites, official recognition or qualifications on river trekking, even though it involves particular skills and certain level of risks. In Hong Kong, any natural rivers can be found in the country side, there would be the possible sites for river trekking.

Attractions and Popularity

River trekking is especially popular in Hong Kong because it is totally a surprise that in this highly developed region are preserved a number of excellent geographical features in its rivers in the countryside. Through river trekking, it is possible to access numerous waterfalls, large ponds, pot holes, other special geographical features as well as special species of animals and plants. Also, it is a very cheap activity in comparison with other challenging outdoor activities like rock climbing, rowling and wind-surfing. No training courses are needed because there is no one in Hong Kong who would provide training for river trekking. However, river trekking has long been one of the most popular outdoor activities in Hong Kong, even though most of the river trekking routes or sites are indicated as "danger" or "no entry" by the government. There is a trend that more and more foreigners and even tourists are taking part in this activity.

The Nine Big Rivers

The Nine Big Rivers are the nine rivers that are most popular among river trekkers in Hong Kong. The Nine Big Rivers include:

- Tai Shing River, located in Tsuen Wan
- Wan Chung River, located in Tai Po
- Ng Tung River, located in Tai Po
- Wong Lung River, located on Lantau Island near Tung Chung
- Sheng Luk River, located in Sai Kung
- Man Cheng Po, located in the west of Lantau Island
- Lotus River, located in Tai Lam Country Park
- Ngon Sam River, located on Lantau Island near Great Buddha
- Ping Nam River, located close to the border between Hong Kong and mainland China

Taiwan

This sport is popular throughout Taiwan, where it is generally called river tracing (??).

Rating of Difficuties

As river trekking has a certain level of risk, experienced river trekkers or hiking groups have developed rating systems about difficuties on different rivers. The ratings usually are various from 1 to 5 stars, even though a few rivers can be more than 5 stars because of their extreme difficulties. Such ratings are largely subjective, depends largely on river trekker's own experience. Therefore, different people or hiking groups would give different number of stars on the same river. According to Hong Kong Adverntruer, an English Website about hiking and river trekking in Hong Kong, difficult scale of different rivers as:

- 1 star: can be handled by normal healthy persons
- 2 stars: not too easy
- 3 stars: fairly difficult
- 4 stars: difficult, absolutely not for beginners
- 5 stars: very difficult, very demanding in term of strength and skill

Risk and Danger

River trekking has certain level of risk. There are occasional accidents in river trekking, including falls from steep cliffs or waterfalls, drownings, exhaustion, or getting lost. Risks that should be prepared for include the following:

First, sudden changes in weather, like rainstorms, can cause rapid rises in water levels and speed in the river. Also, the number of viable paths and climbing areas inside the river valley would be reduced suddenly in a very short period. Besides this, bad or misty weather would also cause low visibility. Low visibility may come in to quickly for trekkers to adapt to. Therefore, a torch (flashlight), preferably a head-mounted one, is a must for river trekking.

Second, steep cliffs inside river valleys require a certain level of rock climbing skills. However, because of the moisturing environment inside the river valley, some rock surfaces can be very wet and some rocks can be very loose despite appearing solid. To deal with such wet climbing conditions, a pair of professional river-trekking boots are strongly advised.

Damage to Stream Systems Caused by River Trekking

Due to the increasing popularity of river trekking, the activity has resulted in some damage to certain streams. The most noticeable kinds of damage are:

- Rubbish left by river trekking groups
- Use of aerosol spraypaints to mark route directions on rocks and trees
- Discarded climbing equipment and unnecessary bolting
- Damage to trees and other flora when used as leverage by trekkers
- Graffiti written in paint, ink and correction fluid

Such damage is, unfortunately, quite common in Hong Kong and goes against the philosophy of leave no trace, which most outdoor adventure sports adhere to.

CANYONING

Canyoning (also known as canyoneering) is traveling in canyons using a variety of techniques that may include walking, scrambling, climbing, jumping, abseiling, and/or swimming. Although hiking down a canyon that is non-technical (canyon hiking) is often referred to as canyoneering, the terms canyoning and canyoneering are more often associated with technical descents-those that require rappels (abseils) and ropework, technical climbing or down-climbing, technical jumps, and/or technical swims.

Canyoning is frequently done in remote and rugged settings and often requires navigational, route-finding and other skills and preparation needed for wilderness travel.

Canyons that are ideal for canyoning are often cut into the bedrock stone, forming narrow gorges with numerous drops, beautifully sculpted walls, and sometimes spectacular waterfalls. Most canyons are cut into limestone, granite or sandstone, though other rock types are found. Canyons can be very easy or extremely difficult, though emphasis in the sport is usually on aesthetics and fun rather than pure difficulty. A wide variety of canyoning routes are found throughout the world, and canyoning is enjoyed by people of all ages and skill levels.

Canyoning gear includes climbing hardware, static ropes, helmets, wetsuits, and specially designed shoes, packs, and rope bags. While canyoners have used and adapted climbing, hiking, and river running gear for years, more and more specialized gear is invented and manufactured as canyoning popularity increases.

Canyoning Around the World

In most parts of the world canyoning is done in mountain canyons with flowing water. Countries with established canyoning include: Australia, New Zealand, Spain, France, Ecuador, Japan, Italy, Switzerland, Germany, Austria, Reunion Island, Greece (Crete), Jordan, Canada, Mexico, Brazil, Croatia, Turkey, Israel, Mauritius and the United States. In South Africa, canyons that involve lots of jumping are common, and it is called Kloofing. Even in Hong Kong, where there are numerous stream gorges, a similar activity called stream or river trekking is popular. In Japan and Taiwan it's called river tracing and typically involves traveling upstream. In the United States, descending mountain canyons with flowing water is often referred to as canyoning, and descending non-flowing (though often wet) desert canyons is referred to as canyoneering. Most canyoneering in the United States occurs in the many slot canyons carved in the sandstone found throughout the Colorado Plateau. Outside of the Colorado Plateau, numerous canyoning opportunities are found in the San Gabriel, Sierra Nevada, Cascade, and Rocky Mountain ranges.

Hazards

Canyoning can be dangerous. Escape out the sides of a canyon is often impossible, and completion of the descent is the only possibility. Due to the remoteness and inaccessibility of many canyons, rescue can be impossible for several hours or several days.

High Water Flow / hydraulics

Canyons with significant water flow may be treacherous and require special ropework techniques for safe travel. Hydraulics, undercurrents, and sieves (or strainers) occur in flowing canyons and can trap or pin and drown a canyoner. A 1993 accident in Zion National Park, Utah, USA, in which two leaders of a youth group drowned in powerful canyon hydraulics (and the lawsuit which followed) brought notoriety to the sport.

Flash Floods

A potential danger of many canyoning trips is a flash flood. A canyon "flashes" when a large amount of precipitation falls in the drainage, and water levels in the canyon rise quickly as the runoff rushes down the canyon. In canyons that drain large areas, the rainfall could be many kilometers away from the canyoners, completely unbeknown to them. A calm or even dry canyon can quickly become a violent torrent due to a severe thunderstorm in the vicinity. Fatalities have occurred as a result of flash floods; in one widely-publicized 1999 incident, 21 tourists on a commercial canyoning adventure trip drowned in Saxetenbach Gorge, Switzerland.

Hypothermia and Hyperthermia

Temperature related illnesses are also canyoning hazards. In arid desert canyons, heat exhaustion can occur if proper hydration levels are not maintained and adequate steps are not taken to avoid the intense rays of the sun. Hypothermia can be a serious danger in any canyon that contains water, during anytime of the year. Wetsuits and drysuits can mitigate this danger to a large degree, but when people miscalculate the amount of water protection they will need, dangerous and sometimes fatal situations can occur. Hypothermia due to inadequate cold water protection is cited as a cause of a 2005 incident in which two college students drowned in a remote Utah canyon.

Keeper Potholes

Some canyoneering, especially in sandstone slots, involves escaping from large potholes. Also called "keeper potholes," these features, carved out by falling water at the bottom of a drop in the watercourse, are circular pits that often contain water that is too deep to stand up in and whose walls are too smooth to easily climb out of. Canyoneers use several unique and creative devices to escape potholes, including hooks used for aid climbing attached to long poles and specialized weighted bags that are attached to ropes and tossed over the lip of a pothole.

Very Narrow Slots

Narrow slot canyons, especially those narrower than humans, present difficult obstacles for canyoners. At times a canyoner is forced to climb up (using chimneying or off-width climbing techniques) to a height where one can comfortably maneuver laterally with pressure on both walls of the canyon. This tends to be strenuous and can require climbing high above the canyon floor, unprotected, for long periods of time. Failure to complete the required moves could result in being trapped in a canyon where rescue is extremely difficult.

Narrow sandstone slot canyons tend have abrasive walls which act as sandpaper as a canyoner moves or slides along them. This abrasion tends to rip clothing and gear, and can cause painful skin abrasion.

HIKING

Hiking is a form of walking, undertaken with the specific purpose of exploring and enjoying the scenery. It usually takes place on trails in rural or wilderness areas.

The word 'hiking' is understood in all English-speaking countries, but there are differences in usage. In some places, off-trail hiking is called 'cross-country hiking', 'bushwhacking', or 'bush-bashing'. In the United Kingdom, hiking is a slightly old-fashioned word, with a flavor more of heartiness and exercise than of enjoying the outdoors; the activity described here would be called 'hillwalking' or simply 'walking'. Australians use the term 'bushwalking' for both on-and off-trail hiking. New Zealanders use 'tramping' (particularly for overnight and longer trips), 'walking' or 'bushwalking'. Hiking in the mountainous regions of Nepal and India is sometimes called 'trekking'. Overnight hiking is called 'backpacking' in some parts of the world. Hiking a long-distance trail from end to end is referred to as 'thru-hiking' in some places.

Hiking is one of the fundamental outdoor activities on which many others are based. Many beautiful places can only be reached overland by hiking, and enthusiasts regard hiking as the best way to see nature. It is seen as better than a tour in a vehicle of any kind (or on an animal; see horseback riding) because the hiker's senses are not intruded upon by distractions such as windows, engine noise, airborne dust and fellow passengers. Hiking over long distances or over difficult terrain does require some degree of physical ability and knowledge.

Ecological Impact of Hiking

Hikers often seek beautiful environments in which to hike. Ironically, these environments are often fragile: hikers may accidentally destroy the environment that they enjoy. The action of an individual may not strongly affect the environment. However, the mass effect of a large number of hikers can degrade the environment. For example, gathering wood in an alpine area to start a fire may be harmless once (except for wildfire risk). Years of gathering wood, however, can strip an alpine area of valuable nutrients. Generally, protected areas such as parks have regulations in place to protect the environment. If hikers follow such regulations, their impact can be minimized. Such regulations include forbidding wood fires, restricting camping to established camp sites, disposing or packing out fecal matter, imposing a quota on the number of hikers per day.

Many hikers espouse the philosophy of Leave No Trace: hiking in a way such that future hikers cannot detect the presence of previous hikers. Practitioners of this philosophy obey its strictures, even in the absence of area regulations.

Human waste is often a major source of environmental impact from hiking. These wastes can contaminate the watershed and make other hikers ill. Bacterial contamination can be avoided by digging catholes 10 to 25 cm deep (4 to 10 inches, depending on local soil composition) and covering after use. If these catholes are dug at least 60 m (200 feet) away from water sources and trails, the risk of contamination is minimized. Many hikers warn other hikers about the location of their catholes by marking them with sticks stuck into the ground.

Sometimes, hikers enjoy viewing rare or endangered species. However, some species (such as martens or bighorn sheep) are very sensitive to the presence of humans, especially around mating season. Hikers should learn the habits and habitats of the endangered species, in order to avoid adverse impact. There is one situation where an individual hiker can make a large impact on an ecosystem: inadvertently starting a wildfire. For example, in 2005, a Czech backpacker burned 7% of Torres del Paine National Park in Chile by knocking over an illegal gas portable stove. Obeying area regulations and setting up cooking devices on bare ground will reduce the risk of wildfire.

Etiquette of Hiking

Because hiking is a recreational experience, hikers expect it to be pleasant. Sometimes hikers can interfere with each others' enjoyment, or that of other users of the land, but they can minimize this interference by following good etiquette. For example:

- When two groups of hikers meet on a steep trail, there may be contention for use of the trail. To avoid conflict, a custom has developed in some areas whereby the group moving uphill has the right-of-way. In other situations, the larger of the two groups will usually yield to the smaller.
- Being forced to hike much faster or slower than one's natural pace can be annoying, and difficult to maintain consistently. More seriously, walking unnaturally fast dramatically increases fatigue and exhaustion, and may cause injury. If a group splits between fast and slow hikers, the slow hikers may be left behind or become lost. A common custom is to encourage the slowest hiker to hike in the lead and have everyone match that speed. Another custom is to have an experienced hiker sweep up the rear, to ensure that everyone in the group is safe and nobody straggles.
- Hikers often enjoy the silence and solitude of their surroundings. Loud sounds, such as shouting or loud conversation, disrupt this enjoyment. Some hikers purposely avoid loud sounds, out of deference to other hikers. Staying quiet will also increase the likelihood of encountering wildlife. (This is a hazard if dangerous animals are present; see "Personal safety hazards".)
- Hikers sometimes trespass onto private property from public land or rights of way (easements). Such trespass can alienate the property owners and (in countries where rights of way are not protected by law) close down hiking rights-of-way. To maximize hiking opportunities for everyone, most hikers will either stay on public land and easements, or solicit permission from property owners. Staying on well-marked trails avoids the possibility of trespass.
- Tree branches or other vegetation often hang low across trails. A passing hiker may cause a tree branch to snap back in the face of a hiker behind. While it is courteous

to warn following hikers if a branch is likely to snap back, it is every hiker's responsibility to allow enough space between himself and the hiker ahead to avoid the hazard.

- When two groups of hikers meet, it is considered a common courtesy to exchange greetings (either verbal or physical (e.g. smiles and friendly nods)). To pass another group without such acknowledgement is seen as rude.

Personal Safety Hazards

Hiking may produce threats to personal safety. These threats can be dangerous circumstances while hiking and/or specific accidents or ailments. Dangerous hiking circumstances include losing the way, inclement weather, hazardous terrain, or exacerbation of pre-existing medical conditions.

Specific accidents include metabolic imbalances (such as dehydration or hypothermia), topical injuries (such as frostbite or sunburn), attacks by animals, or internal injuries (such as ankle sprain).

Hikers often propose a set of behavioral prescriptions to minimize these threats. A well-known example of such a set of prescription is the Ten Essentials.

Kinds of hiking:

- Hiking
- Backpacking, also known as trekking, a multi-day, often arduous hike especially in mountainous regions
- Thru-hiking, hiking a trail from end to end
- Hillwalking
- Dog hiking, hiking with dogs
- Naked hiking
- Waterfalling, aka waterfall hunting and waterfall hiking. Hiking with the purpose of finding and enjoying waterfalls.

URBAN EXPLORATION

Urban exploration (often shortened as urbex or UE) is the examination of the normally unseen or off-limits parts of human civilization. Urban exploration is also commonly referred to as infiltration, although some people consider infiltration to be more closely associated with the exploration of active or inhabited sites. In the USA, it may also be referred to as "draining" (when exploring drains) "urban spelunking", and "urban caving", "vadding", "building hacking", "Reality hacking" or "roof and tunnel hacking".

Targets of Exploration

Abandonments

Ventures into abandoned structures are perhaps the most common example of urban exploration. Abandoned sites are generally entered first by locals, and often sport large amounts of graffiti and acts of vandalism. Explorers face various risks in abandoned structures including collapsing roofs and floors, broken glass, guard dogs, the presence of chemicals, other harmful substances, most notably asbes'os, hostile squatters and sometimes motion detectors. Some explorers wear respirators to protect their airways. Exploration targets vary from one country to another, but some of the more popular or high-profile abandonments include amusement parks, grain elevators, factories, missile silos, hospitals, asylums, and sanatoriums.

Many explorers of abandonments find the decay of uninhabited spaces to be beautiful; many of these explorers are also photographers. Some abandonments are heavily guarded with motion sensors and active security. Others are more easily accessible and carry less risk of discovery. Abandonments are also popular among history buffs, 'urban archaeologists,' 'ghost hunters' and fans of graffiti art.

Active Buildings

Another aspect of urban exploration is the practice of exploring active or in use buildings. This includes seeing secured or "member-only" areas, mechanical rooms, roofs, elevator rooms, abandoned floors and other normally unseen parts of such buildings. The term 'infiltration' is often associated with the exploration of active structures.

Catacombs

Catacombs such as those found in Paris, Rome and Naples have been investigated by urban explorers. The catacombs under

Paris, for instance, have been considered the "Holy Grail" by some due to their extensive nature and history.

Sewers and Storm Drains

Entry into storm drains, or draining, is another common form of UE. Groups devoted to the task have arisen, such as the Cave Clan in Australia. Draining has a specialized set of guidelines, the foremost of which is "When it rains, no drains!"

A small subset of explorers enter sanitary sewers. Sometimes they are the only connection to caves or other subterranean feature. Sewers are among the most dangerous locations to explore owing to extremely high risks of poisoning by build up of toxic gases naturally found in all sewers (commonly methane and hydrogen sulphide). There have been large numbers of fatalities from around the world through being overcome by toxic gases from sewers and the only safe way to enter a sewer is if the atmosphere has been tested by a working monitoring device and other confined space entry procedures followed.

Transit Tunnels

The subset of urban exploration deals with exploring active and abandoned subway and underground railway tunnels and bores. Since these are in major cities, they carry stiff penalties if one should be caught while trespassing in these, especially after the September 11, 2001 attacks. As a result, this type of exploration is rarely publicized. Although they exist worldwide, those who partake in this often reside near New York City, Toronto, London, Sydney and Moscow, along with many other major cities throughout the world.

Utility Tunnels

Universities and other large institutions, such as hospitals, often distribute steam for heating buildings from a central heating plant. These steam ducts are generally run through utility tunnels, which are often accessible solely for the purposes of maintenance. Many of these steam tunnels, such as those on college campuses, often also have a tradition of exploration by students. This was once called vadding at MIT, though students there now refer to it as roof and tunnel hacking.

Steam tunnels in general have been getting more secure in recent years, due to their use for carrying network backbones and perceived risk of their use in terrorist activities, safety and liability.

Some steam tunnels have dirt floors, no lighting and can have temperatures upwards of 115 degrees Fahrenheit (46° C). Others have concrete floors, bright light, and can even be quite nice and feature a cool temperature. Most steam tunnels have large intake fans to bring in fresh air, and push all of the hot air out the back.

Ethics

Most urban explorers understand the risks they face if caught while trespassing or breaking and entering. The crime is generally seen as a means to an end, however, rather than being the focal point of the hobby. There are some urban explorers that tend to stick to a basic set of "ethical practices" out of respect for the locations that they visit, as well as for any other explorers who may want to visit later. The hobby, however, is still ultimately an unstructured one, and there are rarely two explorers who share the same views on ethics. As such, there are many exceptions to these "practices".

To some, the idea behind these "ethical practices" is to leave buildings in the same state that they were in before they were visited. The common, but not always entirely accurate catchphrase for this ethical standpoint is the Sierra Club's motto: "take nothing but pictures, leave nothing but footprints." Some try and adhere to this motto which frowns heavily upon theft, vandalism, tagging, graffiti, and any other crime except for trespassing.

Some explorers, though, remove items from abandoned sites to preserve them or to keep as souvenirs. More often than not, these explorers save these items from further decay or destruction when a location has become a target of vandalism or is being demolished.

Another counterpoint to the "leave no trace" ethic is tagging. Graffiti in drains is sometimes condoned or encouraged as long as speleothems and other features aren't damaged. Drainers may use it to indicate how far down the drain a given explorer has been. Similarly, tags may be left in very inaccessible places such as inside false ceilings, at the tops of elevator shafts, and so on.

Some locations contain a small area reserved for leaving tags, known as a guest book. These vary from actual books to blackboards to pieces of scrap metal or wood, or even the dust on an old piece of machinery. Rarely, employee guest books will be found, made before the business in question closed. Tags, especially those left in guest books, are sometimes referred to as "sign-ins", and the process of leaving them is "signing in". In marked contrast to the values of mainstream U.S. urban graffiti, tags are generally made to be unobtrusive, being written in conventional or slightly enlarged handwriting with pens or markers rather than larger markings made with paint.

As with many other cases of ethical principles, it is primarily up to the individual to make their own decisions based on their viewpoints and their current situation.

Popularity

The rise in the popularity of urban exploration can be attributed to its increased media attention. Recent television shows, such as "Urban Explorers" on the Discovery Channel, MTV's Fear, and the ghost hunting exploits of The Atlantic Paranormal Society have packaged the hobby for a popular audience; Talks and exhibits on urban exploration have appeared at the 5th and 6th Hackers on Planet Earth Conference, complementing numerous newspaper articles and interviews. With the advent rise in the relative popularity of the hobby due to this increased focus, there has been increasing discussion on whether the extra attention has been beneficial to urban exploration as a whole.

The growing popularity of the activity has resulted not just in increased attention from explorers, but also from vandals and law enforcement. The illicit aspects of urban exploring, which may include trespassing and breaking and entering, have brought along with them critical articles in mainstream newspapers. In one recent article, web-postings and photographs from the website Urban Exploration Resource were cited as evidence that explorers were trespassing in a closed prison in Northern Virginia. Users had posted specific details on entry points and how "easy" it was to gain entry to the disused facility.

In that regard, some explorers have become wary of posting information and photographs on UE-related websites for fear of being prosecuted for trespassing. Recently there has been a conflict of interest between explorers about this issue. Additionally, arguments focus on whether online listings of explorable structures undermine the "underground" aspect of urban exploration.

Along with the rise in the popularity of urban exploring, numerous events have been hosted throughout the world. These organized meetings have included campouts, barbeques, day-long explorations, and tours of active and abandoned sites. While most of these are illegal in the sense that they involve trespassing or breaking and entering, a handful of meets, such as a recent event held at the West Virginia State Penitentiary, involve tours or lock-ins. Others include UE-related gatherings, such as a meet held by an urban explorer who calls himself Shiroi in which stunts were performed in an abandoned structure. This has received mixed criticism from the urban exploration community.

5

Tourism : A Rapidly Growing Business

AGRITOURISM

Agritourism is a style of vacation in which hospitality is offered on farms. This may include the opportunity to assist with farming tasks during the visit. Agritourism is often practiced in wine growing regions, as in Italy, France and Spain. In America, Agritourism is wide-spread and includes any farm open to the public at least part of the year. Tourists can pick fruits and vegetables, ride horses, taste honey, learn about wine, shop in gift shops and farm stands for local and regional produce or hand-crafted gifts, and much more. Agritourism is being developed as a valuable component of a business model to support many agricultural entities when the farm products they produce are no longer economically competitive otherwise. To help promote the single agritourism operations, some farms get together to form festivals, tours or other events.

People are more interested in how their food is produced and want to meet the producers and talk with them about what goes into food production. Children who visit the farms often have not seen a live duck, or goat, and have not picked an apple right off the tree. This form of expanded agri-tourism has given birth to what are often called "entertainment farms." These farms cater to the pick-your-own crowd, offering not only regular farm products, but also food, mazes, open-pen animals, train rides, picnic facilities and pick-your-own produce. Dude ranches offer tourists the chance to work on cattle ranches and sometimes include cattle drives.

ARCHAEOLOGICAL TOURISM

Archaeotourism or Archaeological tourism is an alternative form of cultural tourism, which aims to promote the passion for historical-archaeology and the conservation of historical sites.

Establishment

Investigator Georgeos Diaz-Montexano, who initiated a series of publications in 1995 about ArchaeoTourism, such as "Arqueología y Enigmas de la Historia", "Arqueología Sin Fronteras", "La Esfinge. Revista de Egiptologia" and "ArqueoHistoria", brought awareness to the concept of archaeological tourism. Shortly after writing these publications, he founded the first specialized society on Archaeotourism, ArqueoTour (2000). For these efforts, he is considered by some to be the founder of archaeotourism.

Like Ecological tourism (or Ecotourism), Archaeological tourism is promoted to encourage the development of cultural associations, and companies and cooperatives can be found that dedicate themselves to offer this type of service.

The best definition of archaeotourism can be found in the words of its founders:

The passion by the past is something inherent to the human being. As it says well: "Town that does not know from where town comes that does not know to where it goes".

The Archaeotourism or archaeological tourism is ideal for which they look for a higher knowledge and sublimates, tie to the meditation and the relaxation, in perfect syntony with the surroundings or ecosystem that is, integration with the Mother Nature, but always in old places, next to the ruins of the "enigmatic missing civilizations".

Sites and places magician-monks or asylums. From the most remote prehistoric times. From the era of the dinosaurios to the Medieval Age. In order to develop his activities it has a nourished group of authentic experts in each one of the matters.

Therefore, archaeologists, paleontologists, anthropologists, historians and specialists in trips will unite their knowledge under a same objective: to offer to the traveller a wonderful and unforgettable experience, an intensive course and of introduction to each one of these manifestations of the human knowledge. This way the visitor will not be a simple traveller, will be in addition an apprentice in sciences to the past.

Some times will feel a paleontologist discovering tracks of dinosaurious and others will feel like Indiana Jones in the Damn Temple, mainly when penetrating in the mysterious caverns and artificial caves that long ago served from temples our ancestors. Enigmatic places loaded of an atmosphere of magic and mystery that, sometimes, surpass to all fiction created by the cinema...

Other Definitions

Archaeological tourism can include all products associated with public archaeological promotion, including visits to archaeological sites, museums, interpretation centers, reinactment of historical occurrences, the rediscovery of native products, festivals, or theater.

Although archaeological tourism is quite recent, many international institutions and governments have already begun to contemplate viable alternative activity for the sustainable economic-social development. Several countries have for years had programs resembling the main points of Archaeological tourism for economic income, including Egypt, Mexico and Peru.

BOOKSTORE TOURISM

Bookstore tourism is a type of cultural tourism that promotes independent bookstores as a group travel destination. It started as a grassroots effort to support locally owned and operated bookshops, many of which have struggled to compete with large bookstore chains and online retailers.

The project was initiated in 2003 by Larry Portzline, a writer and college instructor in Harrisburg, Pennsylvania who led "bookstore road trips" to other cities and recognized its potential as a group travel niche and marketing tool. He promoted the concept with a how-to book and a web site, and groups around the U.S. soon began offering similar excursions, usually via a chartered bus, and often incorporating book signings, author home tours, and historical sites. In 2005-06, the Southern California Booksellers Association and Northern California Independent Booksellers Association embraced bookstore tourism, offering trips to independent bookstores in Los Angeles, San Diego and San Francisco. The Bookstore Tourism movement encourages schools, libraries, reading groups, and organizations of all sizes to create day-trips and literary outings to cities and towns with a concentration of independent bookstores. It also encourages local booksellers to attract bibliophiles to their communities by employing bookstore tourism as an economic development tool. Others benefiting include local retailers, restaurants, bus companies, and travel professionals.

The effort also provides organizations with an outreach opportunity to support reading and literacy. Portzline has traveled across the country to promote the concept. In Fall 2006 he launched the National Council on Bookstore Tourism (NCBT), a nonprofit organization and trade association that will partner with booksellers, libraries, educators, literary festivals, the travel industry and economic development agencies at the national, state and local levels. In 2006 he created a promotional video featuring group "bookstore road trips" in New York City's Greenwich Village and in Los Angeles area "beach towns" and posted it on the NCBT website.

CULTURAL TOURISM

'Cultural tourism' (or culture tourism) is the subset of tourism concerned with a country or region's culture, especially its arts. It generally focuses on traditional communities who has diverse customs, unique form of art and distinct social practices, which basically distinguishes it from other types/forms of culture. Cultural tourism includes tourism in urban areas, particularly historic or large cities and their cultural facilities such as museums and theatres. It can also include tourism in rural areas showcasing the traditions of indigenous cultural communities (i.e. festivals, rituals), and their values and lifestyle. It is generally agreed that cultural tourists spend substantially more than standard tourists do. This form of tourism is also becoming generally more popular throughout Europe.

Destination

Definition

By definition, the term destination refers broadly to any given area where tourism is a relatively important activity, like for instance having an economy significantly influenced by tourism revenues. However, it is complicated by the fact that a single, recognizable destination may include several cities, towns or municipalities, provinces, or other government entities-in island archipelago it may be the entire country.

Types

Living Cultural Areas

Due to globalization, technology and the onset of cultural tourism and ecotourism, the number of living cultural areas is continually declining. For an indigenous culture that has stayed largely separated from the surrounding majority, tourism can present both advantages and problems. On the positive side are the unique cultural practices and arts that attract the curiosity of tourists and provide opportunities for tourism and economic development. On the negative side is the issue of how to control tourism so that those same cultural amenities are not destroyed and the people do not feel violated.

Prominent Examples

Chiloé, Chile

Chiloé is Chile's largest island, located at the midway point between the capital, Santiago, and the country's extreme south at Tierra del Fuego. Chiloé is the site of the Chiloé Model Forest, member of the same network as the Calakmul and Eastern Ontario Model Forests. Having evolved for centuries isolated from mainland Chile, the "Chilotes" developed a strong, self-reliant culture, rich in folklore, mythology and tradition. This very identity is what constitutes the island's major attraction for domestic tourists in Chile and increasingly, for international tourists.

As in the Calakmul case above, tourism to Chiloé is very strongly based on the island's cultural heritage, predominantly consisting of crafts markets, appreciation of cultural landscapes, museum exhibitions, seafood cuisine and architectural heritage (Chiloé's old churches). However, the average tourist to the island will have little opportunity to see Chilotes involved in their living cultural activities, such as the elaborate preparation of the islands famous "curanto" meal, rich in shellfish, meat and potatoes, the management practices of their farm and forest lands, boat building and more.

In order to overcome the cultural and organizational barriers that keep suppliers of living cultural heritage and tour operators apart, the Chiloé diocese of Ancud established a private foundation called "Fundación con Todos" (One for All Foundation). Among other activities, the Foundation has played a key role in helping a number of Chilote households organize themselves into an "agrotourism" network. The Foundation helped Chilote households make the preparation required to accommodate tourists (including training in sanitation and maintenance of facilities, the provision of basic infrastructure) and complemented this effort with a professional marketing campaign. These works were undertaken with the financial support of other agencies.

Again, in cooperation with the EOMF and the Chiloé Model Forest, a cultural and natural heritage tour was organized to Argentina and Chile, including a three-day visit to Chiloé, permitting some of the Chilote households to host a group of cultural heritage tourists for the first time. The visits were very successful and should be the first of more to come, helping establish the credibility of Chiloé's agrotourism network among other tour operators.

Orrissa Tribes

Nestling on the eastern coast of India, Orissa is one of the most exquisite regions dominated by exotic sandy beaches, plenteous wild life, and holy temples famous for their architectural splendor and primitive lifestyle. The charm of the city is still well-nigh chaste and unrevealed by the visitors, up to its full extent. The other lure of the city lies in its tribal population dotted with more than 62 tribal communities. The tribal communities of Orissa constitute about 23% of its total population. Orissa is inhabited by tribes like Saora or Sabar that had a respectable mentioning in the epic of Mahabharata.

Mostly the Orissa tribes are high land habitats with opulent ethnic trait, cultures and customs dominated by varying languages. The culture conscious tribes are able to preserve their social customs and dignified values. The most primitive tribes are Bondas, Gadabas, Koyas, Kondhas and Sauras.

The culture of tribal Orissa is affluent with their own folk songs and dances, their tattoos. Tribal culture of Orissa is well depicted in its modern city in form of poems, art and craft or music. The tribes have adapted the Hindu traditions and culture from centuries, which is mixed with their own culture giving a distinct zest to the entire racial. Songs and dances are the essence of the tribal culture of Orissa. The traditions and the ceremonies for wedding, birth and death all are represented by singing songs, rural dances along with feasts.

The Tribal Folk Orissan tribes are strong, assiduous and simple hospitable tribes, normally like to be reserved and maintain distance from the people of other communities, as they are too shy. The major occupation of these tribes is agriculture and fishing and hunting. Men usually wear loin attire and women rap long stretch of cloth around them. Women are adorned with ornaments like bangles, armlets, bracelets, necklaces, rings, hairpins etc usually made of silvers, aluminum, and brass. The practice of tattooing is prevalent among women folk. Girls above 5 years are found with tattoo mark on their faces and hands.

Festival Celebration Numbers of deities are worshiped by the tribes for their happy life. Many festivals are also celebrated with much of enthusiasm and excitement. The ceremony rituals are observed through out the year in order to appease their deities and ascendant.

The most significant festival of the year are the chaita parab and push parab-this day all able men of the village go on a hunting expedition. The tribes with their cultural dance, song and music all distinguish custom of their artistic life, which demarcate them from the other non tribal groups.

Orissa acquire every thing Orissa is a state, embellished with hilly terrain of the Eastern Ghats, where primitive tribes dwell and a beautiful stretch of the Indo-Aryans coast where modern life persists. A blend of 2 discrete civilization with contrast cultures, beautiful landscapes, beaches, rich wildlife, offers the best of India to its visitors.

Destination Planning

As the issue of globalization takes place to this modern time, the challenge of preserving the few remaining cultural community around the world is becoming hard. In a tribal based community, reaching economic advancement with minimal negative impacts is an essential objective to any destination planner.

Since they are using the culture of the region as the main attraction, sustainable destination development of the area is vital for them to prevent the negative impacts (i.e. destroying the authentic identity of the tribal community) due to tourism.

Management Issues

Certainly, the principle of "one size fits all" doesn't apply to destination planning. The needs, expectations, and anticipated benefits from tourism vary greatly from one destination to another. This is clearly exemplified as local communities living in regions with tourism potential (destinations) develop a vision for what kind of tourism they want to facilitate, depending on issues and concerns they want to be settled or satisfied.

Destination Planning Resources

Planning Guides

It is important that the destination planner takes into account the diverse definition of culture as the term is subjective. Satisfying tourists' interests such as landscapes, seascapes, art, nature, traditions, ways of life and other products associated to them-which may be categorized cultural in the broadest sense of the word, is a prime consideration as it marks the initial phase of the development of a cultural destination.

The quality of service and destination, which doesn't solely depend on the cultural heritage but more importantly to the cultural environment, can further be developed by setting controls and policies which shall govern the community and its stakeholders. It is therefore safe to say that the planner should be on the ball with the varying meaning of culture itself as this fuels the formulation of development policies that shall entail efficient planning and monitored growth (e.g. strict policy on the protection and preservation of the community).

Local community, tourists, the destination and sustainable tourism.

While satisfying tourists' interests and demands may be a top priority, it is also imperative to ruminate the subsystems of the destination's (residents). Development pressures should be anticipated and set to their minimum level so as to conserve the area's resources and prevent a saturation of the destination as to not abuse the product and the residents correspondingly. The plan should incorporate the locals to its gain by training and employing them and in the process encourage them to participate to the travel business. Keep in mind that the plan should make travellers not only aware about the destination but also concern on how to help it sustain its character while broadening their travelling experience.

Planning Tools

The core of a planner's job is to design an appropriate planning process and facilitate community decision. Ample information which is a crucial requirement is contributed through various technical researches and analyzes. Here are some of the helpful tools commonly used by planners to aid them:

1. Key Informant Interviews
2. Libraries, Internet, and Survey Research
3. Census and Statistical Analysis
4. Spatial Analysis with Geographical Information System (GIS) and Global Positioning System (GPS) technologies

Key Institutions

Participating structures are primarily led by the government's local authorities and the official tourism board or council, with the involvement of various NGOs, community and indigenous representatives, development organizations, and the academe.

Case Studies

Cultural and Ecotourism in the Mountainous Regions of Central Asia and in the Himalayas

Tourism is coming to the previously isolated but spectacular mountainous regions of Central Asia, the Hindu Kush and the Himalayas. Closed for so many years to visitors from abroad, it now attracts a growing number of foreign tourists by its unique culture and splendid natural beauty. However, while this influx of tourists is bringing economic opportunities and employment to local populations, helping to promote these little-known regions of the world, it has also brought challenges along with it: to ensure that it is well-managed and that its benefits are shared by all.

As a response to this concern, the Norwegian Government, as well as the UNESCO, organized an interdisciplinary project called the Development of Cultural and Eco-tourism in the Mountainous Regions of Central Asia and the Himalayas project. It aims to establish links and promote cooperation between local communities, national and international NGOs, and tour agencies in order to heighten the role of the local community and involve them fully in the employment opportunities and income-generating activities that tourism can bring.

Project activities include training local tour guides, producing high-quality craft items and promoting home-stays and bed-and-breakfast type accommodation.

As of now, the project is drawing on the expertise of international NGOs and tourism professionals in the seven participating countries, making a practical and positive contribution to alleviating poverty by helping local communities to draw the maximum benefit from their region's tourism potential, while protecting the environmental and cultural heritage of the region concerned.

DARK TOURISM

Dark tourism or Grief tourism is tourism involving travel to sites associated with death and suffering. Thanatourism, derived from the Ancient Greek word thanatos for the personification of death, is associated with dark tourism but refers more specifically to violent death; it is used in fewer contexts than the terms dark tourism and grief tourism.

This includes sites of pilgrimage such the site of St Peter's death in Rome; castles and battlefields such as Culloden near Inverness, Scotland; sites of disaster, either natural or man made such as Ground Zero in New York; prisons now open to the public such as Beaumaris Prison in Anglesey, Wales; and purpose built centers such as the London Dungeon.

One of the most notorious destinations for dark tourism is the Nazi extermination camp at Auschwitz in Poland.

DISASTER TOURISM

Disaster tourism is the act of traveling to a disaster area as a matter of curiosity. The behavior can be a nuisance if it hinders rescue, relief, and recovery operations.

Hurricane Katrina

Disaster tourism took hold in the Greater New Orleans Area in the aftermath of Hurricane Katrina. There are now guided bus tours to neighborhoods that were severely damaged by storm-related flooding. Some local residents have criticized these tours as unethical, because the tour companies are profiting from the misery of their communities and families. The Army Corp of Engineers has noted that traffic from tour buses and other tourist vehicles have interfered with the movement of trucks and other cleanup equipment on single-lane residential roads. Furthermore, during the first six months after the storm, most of these neighborhoods lacked electricity, phone access, street signs, or access to emergency medical or police assistance. Simply traveling to these neighborhoods was hazardous. For these reasons, organized disaster tours are now banned from two of the most severely damaged areas in the city, the Lower 9th and St. Bernard Parish near the Industrial Canal.

On the other hand, such communities as Gentilly and Lakeview, along the 17th Street Canal, have welcomed organized tour groups as a means to publicize the scale of the destruction and attract more aid to the city. Much of the recovery effort in the New Orleans relies on out-of-state volunteers and donations.

Numerous non-profit organization, including Habitat for Humanity International and Catholic Charities, have converged on the city to gut and rebuild homes. There is also a movement by local residents to bring congressmen and other national leaders to the city and view the damage in person, since

recovery efforts have been hampered by the failure of many homeowners and businesses to receive claims from their insurance providers.

DRUG TOURISM

Drug tourism is travel for the purpose of obtaining or using drugs for personal use that are unavailable or illegal in one's home jurisdiction. This would include crossing a national border to obtain drugs over the counter that are not sold in one's own country, or traveling to another country in order to obtain or use narcotics that are illegal in one's own country, or even traveling from one U.S. state to another in order to buy alcohol or tobacco more easily (although this last situation is often considered too trivial to qualify as drug tourism).

Drug tourism has many legal implications, and persons engaging in it sometimes risk prosecution for drug smuggling or other drug-related charges in their home jurisdictions or in the jurisdictions they are visiting, especially if they bring their purchases home rather than using them abroad. The act of traveling for the purpose of buying or using drugs is itself a criminal offense in some jurisdictions.

Amsterdam is a popular destinations for drug tourists, due to the Dutch government's acceptance of marijuana use and possession. Another Dutch city which is visited frequently by drug tourists is Maastricht because of its position close to the borders of Germany and Belgium.

Other popular destinations include Southeast Asia and South America. Drug tourism thrives because legislation controlling the sale, possession, and use of drugs varies dramatically from one jurisdiction to another.

ECOTOURISM

Ecotourism, also known as ecological tourism, is a form of tourism which appeals to the ecologically and socially conscious. Generally speaking, ecotourism focuses on local culture, wilderness adventures, volunteering, personal growth, and learning new ways to live on the planet; typically involving travel to destinations where flora, fauna, and cultural heritage are the primary attractions.

Responsible ecotourism includes programs that minimize the negative aspects of conventional tourism on the environment, and enhance the cultural integrity of local people. Therefore, in addition to evaluating environmental and cultural factors, an integral part of ecotourism is in the promotion of recycling, energy efficiency, water conservation, and creation of economic opportunities for the local communities.

Many global environmental organizations and aid agencies believe that ecotourism has great potential for sustainable development.

Ideally, ecotourism should satisfy several criteria, such as:

- conservation of biological diversity and cultural diversity, through ecosystem protection
- promotion of sustainable use of biodiversity, by providing jobs to local populations
- sharing of socio-economic benefits with local communities and indigenous people by having their informed consent and participation in the management of ecotourism enterprises.
- increase of environmental & cultural knowledge
- minimization of tourism's own environmental impact
- affordability and lack of waste in the form of luxury
- local culture, flora and fauna being the main attractions

For many countries, ecotourism is not simply a marginal activity to finance protection of the environment but as a major industry of the national economy. For example, in places such as Costa Rica, Ecuador, Nepal, Kenya, Madagascar, and Antarctica, ecotourism represents a significant portion of the gross domestic product and economic activity.

The concept of ecotourism is widely misunderstood, and in practice is often used as a marketing tool to promote tourism that is related to nature. Critics claim that ecotourism as practiced and abused often consists of placing a hotel in a splendid landscape, to the detriment of the ecosystem. According to them, ecotourism must above all sensitize people with the beauty and the fragility of nature. They condemn some operators as "greenwashing" their operations; using the label of "ecotourism" and "green-friendly", while behaving in environmentally irresponsible ways. Although academics disagree about who can be classified as an ecotourist and there is precious little statistical data, some estimate that more than five million ecotourists-the majority of the ecotourist population-come from the United States, with others from Western Europe, Canada, and Australia.

Currently there are various moves to create national and international ecotourism accrediation programs, although the process is also controversial. Ecotourism certificates have been put in place at Costa Rica, although some critics have dismissed these programs as greenwashing.

History

Ecotourism, responsible tourism, and sustainable development have become prevalent concepts since the late 1980s, and ecotourism has experienced arguably the fastest growth of all sub-sectors in the tourism industry. The popularity represents a change in tourist perceptions, increased environmental awareness, and a desire to explore natural environments. Such changes have become a statement affirming one's social identity, educational sophistication, and disposable income as it has about preserving the Amazon rainforest or the Caribbean reef for posterity.

With its great potential for environmental protection, the United Nations celebrated the "International Year of Ecotourism" in 2002.

Criticisms

Definitional Problems and Greenwashing

To approach an understanding of the problem, a clear definition must delineate what is, and is not, ecotourism. Ideally, ecotourism satisfies several general criteria, including the conservation of biological diversity and cultural, diversity through ecosystem protection, promotion of sustainable use of biodiversity, share of socio-economic benefits with local communities through informed consent and participation, increase in environmental and cultural knowledge, affordability and reduced waste, and minimization of its own environmental impact. In such ways, it contributes to the long term benefits to both the environment and local communities.

However, in the continuum of tourism activities that stretch from conventional tourism to ecotourism proper, there has been a lot of contention to the limit at which biodiversity preservation, local socio-economic benefits, and environmental impact can be considered "ecotourism". For this reason, environmentalists, special interest groups, and governments define ecotourism differently. Environmental organizations have generally insisted that ecotourism is nature-based, sustainably managed, conservation supporting, and environmentally educated. The tourist industry and governments, however, focus more on the product aspect, treating ecotourism as equivalent to any sort of tourism based in nature. As a further complication, many terms are used under the rubric of ecotourism. Nature tourism, low impact tourism, green tourism, bio-tourism, ecologically responsible tourism, and others have been used in literature and marketing, although they are not necessary synonymous with ecotourism.

The problems associated with defining ecotourism have led to confusion among tourists and academics alike. Definitional problems are also subject of considerable public controversy and concern because of greenwashing, a trend towards the commercialization of tourism schemes disguised as sustainable, nature based, and environmentally friendly ecotourism. According to McLaren, these schemes are environmentally destructive, economically exploitative, and culturally insensitive at its worst. They are also morally disconcerting because they mislead tourists and manipulate their concerns for the environment. Despite objections, greenwashing continues to grow unabated. The Nature's Sacred Paradise, a theme park in Quintana Roo, Mexico, is responsible for displacing local Mayan communities and illegally keeping endangered species in captivity to attract visitors. The development and success of such large scale, energy intensive, and ecologically unsustainable schemes are a testament to the tremendous profits associated with being labeled as ecotourism.

The Negative Psycho-social Impact of Ecotourism

Ecotourism is the trend towards the commercialization of tourism throughout the nation. This trend has become one of the fastest growing sectors of the tourism industry growing annual 10-15% worldwide (Kamuaro, 2007). Ecotourism was first introduced in Africa in the 1950's with the legalization of hunting (Kamuaro, 2007). This need for recreational hunting zones lead to the creation of protected areas, national parks, and game reserves. Today these areas have become important revenue-earning venues with the establishment of lodges and tourist campsites. One definition of ecotourism is "the practice of low-impact, educational, ecologically and culturally sensitive travel that benefits local communities and host countries" (Honey, 1999). Many of the ecotourism projects are not meeting these standards. Even if some of the guidelines are being executed, the local communities are still facing other negative impacts. South Africa is one of the countries that are reaping significant economic benefits from ecotourism, but negative effects including, physical displacement of persons, gross violation of fundamental rights, and environmental hazards far out weigh the medium-term economic benefits (Kamuaro, 2007). A tremendous amount of money is being spent and human resources continue to be used for ecotourism despite the lack of success stories, and even more money is put into public relation campaigns to dilute the effects of the criticism. Ecotourism channels resources away from other projects that could contribute more sustainable and realistic solutions to pressing social and environmental problems. "The money tourism can generate often ties parks and managements to eco-tourism" (Walpole et al. 2001).

But there is a tension in this relationship because eco-tourism often causes conflict and changes in land-use rights, fails to deliver promises of community-level benefits, damages environments, and has plenty of other social impacts. Indeed many argue repeatedly that eco-tourism is neither ecologically nor socially beneficial, yet it persists as a strategy for conservation and development (West, 2006). While several studies are being done on ways to improve the ecotourism structure, these examples provide reason that it should just stop all together.

The ecotourism system exercises tremendous financial and political influence. The evidence above shows that at the very least a strong case exists for restraining such activities. Funding could be used for field studies aimed at finding alternative solutions to tourism and the diverse problems Africa faces in result of urbanization, industrialization, and over exploitation of agriculture (Kamuaro, 2007). At the local level ecotourism has become a source of conflict over control of land, resources, and tourism profits. There are many problems with the idea of ecotourism. Environmental, the effects on the local people, and conflicts over profit distribution are only a few of the negative effects of ecotourism. In a perfect world more efforts would be made towards educating tourists of the environmental and social effects of their travels. Very few regulations or laws stand in place as boundaries for the investors in ecotourism. These should be implemented to prohibit the promotion of unsustainable ecotourism projects and materials which project false images of destinations, demeaning local and indigenous cultures.

Direct Environmental Impacts

Ecotourism operations typically fail to live up to conservation ideals. It is often overlooked that ecotourism is a highly consumer-centered activity, and that environmental conservation is only a means to further economic growth.

Although ecotourism is intended for small groups, even a modest increase in population, however temporary, puts extra pressure on the local environment and necessitates the development of additional infrastructure and amenities. The construction of water treatment plants, sanitation facilities, and lodges come with the exploitation of non-renewable energy sources and the utilization of already limited local resources. The conversion of natural land to such tourist infrastructure is implicated in deforestation and habitat deterioration of butterflies in Mexico and squirrel monkeys in Costa Rica. In other cases, the environment suffers because local communities are unable to meet the infrastructure demands of ecotourism. The lack of adequate sanitation facilities in many East African parks results in the disposal of campsite sewage in rivers, contaminating the wildlife, livestock, and people who draw drinking water from it.

Aside from environmental degradation with tourist infrastructure, population pressures from ecotourism also leaves behind garbage and pollution associated with the Western lifestyle. Although ecotourists claim to be educationally sophisticated and environmentally concerned, they rarely understand the ecological consequences of their visits and how their day-to-day activities append physical impacts on the environment.

As one scientist observes, they "rarely acknowledge how the meals they eat, the toilets they flush, the water they drink, and so on, are all part of broader regional economic and ecological systems they are helping to reconfigure with their very activities." Nor do ecotourists recognize the great consumption of non-renewable energy required to arrive at their destination, which is typically more remote than conventional tourism destinations.

For instance, an exotic journey to a place 10,000 kilometers away consumes about 700 liters of fuel per person.

Ecotourism activities are, in of itself, issues in environmental impact because they disturb fauna and flora. Ecotourists believe that because they are only taking pictures and leaving footprints, they keep ecotourism sites pristine, but even harmless sounding activities such as a nature hike can be ecologically destructive.

In the Annapurna Circuit in Nepal, ecotourists have worn down the marked trails and created alternate routes, contributing to soil impaction, erosion, and plant damage. Where the ecotourism activity involves wildlife viewing, it can scare away animals, disrupt their feeding and nesting sites, or acclimate them to the presence of people. In Kenya, disruption of wildlife observers drive cheetahs off their reserves, increasing the risk of inbreeding and further endangering the species.

Environmental Hazards

We already understand that biodiversity and environmentally intact lands form the basis of ecological stability. Unfortunately, industrialization, urbanization, and unsustainable agriculture practices have all had serious effects on the environment. Ecotourism is now also playing a role in this depletion. While the term ecotourism may sound relatively benign, one of its most serious impacts is its consumption of virgin territories (Kamuaro, 2007). These invasions often include deforestation, disruption of ecological life systems and various forms of pollution, all of which contribute to environmental degradation. The number of motor vehicles crossing the park increases as tour drivers search for rare species. The number of roads has disrupted the grass cover which has serious effects on plant and animal species. These areas also have a higher rate of disturbances and invasive species because of all the traffic moving off the beaten path into new undiscovered areas (Kamuaro, 2007). Ecotourism also has an affect on species through the value placed on them. "Certain species have gone from being little known or valued by local people to being highly valued commodities. The commodification of plants may erase their social value and lead to overproduction within protected areas. Local people and their images can also be turned into commodities" (West, 2006). Kamuaro brings up a relatively obvious contradiction, any commercial venture into unspoiled, pristine land with or without the "eco" prefix as a contradiction in terms. To generate revenue you have to have a high number of traffic, tourists, which inevitably means a higher pressure on the environment.

Local Peoples

Most forms of ecotourism are owned by foreign investors and corporations that provide few benefits to local communities. An overwhelming majority of profits are put into the pockets of investors instead of reinvestment into the local economy or environmental protection. The limited numbers of local people who are employed in the economy enter at its lowest level, and are unable to live in tourist areas because of meager wages and a two market system. In some cases, the resentment by local people results in environmental degradation. As a highly publicized case, the Maasai nomads in Kenya killed wildlife in national parks to show aversion to unfair compensation terms and displacement from traditional lands. The lack of economic opportunities for local people also constrains them to degrade the environment as a means of sustenance. The presence of affluent ecotourists encourage the development of destructive markets in wildlife souvenirs, such as the sale of coral trinkets on tropical islands and animal products in Asia, contributing to illegal harvesting and poaching from the environment. In Surinam, sea turtle reserves use a large portion of their budget to guard against these activities.

Displacement of People

One of the most powerful examples of communities being moved in order to create a park is the story of the Masai. About 70% of national parks and game reserves in East Africa are on Masai land (Kamuaro, 2007). The first undesirable impact of tourism was that of the extent of land lost from the Masai culture. Local and national governments took advantage of the Masai's ignorance on the situation and robbed them of huge chunks of grazing land, putting to risk their only socioeconomic livelihood. In Kenya the Masai also have not gained any economic benefits. Despite lose of their land, employment favors better educated workers. Further more the investors in this area are not local and have not put profits back into local economy. In some cases game reserves can be created without informing or consulting local people, who come to find out about the situation when an eviction notice is delivered (Kamuaro, 2007).

Another source of resentment is the manipulation of the local people by their government. "Eco-tourism works to create simplistic images of local people and their uses and understandings of their surroundings. Through the lens of these simplified images, officials direct policies and projects towards the local people and the local people are blamed if the projects fail" (West, 2006). Clearly tourism as a trade is not empowering the local people who make it rich and satisfying. Instead ecotourism exploits and depletes, particularly in African Masai tribes. It has to be reoriented to serve useful to local communities and to become sustainable.

Threats to Indigenous Cultures

Ecotourism often claims that it preserves and "enhances" local cultures. However, evidence shows that with the establishment of protected areas local people have illegally lost their homes, and most often with no compensation (Kamuaro, 2007). What about pushing people onto marginal lands with harsh climates, poor soils, lack of water, and infested with livestock and disease is "enhancing"? The establishment of parks does nothing but create harsh survival realities and deprives the people of their traditional use of land and natural resources. Ethnic groups are increasingly being seen as a "backdrop" to the scenery and wildlife. The local people struggle for cultural survival and freedom of cultural expression while being "observed" by tourists. Local indigenous people also have strong resentment towards the change, "Tourism has been allowed to develop with virtually no controls. Too many lodges have been built, too much firewood is being used and no limits are being placed on tourism vehicles. They regularly drive off-track and harass the wildlife. Their vehicle tracks crisscross the entire Masai Mara. Inevitably the bush is becoming eroded and degraded" (Kamuaro, 2007).

Mismanagement of Ecotourism Sites

While governments are typically entrusted with the administration and enforcement of environmental protection, they often lack the commitment or capability to manage ecotourism sites effectively. The regulations for environmental protection may be vaguely defined, costly to implement, hard to enforce, and uncertain in effectiveness. Government regulatory agencies, as political bodies, are susceptible to making decisions that spend budget on politically beneficial but environmentally unproductive projects. Because of prestige and conspicuousness, the construction of an attractive visitor's center at an ecotourism site may take precedence over more pressing environmental concerns like acquiring habitat, protecting endemic species, and removing invasive ones. Finally, influential groups can pressure and sway the interests of the government to their favor. The government and its regulators can become vested in the benefits of the ecotourism industry which they are supposed to regulate, causing restrictive environmental regulations and enforcement to become more lenient.

Management of ecotourism sites by private ecotourism companies offers an alternative to the cost of regulation and deficiency of government agencies. It is believed that these companies have a self interest in limited environmental degradation, because tourists will pay more for pristine environments, which translates to higher profit. However, theory indicates that this practice is not economically feasible and will fail to manage the environment.

The model of monopolistic competition states that distinctiveness will entail profits, but profits will promote imitation. A company that protects its ecotourism sites is able to charge a premium for the novel experience and pristine environment. But when other companies view the success of this approach, they also enter the market with similar practices, increasing competition and reducing demand. Eventually, the demand will be reduced until the economic profit is zero. A cost-benefit analysis shows that the company bears the cost of environmental protection without receiving the gains. Without economic incentive, the whole premise of self interest through environmental protection is quashed; instead, ecotourism companies will minimize environment related expenses and maximize tourism demand.

The tragedy of the commons offers another model for economic unsustainability from environmental protection, in ecotourism sites utilized by many companies. Although there is a communal incentive to protect the environment, maximizing the benefits in the long run, a company will conclude that it is in their best interest to utilize the ecotourism site beyond its sustainable level. By increasing the number of ecotourists, for instance, a company gains all the economic benefit while paying only a part of the environmental cost. In the same way, a company recognizes that there is no incentive to actively protect the environment; they bear all the costs, while the benefits are shared by all other companies. The result, again, is mismanagement.

Taken together, the mobility of foreign investment and lack of economic incentive for environmental protection means that ecotourism companies are disposed to establishing themselves in new sites once their existing one is sufficiently degraded.

IMPROVING SUSTAINABILITY

Regulation and Accreditation

Because the regulation of ecotourism is poorly implemented or nonexistent, ecologically destructive greenwashed operations like underwater hotels, helicopter tours, and wildlife theme parks are categorized as ecotourism along with canoeing, camping, photography, and wildlife observation. The failure to acknowledge responsible, low impact ecotourism puts these companies at a competitive disadvantage.

Many environmentalists have argued for a global standard of accreditation, differentiating ecotourism companies based on their level of environmental commitment. A national or international regulatory board would enforce accreditation procedures, with representation from various groups including governments, hotels, tour operators, travel agents, guides, airlines, local authorities, conservation organizations, and non-governmental organizations. The decisions of the board would be sanctioned by governments, so that non-compliant companies would be legally required to disassociate themselves from the use of the ecotourism brand.

Crinion suggests a Green Stars System based on criteria including a management plan, benefit for the local community, small group interaction, education value, and staff training. Ecotourists who consider their choices would be confident of a genuine ecotourism experience when they see the higher star rating.

In addition, environmental impact assessments could be used as a form of accreditation. Feasibility is evaluated from a scientific basis, and recommendations could be made to optimally plan infrastructure, set tourist capacity, and manage the ecology. This form of accreditation is more sensitive to site specific conditions.

Guidelines and Education for Ecotourists

An environmental protection strategy must address the issue of ecotourists removed from the cause-and-effect of their actions on the environment. More initiatives should be carried out to improve their awareness, sensitize them to environmental issues, and care about the places they visit.

Tour guides are an obvious and direct medium to communicate awareness. With the confidence of ecotourists and intimate knowledge of the environment, they can actively discuss conservation issues. A tour guide training program in Costa Rica's Tortuguero National Park has helped mitigate negative environmental impacts by providing information and regulating tourists on the parks' beaches used by nesting endangered sea turtles.

Small Scale, Slow Growth, Locally based Ecotourism

The underdevelopment theory of tourism describes a new form of imperialism by multinational corporations that control ecotourism resources. These corporations finance and profit from the development of large scale ecotourism that causes excessive environmental degradation, loss of traditional culture and way of life, and exploitation of local labor. In Zimbabwe and Nepal's Annapurna region, where underdevelopment is taking place, more than 90 percent of ecotourism revenues are expatriated to the parent countries, and less than 5 percent go into local communities.

The lack of sustainability highlights the need for small scale, slow growth, and locally based ecotourism. Local peoples have a vested interest in the well being of their community, and are therefore more accountable to environmental protection than multinational corporations. The lack of control, westernization, adverse impacts to the environment, loss of culture and traditions outweigh the benefits of establishing large scale ecotourism.

The increased contributions of communities to locally managed ecotourism create viable economic opportunities, including high level management positions, and reduce environmental issues associated with poverty and unemployment. Because the ecotourism experience is marketed to a different lifestyle from large scale ecotourism, the development of facilities and infrastructure does not need to conform to corporate Western tourism standards, and can be much simpler and less expensive. There is a greater multiplier effect on the economy, because local products, materials, and labor are used. Profits accrue locally, and import leakages are reduced. However, even this form of tourism may require foreign investment for promotion or start up. When such investments are required, it is cruical for communities for find a company or non-governmental organization that reflects the philosophy of ecotourism; sensitive to their concerns and willing to cooperate at the expense of profit.

The basic assumption of the multiplier effect is that the economy starts off with unused resources, for example, that many workers are cyclically unemployed and much of industrial capacity is sitting idle or incompletely utilized. By increasing demand in the economy it is then possible to boost production. If the economy was already at full employment, with only structural, frictional, or other supply-side types of unemployment, any attempt to boost demand would only lead to inflation. For various laissez-faire schools of economics which embrace Say's Law and deny the possibility of Keynesian inefficiency and under-employment of resources, therefore, the multiplier concept is irrelevant or wrong-headed.

As an example, consider the government increasing its expenditure on roads by $1 million, without a corresponding increase in taxation. This sum would go to the road builders, who would hire more workers and distribute the money as wages and profits. The households receiving these incomes will save part of the money and spend the rest on consumer goods. These expenditures in turn will generate more jobs, wages, and profits, and so on with the income and spending circulating around the economy.

The multiplier effect arises because of the induced increases in consumer spending which occur due to the increased incomes—and because of the feedback into increasing business revenues, jobs, and income again. This process does not lead to an economic explosion not only because of the supply-side barriers at potential output (full employment) but because at each "round", the increase in consumer spending is less than the increase in consumer incomes. That is, the marginal propensity to consume (mpc) is less than one, so that each round some extra income goes into saving, leaking out of the cumulative process. Each increase in spending is thus smaller than that of the previous round, preventing an explosion.

EXTREME TOURISM

Extreme tourism or shock tourism is a type of niche tourism involving travel to dangerous places (mountains, jungles, deserts, caves, etc.) or participation in dangerous events. Extreme tourism overlaps with extreme sport. The two share the main attraction, "adrenaline rush" caused by an element of risk, and differing mostly in the degree of engagement and professionalism.

Extreme tourism is a growing business in the countries of the former Soviet Union (Russia, Ukraine, Armenia, etc.) and in South American countries like Peru, Chile and Argentina. The mountainous and rugged terrain of Northern Pakistan has also developed into a popular extreme tourism location.

While traditional tourism requires significant investments in hotels, roads, etc., extreme tourism requires much less to jump-start a business. In addition to traditional travel-based tourism destinations, various exotic attractions are suggested, such as flyovers in MiGs at 2.5 Mach, ice diving in the White Sea, or travelling across the Chernobyl zone.

FEMALE SEX TOURISM

Female sex tourism is travel by women, partially or fully for the purpose of having sex.

Overview

Female sex tourism differs from male sex tourism in that women do not use bars, sex shows and formal tours to meet foreign men. There are "de facto" tours, however, such as airplanes bound to the Gambia in West Africa full of British and Scandinavian women seeking affairs with beach boys.

Often such trips are referred to by women as "romance tourism."

Women usually give clothes, meals, cash and gifts to their male prostitutes. In some destinations, there are "going rates" for male companionship, ranging from $50 to $200. In few destinations, especially in Southern Europe, Turkey, Bali and the French Caribbean, men do not expect to be compensated.

Destinations

While men tend to go to Asia for sex tourism, women tend to head to the Caribbean, Southern Europe, and Africa. The patterns have been explored by Michel Houellebecq in Platform and in the non-fiction work Romance on the Road, and are important in that they support the idea that sex tourism by both men and women reflects serious problems in the tourists' home countries, including a dating war, or profound conflict between the sexes.

Thailand, the Dominican Republic and Cuba are exceptional in that both male and female sex tourists find these places all-purpose sexual emporia.

The primary destinations for female sex tourism are Southern Europe (mainly Italy, Greece, Turkey, Croatia and Spain), the Caribbean (led by Jamaica, Barbados and the Dominican Republic), Ghana and Kenya in Africa, Bali in Indonesia and Phuketin Thailand. Lesser destinations include Nepal, Morocco, Fiji, Ecuador and Costa Rica.

Lesbian sex tourism is nascent but evident in Lesbos (Mytilini) in Greece; Bangkok and Pattaya in Thailand, and on Bali in Indonesia.

Terms used for Female Sex Tourists

Tourist women are called Shirley Valentines (if British), longtails (in Bermuda), yellow cabs (Japan) and, in Jamaica, milk bottles if newly arrived or Stellas if black. Female sex tourism in Barbados has been dubbed "Canadian secretary syndrome."

The men who chase tourist women are kamakia ("fishing harpoons," Greece),galebovi ("seagulls,"Croatia), sharks (Costa Rica), rent-a-dreads, rent-a-rastas, rent-a-gents and the Foreign Service (Caribbean), Kuta Cowboys or pemburu-bule ("whitey hunters," Bali), Marlboro men (Jordan), bomsas or bumsters (the Gambia), sanky pankies (Dominican Republic), "gringa hunter" in Ecuador and "brichero" in Peru.

History

Barring some isolated cases of women traveling for sex among North American Indian tribes and within Turkey, female travel sex (involving American and English women) began in Rome in the late 1840s, at the same time as feminism's first wave, which encouraged independence and travel.

Affairs and intrigues, particularly between American heiresses and down-on their luck European aristocrats, continued steadily until World War I and inspired Henry James's Daisy Miller, Joaquin Miller's The One Fair Woman, and much of the early output of E.M. Forster.

Female sex travel declined from the time of the Depression until the 1960s, with the exception of India, Nepal and Thailand, where intrepid women from England, France, Czechoslovakia, the United States and elsewhere continued to attract the attention of maharajas and other Asian royals, despite the uproar of World War II.

Coincident with the explosion of leisure travel in the 1960s and feminism's second wave, sex tourism by women re-ignited, first via French Canadian women traveling to Barbados and Swedish and Northern European women to Spain, Greece, Yugoslavia and the Gambia. Female sex travel became ubiquitous throughout the Caribbean, from the tiniest islands through the big destinations of Jamaica, the Dominican Republic and Barbados.

In the 1990s, women from Japan and Taiwan began to appear on the beaches of Bali and Phuket in Thailand.

Today, many other destinations are popular, including Morocco, Nepal, Thailand, Ecuador, Costa Rica, Mexico—everywhere with beaches (or in Nepal's case, mountains) and a surplus of underemployed men.

Reasons

Female sex tourism's first and second waves coincided not only with feminism but with Victorian-era man shortages that began in England and later cropped in continental Europe and the United States.

Other societal reasons for women seeking intimate companionship abroad include the dating war, as typified by extreme competition between the sexes in schools, the workplace, while dating, in marriages, and even in contentious divorces. The dating war appears to especially drive sex tourism by Australian and Japanese women, and to a lesser extent, German and Scandinavian female tourists.

Another factor in women engaging in holiday romance is identity loss. Many women behave while traveling in a way at odds to how they behave at home, where fear of the "slut" label curbs the kind of hedonistic behavior seen on holiday. Traveling and expatriate women often try on a new, more experimental identity when away from family and friends.

Additional reasons include:

- sexual connoisseurship—an interest in experiencing a variety of men
- a search for healing after a divorce or breakup (see Michelle Thomas, in Major academic publications, below)
- prolonged involuntary celibacy
- the commodification of sex, whereby affection is now something that can be purchased by women, as well as men, as well as the globalization of sex and affection markets
- interest in fulfilling sexual fantasies

Depictions

Non-fiction books include Anne Cumming's The Love Habit and The Love Quest, Fiona Pitt-Kethley's The Pan Principle and Journeys to the Underworld, Cleo Odzer's Patpong Sisters and Lucretia Stewart's The Weather Prophet.

Female sex tourists have been notoriously difficult to find and interview on the record (see de Albuquerque, 1998, in "Major academic publications" subheading, below). Thus some observers have turned to film and fiction to examine the motivations of women who travel for sex, love and affection. Movies include Heading South (Vers le Sud), with Charlotte Rampling which depicts three Western tourists in Haiti in the 1970s, taking their pleasure with local men. Earlier film depictions include How Stella Got Her Groove Back and Shirley Valentine. Stella led to a quantifiable increase in trips by women to Jamaica, according to Michele Faul's Associated Press article, 12/6/1998, " 'Stella' the Movie Attracting Single Women to Jamaica."

SEX TOURISM

Sex tourism is travel to engage in sexual intercourse or sexual activity with prostitutes, and is typically undertaken internationally by tourists from wealthier countries whose payment for services may then be rendered either in cash or in kind.

The World Tourism Organization, a specialized agency of the United Nations, defines sex tourism as "trips organized from within the tourism sector, or from outside this sector but using its structures and networks, with the primary purpose of effecting a commercial sexual relationship by the tourist with residents at the destination". The U.N. opposes sex tourism citing health, social and cultural consequences for both tourist home countries and destination countries, especially in situations exploiting gender, age, social and economic inequalities in sex tourism destinations.

Attractions for sex tourists can include reduced costs for services in the destination country, along with either legal prostitution or indifferent law enforcement and access to child prostitution.

Destinations

National destinations for sex tourists include Thailand, Brazil, Dominican Republic, Costa Rica, and Cuba. An individual city or region can have a particular reputation as a sex tourist destination. Many of these coincide with major red-light districts, and include Amsterdam in the Netherlands; Zona Norte in Tijuana, Mexico; Bangkok, Pattaya and Phuket in Thailand; Vladivostok in Russian Far East, destination for Japanese sex tourists, and Angeles City, the site of a former United States military base in the province of Pampanga, Philippines. In the United States, prostitution is largely illegal, with the exception of rural areas of the state of Nevada; these have become a sex tourist destination for some Americans. To a lesser extent, several other large cities in the U.S. are also domestic sex tourist destinations despite legal sanctions on prostitution.

Conversely, prostitution is a legal activity in a growing list of other nations worldwide including in many of these destinations.

Female Sex Tourism Destinations

The primary destinations for female sex tourism are Southern Europe (mainly Italy, former Yugoslavia, Turkey, Greece and Spain), the Caribbean (led by Jamaica, Barbados and the Dominican Republic), parts of Africa, Pattaya or Phuket in Thailand. Lesser destinations include Nepal, Morocco, Fiji, Ecuador and Costa Rica. Female sex tourism differs from male sex tourism, in that women do not usually go to specific bars. Women usually give clothes, meals, cash and gifts to their prostitutes, but not all (especially in Southern Europe) expect compensation.

Criminality and Controversy

Tourism Involving Sex with Minors

Child Wise defines child sex tourism as "the commercial sexual exploitation of children by foreigners", usually referring to:

- travel to other countries to engage in sexual acts with children, or
- foreigners engaging in sexual activity with children while overseas

While most sex tourists only engage in this activity with other adults, some actively look for child prostitutes, while others are not very selective either way regarding age. The WTO makes a distinction between "sex tourism" and "child sex tourism." A tourist who has sex with a child prostitute offends the spirit of the international Convention on the Rights of the Child and the Optional protocol on the sale of children, child prostitution and child pornography, and, in addition to breaking the law in the host country, might well also be doing so in the country the tourist is a national of. A growing number of countries are enacting laws with extra-territorial reach in order to meet their obligations under the covenants above, and consequently punishing citizens who engage in sex with minors whilst overseas. But being difficult to police and enforce these crimes continue nonetheless.

The term "child" is often used as defined by the international conventions above and refers to any person below the age of consent. Many countries have signed the Worst Forms of Child Labour Convention, 1999 and implemented domestic law making having sex with child prostitutes a criminal offence for their nationals or inhabitants including when practised abroad regardless of whether it is forbidden by the laws of the destination country. Singapore has been criticized for having no such law, in spite of being adjacent to the sex tourism destination of Batam in Indonesia, which has many underage sex workers, many of whom have been forced into prostitution.

In 2004 Canada started to prosecute individuals under the sex tourism law. The first individual charged in Canada under this law was Donald Bakker. Australia has long done so: with a conviction in 1996 after enactment of legislation in 1994. Its Government has, for example, caused an international political incident in pressing for the extradition of suspended Solomon Islands Attorney-General Julian Moti, an Australian citizen, to face possible charges over alleged offences dating back to 1997.

According to the Cambodia minister for Woman's Affairs, it is not tourists who are the prime culprits of pedophilia in her country, but the locals.

Legal Issues in the United States

Federal law (see PROTECT Act of 2003) prohibits United States citizens or permanent residents to engage in international travel with the purpose or effect of having commercial sex with a person under the age of 18, or any sex with a person under the age of 16; facilitating such travel is also illegal. Arrests by Immigration and Customs Enforcement are becoming common, however prosecutions under this law are still very rare.

As of 2005, there has been one effort to prosecute a sex tour operator: Big Apple Oriental Tours of New York was prosecuted for "promotion of prostitution" by the New York State Attorney General after lobbying by feminist human rights groups, however the case has been thrown out twice.

HR 972, the Trafficking Victims Protection Reauthorization Act of 2005 reauthorizes the 2000 law, but it also gives U.S. law enforcement better tools to study human trafficking within the United States and to prosecute those who purchase sex acts. The measure authorizes $50 million for grants to state and local law enforcement to investigate and prosecute persons who engage in the purchase of commercial sex acts.

Scandals

In 2005 it was reported that Philippe Servaty, a newspaper columnist for Le Soir, traveled to Morocco where he persuaded women to engage in sexual activity by promising to marry and bring them to Belgium. He then posted photos online to boast of his conquests, but when his explicit materials were circulated back to Morocco many of the women were arrested, had their lives ruined, committed suicide or disappeared.

Academic Study

University of Leicester sociologists studied this subject as part of a research project for the Economic and Social Research Council and End Child Prostitution and Trafficking campaign. The study included interviews with over 250 Caribbean sex tourists. Among their findings:

- Preconceptions about race and gender influenced their opinions.
- Economically underdeveloped tourist-receiving countries are promoted as being culturally different so that (in the Western tourist's understanding) prostitution and traditional male domination of women have less stigma than similar practices might have in their home countries.

Documentaries

Canadian film makers have been active at reporting on sex tourism. Documentary titles include:

- Falang: Behind Bangkok's Smile by Jordon Clark (2005) (this title at the Internet Movie Database), set in Thailand

- the CBC series, the Lens episode "Selling Sex in Heaven" (2005) (this title at the Internet Movie Database), set in the Philippines.
- Channel 4 Cutting Edge episode "The Child Sex Trade" (2003), set in Romania, Italy

Depictions in Fiction and Popular Culture

- The 2005 film Heading South describes the experiences of a group of middle-aged women in the late 1970s, who travel to Haiti for the purposes of sexual tourism.
- In the animated TV series South Park the character Chef joins the Super Adventure Club which travels the world having sex with children.
- Sex tourism is a major theme of Platform, a novel by Michel Houellebecq.
- In the 2005 film Hostel, directed by Eli Roth, depicts sex tourism in Slovakia
- The film Macho Dancer deals with male sex workers in Manila. It includes characters who are female prostitutes.

TRAFFICKING IN HUMAN BEINGS

Trafficking of human beings is the recruitment, transportation, transfer, harbouring or receipt of people for the purpose of exploitation. Trafficking involves a process of using illicit means such as threat, use of force, or other forms of coercion, of abduction, of fraud, of deception, of the abuse of power or of a position of vulnerability.

Exploitation includes forcing people into prostitution or other forms of sexual exploitation, forced labour or services, slavery or practices similar to slavery, servitude or the removal of organs. For children exploitation may include also, illicit international adoption, trafficking for early marriage, recruitment as child soldiers, for begging or for sports (such as child camel jockeys or football players), or for recruitment for religious cults.

Overview

Human trafficking differs from people smuggling. In the latter, people voluntarily request smuggler's service for fees and there may be no deception involved in the (illegal) agreement.

On arrival at their destination, the smuggled person is usually free. On the other hand, the trafficking victim is enslaved, or the terms of their debt bondage are fraudulent or highly exploitative. The trafficker takes away the basic human rights of the victim. Victims are sometimes tricked and lured by false promises or physically forced. Some traffickers use coercive and manipulative tactics including deception, intimidation, feigned love, isolation, threat and use of physical force, debt bondage, other abuse, or even force-feeding with drugs to control their victims.

In the case of children, such practices are considered child trafficking even if none of the illicit means previously described are used.

Trafficked people usually come from the poorer regions of the world, where opportunities are limited, and are often from the most vulnerable in society, such as runaways, refugees, or other displaced persons, (though they may come from any social background, class or race. People who are seeking entry to other countries may be picked up by traffickers, and-typically-misled into thinking that they will be free after being smuggled across the border. In some cases, they are captured through slave raiding, although this is increasingly rare.

Trafficking of children often involves exploitation of the parents' extreme poverty. The latter may sell children to traffickers in order to pay off debts or gain income or they may be deceived concerning the prospects of training and a better life for their children. In West Africa, trafficked children have often lost one or both parents to the African AIDS crisis.

Women, who form over 80% of trafficking victims, are particularly at risk to become involved in sex trafficking. Potential kidnappers exploit lack of opportunities, promise good jobs or opportunities for study, and then force the victims to become prostitutes, participate in pornography or escort services. Through agents and brokers who arrange the travel and job placements, women are escorted to their destinations and delivered to the employers. Upon reaching their destinations, some women learn that they have been deceived about the nature of the work they will do; most have been lied to about the financial arrangements and conditions of their employment; and all find themselves in coercive and abusive situations from which escape is both difficult and dangerous.

The main motive of a woman (in some cases an underage girl) to accept an offer from a trafficker is better financial opportunities for herself or her family. In many cases traffickers initially offer 'legitimate' work or the promise of an opportunity to study. The main types of work offered are in the catering and hotel industry, in bars and clubs, modeling contracts, or au pair work. Offers of marriage are sometimes used by traffickers as well as threats, intimidation and kidnapping. In the majority of cases, the women end up in prostitution. Also some (migrating) prostitutes become victims of human trafficking. Some women know they will be working as prostitutes, but they have a too-rosy picture of the circumstances and the conditions of the work in the country of destination.

Men are also at risk of being trafficked for unskilled work predominantly involving hard labor. Other forms of trafficking include bonded and sweatshop labor, forced marriage, and domestic servitude. Children are also trafficked for both labor exploitation and sexual exploitation. On a related issue, children are forced to be child soldiers.

Many women are forced into the sex trade after answering false advertisements, and others are simply kidnapped. Thousands of children from Asia, Africa, and South America are sold into the global sex trade every year. Often they are kidnapped or orphaned, and sometimes they are actually sold by their own families.

Extent

United States State Department data "estimated 600,000 to 820,000 men, women, and children [are] trafficked across international borders each year, approximately 80 percent are women and girls and up to 50 percent are minors. The data also illustrate that the majority of transnational victims are trafficked into commercial sexual exploitation." Due to the illegal nature of trafficking and differences in methodology, the exact extent is unknown.

An estimated 14,000 people are trafficked into the United States each year, although again because trafficking is illegal, accurate statistics are difficult. According to the Massachusetts based Trafficking Victims Outreach and Services Networkin Massachusetts alone, there were 55 documented cases of human trafficking in 2005 and the first half of 2006 in Massachusetts. In 2004, the Royal Canadian Mounted Police (RCMP) estimated that 600-800 persons are trafficked into Canada annually and that additional 1,500-2,200 persons are trafficked through Canada into the United States.

In the United Kingdom, 71 women were known to have been trafficked into prostitution in 1998 and the Home Office recognized that the scale is likely greater as the problem is hidden and research estimates that the actual figure could be up to 1,420 women trafficked into the UK during the same period. Trafficking in people is increasing in Africa, South Asia and into North America.

Russia is a major source of women trafficked globally for the purpose of sexual exploitation. Annually, thousands of Russian women end up as prostitutes in China, Japan or South Korea. Russia is also a significant destination and transit country for persons trafficked for sexual and labor exploitation from regional and neighboring countries into Russia, and on to the Gulf states, Europe, Asia, and North America. The ILO estimates that 20 percent of the five million illegal immigrants in Russia are victims of forced labor, which is a form of trafficking. There were reports of trafficking of children and of child sex tourism in Russia. The Government of Russia has made some effort to combat trafficking but has also been criticized for not complying with the minimum standards for the elimination of trafficking.

The majority of child trafficking cases are in Asia, although it is a global problem. In Thailand, non-governmental organisations (NGO) have estimated that up to a third of prostitutes are children under 18, many trafficked from outside Thailand. In Ukraine, a survey conducted by the NGO "La Strada-Ukraine" in 2001-2003, based on a sample of 106 women being trafficked out of Ukraine found that 3% were under 18, and the US State Department reported in 2004 that incidents of minors being trafficked was increasing.

In Asia, Japan is the major destination country for trafficked women, especially from the Philippines and Thailand. The US

State Department has rated Japan as either a 'Tier 2' or a 'Tier 2 Watchlist' country every year since 2001 in its annual Trafficking in Persons reports. Both these ratings implied that Japan was (to a greater or lesser extent) not fully compliant with minimum standards for the elimination of human trafficking trade.

In Ukraine, a survey conducted by the NGO "La Strada-Ukraine" in 2001-2003, based on a sample of 106 women being trafficked out of Ukraine found that 3% were under 18, and the US State Department reported in 2004 that incidents of minors being trafficked was increasing.

In the United Kingdom, Vietnamese human trafficking have been discovered in the past few years. Many Vietnamese people are trafficked to work in illegal Vietnamese cannabis factories throughout the country, as the recent police Operation Keymer showed. Another recent police Operation Pentameter discovered illegal Vietnamese are also smuggled in to work in Vietnamese nail salons. Recently the UK authority planned to deport over 500 children back to Vietnam who had been smuggled into the country.

Reporters have witnessed a rapid increase in prostitution in Cambodia, Bosnia, and Kosovo after UN and, in the case of the latter two, NATO peacekeeping forces moved in. Peacekeeping forces have been linked to trafficking and forced prostitution. Proponents of peacekeeping argue that the actions of a few should not incriminate the many participants in the mission, yet NATO and the UN have come under criticism for not taking the issue of forced prostitution linked to peacekeeping missions seriously enough. In the western world, Canada in particular has a major problem with modern-day sexual slavery. In a 2006 report the Future Group, a Canadian humanitarian organization dedicated to ending human trafficking, ranked eight industrialized nations and gave Canada an F for its "abysmal" record treating victims. The report, titled "Falling Short of the Mark: An International Study on the Treatment of Human Trafficking Victims", concluded that Canada "is an international embarrassment" when it comes to combatting this form of slavery.

The report's principal author Benjamin Perrin wrote, "Canada has ignored calls for reform and continues to re-traumatize trafficking victims, with few exceptions, by subjecting them to routine deportation and fails to provide even basic support services."

In the report, the only other country to flunk was the United Kingdom, which received a D, while the United States received a B+ and Australia, Norway, Sweden, Germany and Italy all received grades of B or B-. The report criticizes former Liberal Party of Canada cabinet ministers Irwin Cotler, Joe Volpe and Pierre Pettigrew for "passing the buck" on the issue. Commenting on the report, the then Minister of Citizenship and Immigration, Monte Solberg told Sun Media Corporation, "It's very damning, and if there are obvious legislative or regulatory fixes that need to be done, those have to become priorities, given especially that we're talking about very vulnerable people."

Cause of Trafficking

Some causes of trafficking include:

- poverty
- perceived higher standards of life elsewhere
- lack of employement opportunities
- organised crime and presence of organised criminal gangs
- regional imbalances
- economic disparities
- social discrimination
- corruption in governement
- political instability
- armed conflict
- uprooting of communities because of mega projects without proper Resttlement and Rehabilitation packages.
- Profitability
- Growing deprivation and marginalization of the poor
- Insufficient penalties against traffickers
- According to the UN a major factor that has allowed the growth of sexual trafficking is "Governments and human rights organizations alike have simply judged the woman guilty of prostitution and minimized the trafficker's role."

- Driven by demand; demand is high for prostitutes and other forms of labor in host countries; therefore there is a very profitable market available to those who wish to become handlers.

Trafficking in people has been facilitated by porous borders and advanced communication technologies, it has become increasingly transnational in scope and highly lucrative. Unlike drugs or arms, people can be "sold" many times. The opening up of Asian markets, porous borders, the end of the Soviet Union and the collapse of the former Yugoslavia have contributed to this globalization.

Government Action against Human Trafficking

A human trafficking awareness poster from the Canadian Department of Justice Actions taken to combat human trafficking vary from government to government. Some have introduced legislation specifically aimed at making human trafficking illegal. Governments can also develop systems of co-operation between different nation's law enforcement agencies and with non-government organisations (NGOs).

Other actions governments could take is raise awareness. This can take on three forms. Firstly in raising awareness amongst potential victims, in particular in countries where human traffickers are active. Secondly, raising awareness amongst police, social welfare workers and immigration officers. And in countries where prostitution is legal or semi-legal, raising awareness amongst the clients of prostitution, to look out for signs of a human trafficking victim.

Laws against trafficking in the United States are prosecuted at the federal level. The overwhelming majority of states do not have laws against human trafficking. For example, in Maryland it is a felony to have sex with a minor, but only a misdemeanor for making it available to those who wish to have sex with a minor. Raising awareness can take on different forms. One method is through the use of awareness films or through posters.

Criticism of Bangladesh on Human Trafficking

In June 2006, the government of Bangladesh issued a restraining order preventing Sigma Huda, U.N. special reporter on trafficking in persons, from leaving the country to deliver a key report on trafficking before the Human Rights Council in Geneva on June 11, 2007. U.N. High Commissioner for Human Rights Louise Arbour has asked Bangladesh to clarify corruption charges against a U.N. human rights investigator, which will prevent her from addressing the main U.N. rights body. The Coalition Against Trafficking in Women issued a statement calling this "an outrage and a violation of her right to freedom of movement and freedom of speech."

International Law

In 2000 the United Nations adopted the Convention against Transnational Organized Crime, also called the Palermo Convention and two Palermo protocols thereto:

- Protocol to Prevent, Suppress and Punish Trafficking in Persons, especially Women and Children; and
- Protocol against the Smuggling of Migrants by Land, Sea and Air.

All of these instruments contain elements of the current international law on trafficking in human beings.

Council of Europe

The Council of Europe Convention on Action against Trafficking in Human Beings was adopted by the Council of Europe on 16 May 2005. The aim of the convention is to prevent and combat the trafficking in human beings. Of the 46 members of the Council of Europe, so far 31 have signed the convention and 1 has ratified it.(29 June 2006).

United States Federal Law

The United States federal government has taken a firm stance against human trafficking both within its borders and beyond. Domestically, human trafficking is prosecuted through the Civil Rights Division, Criminal Section of the United States Department of Justice. Older statutes used to protect 13th Amendment rights within United States borders are Title 18 U.S.C., Sections 1581 and 1584. Section 1584 makes it a crime to force a person to work against his will. This compulsion can be effected by use of force, threat of force, threat of legal coercion or by "a climate of fear", that is, an environment wherein individuals believe they may be harmed by leaving or refusing to work. Section 1581 similarly makes it illegal to force a person to work through "debt servitude".

New laws were passed under the Victims of Trafficking and Violence Protection Act of 2000. The new laws responded to a changing face of trafficking in the United States. It allowed for greater statutory maximum sentences for traffickers, provided resources for protection of and assistance for victims of trafficking and created avenues for inter-agency cooperation in the field of human trafficking. It also allows many trafficking victims to remain in the United States and apply for permanent residency. This law also attempted to encourage efforts to prevent human trafficking internationally, by creating annual country reports on trafficking, as well as by tying financial non-humanitarian assistance to foreign countries to real efforts in addressing human trafficking.

International NPOs, such as Human Rights Watch and Amnesty International, have called on the United States to improve its measures aimed at reducing trafficking. They recommend that the United States more fully implement the "United Nations Protocol to Prevent, Suppress and Punish Trafficking in Persons, Especially Women and Children" and the "United Nations Convention against Transnational Organized Crime" and for immigration officers to improve their awareness of trafficking and support the victims of trafficking.

United States State Law on Trafficking Several states have also written laws to address human trafficking in their borders. Florida has written trafficking statutes criminalizing forced labor, sex trafficking, and document servitude. Florida also provides for mandatory law enforcement trainings and victim services.

On May 8, 2006, Connecticut passed an act addressing human trafficking that criminalized coerced work, and made trafficking a violation of the Connecticut RICO Act.

Human Trafficking in Popular Culture

Lilya 4-ever, a film based loosely on the real life of Dangoule Rasalaite, portrays a young woman from the former Soviet

Union who is deceived into being trafficked for exploitation in Sweden. Human trafficking has also been portrayed in the Canadian/UK TV drama Sex Traffic. Based on true events, Svetlana's Journey by Michael Cory Davis depicts the trials of a 13-year-old who loses her family and is sold to human traffickers by her adoptive family. Drugged, raped, and forced to endure continuous abuse by her 'clients' and traffickers, she finally commits suicide.

The 2007 film Trade deals with human trafficking out of Mexico and a brother's attempt to rescue his kidnapped and trafficked young sister. It is based on Peter Landesman's article about sex slaves, which was featured as the cover story in the January 24, 2004 issue of New York Times Magazine.

The film The Transporter deals with the hero, Frank Martin, played by Jason Statham, trying to stop a container full of men and women being illegally transported. Human Trafficking (2005) (TV) by Christian Duguay stars Mira Sorvino, Donald Sutherland, and Richard Carlyle. A sixteen-year-old girl from the Ukraine, a single mother from Russia, an orphaned seventeen-year-old girl from Romania, and a twelve-year-old American tourist become the victims of international sex slave traffickers. Sorvino and Sutherland are the Immigration and Customs Enforcement (ICE) agents who struggle to save them.

FREE INDEPENDENT TRAVELER/TOURIST (FIT)

With world travel market having undergone significant changes over the last few years a new type of tourist has emerged known as the Free Independent Traveler or Tourist (FIT). The definition is broad but tends to refer to people over 35, often, though not necessarily, of above average income who like to travel in small groups, usually couples. They eschew mass tourism and the holiday package concept promoted by Travel operators, in favour of a more individualistic approach to travel.

There are two implications to the idea of the Free Independent Traveler. One is important in the context of a marketing niche with a distinct economic behaviour whilst the other concentrates more on the philosophy of travel. This distinction can be summarised in how they are described. For the economic importance of tourism and for marketing purposes they are Free

Independent Travelers (Upper case as they are an identifiable group within the market) whilst the people themselves are perhaps more attracted to the possibilities and lack of limitations in the concept of being a free, independent traveler.

Free Independent Travelers as an Alternative Movement

They tend to be environmentally aware, enjoy experiencing new ways of life and are enthusiastic, off the beaten track explorers practising for travel what the Slow Food Movement does for eating. They enjoy good food, architecture, and the heritage of local cultures. They tend to reject the traditional Package holiday model and even the Dynamic packaging system of doing things. People may garner information from a wide variety of sources or tips. The Guardian Newspaper's ivebeenthere site or Lonely Planet's forum are all examples and represent the fundamental difference between the FIT and other types of travel that this is about sharing and passing on of ideas and knowledge in accordance with the much talked about Web 2.0. The FIT vacation is a custom built cocktail then with suggestions from friends, forums, speciality providers or others creating the idea around which the vacation is built. The FITs themselves are responsible for adding components in place of the traditional package operators. The rise of low cost airlines in the US and Europe has also increased the supply of alternative and lower cost short haul destinations fueling demand for these newly available markets. Southwest Airlines in the US, Ryanair and easyJet in Europe and later Spanish, German and nationally orientated airlines grew up adding destinations and creating an internationally networked portfolio of air-routes delivering people to destinations that were not previously available at a commercial, international level.

The internet is fundamental to the rise of the FIT, offering them the suggestions, for example, of a good meal out in Rome from a fellow FIT, across the globe, who ate there last week.

Free Independent Travelers as an Economic Phenomenon

Here they are an important and growing sector in the market. Governments, regional tourist boards and other public sectors responsible for tourism development try to attract them.

Why? The basic principle is economics. FITs spread their money around in a more efficient fashion. Fifteen FITs will eat, sleep, snack, take a coffee, go to theatres/art shows/opera festivals/ football games/rural villages in fifteen different locations and introduce their money in hundreds of different channels harnessing the power of Keynes' multiplier effect in a much more efficient manner.

Contrast this with a group tour of another 15 people run by Tour Operator 1 based in and delivering share-holder profit to Country A. Their tour to Country B is less efficient from an economic development point of view as the Tour Operator controls so many of the components in the chain. Also those 15 sleep in the same hotel and eat in the same restaurants ensuring that though their money stimulates the local economy it tends to do so in a less than optimally efficient manner.

GARDEN TOURISM

Garden tourism is a type of niche tourism involving visits or travel to botanical gardens and places which are significant in the history of gardening. Garden tourists often travel individually in countries with which they are familiar but often prefer to join organized garden tours in countries where they might experience difficulties with language, travel or finding accommodation in the vicinity of the garden.

The list of famous gardens which attract garden tourists from afar includes: Sissinghurst Castle Garden and Stourhead in England, Versailles and Giverny in France, Keukenhof in Holland, Villa d'Este and Villa Lante in Italy, Alhambra in Spain, Longwood Gardens and Filoli in the USA, Taj Mahal in India, Ryoan-ji in Japan. In the year 2000 the Alhambra and the Taj Mahal both received over 2 million visitors. This poses problems for the landscape manager.

Michel de Montaigne was one of the earliest garden tourists to record his impressions of gardens (c1580). John Evelyn also recorded his visits to gardens in France and Italy, as did Fynes Moryson. At the start of the twenty-first century Britain had the largest number of gardens open to the public for tourist visits: over 3,500 gardens are listed in Gardens of England and Wales Open for Charity (the 'Yellow Book').

GUEST RANCH

The guest ranch, also known as a dude ranch, is a type of ranch oriented towards visitors or tourism. It is a phenomenon of the romanticization of the American West after the official closing of the United States frontier in the late 19th century. The Western adventures of hardy aristocrats like Theodore Roosevelt were made available to paying guests from cities or the East, called "tenderfeet," "greenhorns," or "dudes" in the West. After World War I, the transcontinental railroad network brought these paying visitors to the local depot, where a wagon would be waiting for them. Some guest ranch visitors expected a somewhat edited version of the "cowboy life," while others were more tolerant of the odors and timetable of a working ranch. Guest ranches have also become a feature of the Australian Outback.

In the United States, guest ranches are a long-established tradition and continue to be a popular vacation destination. Depending on the climate, some guest ranches are open only in the summer or winter, others offer "year-round" service in all four seasons. College students are often recruited to work at guest ranches during the summer months. Common jobs offered to college students include: housekeeping, wrangler, dining staff, and office staff or babysitters.

Hunting Ranches

Some guest ranches cater to hunters. Some feature native wildlife such as whitetail deer, mule deer, bison or elk. Others feature exotic species imported from other nations such as Africa and India. Both types of ranches are highly controversial. While many traditional ranches allow hunters and outfitters on their land to hunt native game, the act of confining game to guarantee a kill is considered unsporting by some people.

The introduction of non-native species on ranches is even more controversial because of concerns that these "exotics" may escape and contaminate the gene pool of native species or spread previously unknown disease. The advocates of hunting ranches argue in turn that they help protect native herds from over-hunting and the stocking of exotic species actually increases their numbers and may help save them from extinction.

HERITAGE TOURISM

Cultural heritage tourism (or just heritage tourism) is a branch of tourism oriented towards the cultural heritage of the location where tourism is occurring. Culture has always been a major object of travel, as the development of the Grand Tour from the 16th century onwards attests. In the 20th century, some people have claimed, culture ceased to be the objective of tourism: tourism is now culture. Cultural attractions play an important role in tourism at all levels, from the global highlights of world culture to attractions that underpin local identities. (Richards, 1996)

According to the Weiler and Hall, culture, heritage and the arts have long contributed to appeal of tourist destination. However, in recent years 'culture' has been rediscovered as an important marketing tool to attract those travellers with special interests in heritage and arts. According to the Hollinshead, cultural heritage tourism defines as cultural heritage tourism is the fastest growing segment of the tourism industry because there is a trend toward an increase specialization among tourist. This trend is evident in the rise in the volume of tourists who seek adventure, culture, history, archaeology and interaction with local people.

Cultural heritage tourism is important for various reasons; it has a positive economic and social impact, it establishes and reinforces identity, it helps preserve the cultural heritage, with culture as an instrument it facilitates harmony and under-standing among people, it supports culture and helps renew tourism (Richards, 1996).

Cultural heritage tourism has a number of objectives that must be met within the context of sustainable development such as; the conservation of cultural resources, accurate interpretation of resources, authentic visitors experience, and the stimulation of the earned revenues of cultural resources. We can see therefore, that cultural heritage tourism is not only concerned with identification, management and protection of the heritage values but it must also be involved in understanding the impact of tourism on communities and regions, achieving economic and social benefits, providing financial resources for protection, as well as marketing and promotion. (J. M. Fladmark, 1994)

Heritage tourism involves visiting historical or industrial sites that may include old canals, railways, battlegrounds, etc. The overall purpose is to gain an appreciation of the past. It also refers to the marketing of a location to members of a diaspora who have distant family roots there. Decolonization and immigration form the major background of much contemporary heritage tourism. Falling travel costs have also made heritage tourism possible for more people.

Another possible form involves religious travel or pilgrimages. Many Catholics from around the world come to the Vatican and other sites such as Lourdes or Fátima. Large numbers of Jews have both visited Israel and emigrated there. Many have also gone to Holocaust sites and memorials. Islam commands its followers to take the hajj to Mecca, thus differentiating it somewhat from tourism in the usual sense, though the trip can also be a culturally important event for the pilgrim. Heritage Tourism can also be attributed to historical events that have been dramatised to make them more entertaining. For example a historical tour of a town or city using a theme such as ghosts or vikings.

LITERARY TOURISM

Literary Tourism is a type of cultural tourism that deals with places and events from fictional texts as well as the lives of their authors. This could include following the route a fictional character charts in a novel, visiting particular settings from a story or tracking down the haunts of a novelist. Literary tourists are specifically interested in how places have influenced writing and at the same time how writing has created place. In order to become a literary tourist you only need a novel and an inquisitive mind-set, however there are literary guides, literary maps and literary tours to help you on your way. In addition to visiting author and book sites, literary tourists often engage in bookstore tourism, browsing local bookshops for titles specifically related to the sites as well as other regional books and authors.

Literary Tourism in KwaZulu-Natal

'Literary Tourism in KwaZulu-Natal' is a National Research Foundation funded project that is working on a Literary Map that connects authors whose lives or work is tied in some significant way to specific places in KwaZulu-Natal, South Africa. Each author entry contains a short biography, a selected bibliography and an excerpt from the author's work that relates to the place identified in the map. The map can be viewed here:

MUSIC TOURISM

Music tourism is the act of visiting a city or town in order to see a gig or festival. With the presence of the tourist, money is spent and the local economy benefits. This sort of tourism is particularly important to small villages such as Glastonbury, as well as large cities like Glasgow.

NAKED HIKING

Naked walking, naked hiking, or Freehiking is a sub-set of the modern form of social nudity. For some people, naked hiking may appear to be some form of energetic sport; however, for most it is simply a pleasant recreational pastime, with no social agenda.

Context

Naturism has traditionally been an activity engaged in a private space or landed club environment. Modern naturism is moving towards a public space, as well including a more active component. Although naturists have always been interested in health and fitness, indeed this was a prerequisite to many early gatherings, and most clubs have volleyball nets and table tennis tables, there has always been a slight reluctance to walk, run or cycle naked. One reason for this has been the secluded nature of the early clubs, private from prying eyes and textiles, and the limited area in which the early pioneers had to work with.

Modern naturism in nude-tolerant societies is moving out of the private enclosure and towards the arena of public nudity, where it is deemed ok to be not only naked in public, but where it is also ok to be active (from a stroll to action sports) in the nude. The point about being active is that many people appear to find static nudity acceptable, for example in the media (porn magazines or page 3 girls in newspapers), and theatre (non-moving Greek-statue-like nudity), but moving nudity, in contrast, seems to generate heated feeling.

Attention and Opinion

Naked outdoor activity is a subject expounded clearly in the publications of the Nacktiv site. People simply go about their normal day to day business, or recreational activities, naked. The more naked bodies people see in a public setting the more likely they are to question the advertising and media industries' onesided linking of sex with nudity. Public active nudists go out of their way to be discreet, and are to be seen walking in remote mountain areas, through quiet forests and woods, across distant fields and scrubland, and not in densely populated areas, often not meeting anyone else at all.

In the United Kingdom, Steve Gough, known as The Naked Rambler, received much media coverage for walking naked from Land's End to John o' Groats in 2003-2004 and again in 2005-2006. He was arrested and imprisoned several times during both his walks. In both 2005 and 2006 the European Alps were crossed naked during a one week hiking (tour), there was little media coverage and no-one was arrested or troubled.

Special Considerations

Although extremists might insist that naked hiking should be all-naked, and nothing but naked, as in all things one should remain practical and sensible about such activities.

Sensible footwear might mean bare feet on the beach, but wearing mountain boots in the mountains. Sunstroke or sunburn is a danger by any activity, naked or not, but naked hiking in the high mountains exposes the body to an increased level of sunshine not found at sea level, so sunscreen and a sun hat are essential items. Bugs, such as mosquitoes and midges, can be particularly troublesome, especially in sensitive areas, so anti-bug formulas are often needed by participants in this activity. Walking through a bunch of stinging nettles, or a field full of high thistles, can be an interesting experience (even with shorts on). Naturally, extra care must be taken.

NEO TOURISM

Neo Tourism is a term coined by the Korea tourism organization that comprehensively describes the newly changing trend of the tourism.

Definition of Neo Tourism

Following the changes in the economic, social and cultural paradigm of the last century, the form of tourism is changing as well. "Neo Tourism" is a term that comprehensively describes the new aspects of such changes and diversification of the tourism. The "Neo Tourism" incorporates concepts such as 'Sustainable tourism' which puts emphasis on the environmental sustainability and 'Special Interest Tourism (SIT)' which reflects postmodern social phenomenon.

The Origin of Neo Tourism

Initially the term "Neo Tourism" was generated to explain a form of tourism which has not existed before, to say, "New Tourism". However, with continuous advents of various types of tourism, it has become necessary to categorize those concepts in further details and eventually the "Neo Tourism" has taken more concrete meaning as such including the essential key words in the category. Those essential key words are as follows.

- Postmodernism
- Sustainability
- Digitalization

Application of Neo Tourism

The term of "Neo Tourism" can explain the following types of tourism.

- Tourism that satisfies individual interests and purposes appearing with post-modern social change
- Tourism that avoids the environmental destruction and ensure experiencing the untouched nature
- Tourism that manages various matters such as gathering information and making reservation through Internet.

The term "Neo Tourism" can be used from the suppliers' point of view as well as the customers' in the following concepts.

- Creating a new type of tourism product by connecting tourism industry with other industries. (ex. Medical tourism, Edu Tourism)
- Developing environmentally and socially sustainable tourist attractions

- Utilizing IT technology such as internet and ubiquitous systems to promote and sale the tourism products

POP-CULTURE TOURISM

Pop-culture tourism is the act of traveling to locations featured in literature, film, music, or any other form of popular entertainment.

Popular destinations have included:

- Los Angeles, California film studios.
- the Iowa cornfields featured in Field of Dreams
- New Zealand after The Lord of the Rings was filmed there
- The Louvre in which the book and movie The Da Vinci Code takes place
- Tom's Restaurant which is known to many as Monk's from Seinfeld
- Prince Edward Island, in which the Canadian novel Anne of Green Gables takes place, is a popular attraction for tourists, notably from Japan.
- South Korea because of the recent Hallyu phenomenon in East Asia.
- Japan for japanophiles or lovers of Japanese pop-culture.
- North Bend, Washington and in particular Twede's Cafe where much of the television show Twin Peaks was shot.
- Roslyn, Washington, which stood in for Cicely Alaska in the television show Northern Exposure.
- Tunisia, location of the filming of the Star Wars movies.

Pop-culture tourism is in some respects akin to pilgrimage, with its modern equivalents of places of pilgrimage, such as Elvis Presley's Graceland and the grave of Jim Morrison in Père Lachaise Cemetery. Another pop-culture tourism destination is Vulcan, Alberta Canada. In the early 1990s this small rural community began to explore ways it could capitalize on the coincidence of the Town's name being the same as popular Star Trek Character, Mr. Spock's home planet: Vulcan, to develop its local tourism industry.

PERPETUAL TRAVELER

The term perpetual traveler (PT, permanent tourist or prior taxpayer) refers to both a lifestyle and a philosophy.

Background

In practical terms, perpetual travelers are people who live in such a way that they are not considered a legal resident of any of the countries in which they spend time. In this way, they seek to avoid the legal obligations which may accompany residency, such as taxes, jury duty, and military service. For example, while PT's may hold citizenship in one or more countries that impose taxes based solely on residency, their legal residence will most likely be in a tax haven. They may spend the majority of their time in other countries, never staying long enough to be considered a resident.

Tax Avoidance

It is possible to live for several months, and in some cases even own property, in many countries without paying income tax. For example, one can spend up to 122 days each year in the United States without being considered a resident or being required to file a US tax return.

Some PT's are wealthy individuals whose primary motivation is tax avoidance. By exploiting the rules in place for tourists and travelers, individuals may be able to legally reduce or eliminate their tax burden. However other PT's, such as itinerants, may adopt this lifestyle for purely self-ownership reasons, just to be free from government authority, interference and "The System".

Five Flag Theory

Many perpetual travelers attempt to organize their affairs around the "Five Flags" theory, arranging for different facets of their lives to fall under the jurisdiction of separate countries, or flags. This is an extension of W.G. Hill's original "Three Flags" approach. Whether to minimize governmental interference (via taxes or otherwise), or to maximize privacy, the theory proposes that you arrange for each of the following to be in a separate country:

1. Passport and Citizenship-in a country that does not tax money earned outside the country

2. Legal Residence-in a tax haven
3. Business Base-where you earn your money
4. Asset Haven-where you keep your money
5. Playgrounds-where you spend your money

Philosophy

On the surface, perpetual tourists have some things in common with world citizens, in that they see themselves as untethered to any one nation. However, PT's generally seem to eschew the humanistic and utopian overtones of world citizenship. Many PT's align themselves closely with the libertarian school of thought, which advocates individual sovereignty-sovereignty vested in the individual rather than in nation-states.

PILGRIMAGE

In religion and spirituality, a pilgrimage is a long journey or search of great moral significance. Sometimes, it is a journey to a sacred place or shrine of importance to a person's beliefs and faith. Members of every major religion participate in pilgrimages. A person who makes such a journey is called a pilgrim.

Buddhism offers four sites of pilgrimage: the Buddha's birthplace at Kapilavastu, the site where he attained Enlightenment Bodh Gaya, where he first preached at Benares, and where he achieved Parinirvana at Kusinagara.

In the kingdoms of Israel and Judah the visitation of certain ancient cult-centers was repressed in the 7th century BC, when the worship was restricted to Jahweh at the temple in Jerusalem. In Syria, the shrine of Astarte at the headwater spring of the river Adonis survived until it was destroyed by order of Emperor Constantine in the 4th century AD.

In mainland Greece, a stream of individuals made their way to Delphi or the oracle of Zeus at Dodona, and once every four years, at the period of the Olympic games, the temple of Zeus at Olympia formed the goal of swarms of pilgrims from every part of the Hellenic world. When Alexander the Great reached Egypt, he put his whole vast enterprise on hold, while he made his way with a small band deep into the Libyan desert, to consult the oracle of Ammun. During the imperium of his Ptolemaic heirs, the shrine of Isis at Philae received many votive inscriptions from Greeks on behalf of their kindred far away at home.

Although a pilgrimage is normally viewed in the context of religion, the personality cults cultivated by communist leaders ironically gave birth to pilgrimages of their own. Prior to the demise of the USSR in 1991, a visit to Lenin's Mausoleum in Red Square, Moscow can be said to have had all the characteristics exhibiting a pilgrimage-for Communists. This type of pilgrimage to a personality cult is still evident today on people who pay visits of homage to Mao Tse Tung, Kim Il Sung, and Ho Chi Minh.

Effects on Trade

Pilgrims contributed an important element to long-distance trade before the modern era, and brought prosperity to successful pilgrimage sites, an economic phenomenon unequalled until the tourist trade of the 20th century. Encouraging pilgrims was a motivation for assembling (and sometimes fabricating) relics and for writing hagiographies of local saints, filled with inspiring accounts of miracle cures. Lourdes and other modern pilgrimage sites keep this spirit alive.

Modern Pilgrimage

Pilgrimages are still made throughout the world: modern-day pilgrimages include the Way of St. James, the Hajj, and the pilgrimage to Mount Kailash. In modern usage, the terms pilgrim and pilgrimage can also have a somewhat devalued meaning as they are often applied in a secular context. For example, fans of Elvis Presley may choose to visit his home, Graceland, in Memphis, Tennessee. Similarly one may refer to a cultural center such as Venice as a "tourists' Mecca".

PILGRIMAGE CENTRES IN VARIOUS TIMES AND CULTURES

Antiquity

Many ancient religions had holy sites, temples and groves, where pilgrimages were made.

- Karnak, Egypt.
- Thebes, Egypt.

- Kurukshetra, India
- Delphi, Greece. Oracle.
- Dodona, Epirus, Greece. Oracle.
- Ephesus Temple of Diana.
- Baalbek Lebanon.

Bahá'í Faith

A Bahá'í pilgrimage currently consists of visiting the holy places in Haifa, Akká, and Bahjí in Northwest Israel. Bahá'ís do not have access to other places designated as sites for pilgrimage.

Bahá'u'lláh decreed pilgrimage in His Motherbook (Kitáb-i-Aqdas) to two places: the House of Bahá'u'lláh in Baghdad, Iraq, and the House of the Báb in Shiraz, Iran. In two separate Tablets, known as Suriy-i-Hajj, He prescribed specific rites for each of these pilgrimages (lifting the injunction regarding the shaving of one's head for pilgrimage in the Kitáb-i-Aqdas). It is obligatory to make the pilgrimage, "if one can afford it and is able to do so, and if no obstacle stands in one's way". Bahá'ís are free to choose between the two Houses, as either has been deemed sufficient. And although women are not bound to perform pilgrimage, they are certainly not prohibited to do so.

Later, 'Abdu'l-Bahá designated the Shrine of Bahá'u'lláh at Bahji (the Qiblih) as a site of visitation. No rites have been prescribed for this.

Buddhism

Gautama Buddha spoke of the four sites most worthy of pilgrimage for his followers to visit:

- Lumbini: birth place (in Nepal)
- Bodh Gaya: place of Enlightenment
- Sarnath: (formally Isipathana) where he delivered his first teaching
- Kusinara: (now Kusinagar, India) where he attained mahaparinirvana (passed away).

Other pilgrimage places in India and Nepal connected to the life of Gautama Buddha are: Savatthi, Pataliputta, Nalanda, Gaya, Vesali, Sankasia, Kapilavastu, Kosambi, Rajagaha, Varanasi.

Other famous places for buddhist pilgrimage in various countries include:

- India: Sanchi, Ellora, Ajanta.
- Thailand: Sukhothai, Ayutthaya, Wat Phra Kaew, Wat Doi Suthep.
- Tibet: Lhasa (traditional home of the Dalai Lama), Mount Kailash, Lake Nam-tso.
- Cambodia: Angkor Wat, Silver Pagoda.
- Sri Lanka: Polonnaruwa, Temple of the Tooth (Kandy), Anuradhapura.
- Laos: Luang Prabang.
- Myanmar: Bagan, Sagaing Hill.
- Nepal: Bodhnath, Swayambhunath.
- Indonesia: Borobudur.
- China: Yung-kang, Lung-men caves.
- Japan: Kyoto, Nara.

Communism

- USSR: Moscow, Mausoleum of Lenin in Red Square.
- China: Peking, Mausoleum of Mao Tse Tung in Tiananmen Square.
- Germany: Trier, Birthplace of Karl Marx in Trier

Christianity

Pilgrimages were first made to sites connected with the birth, life, crucifixion and resurrection of Jesus. Surviving descriptions of Christian pilgrimages to the Holy Land date from the 4th century, when pilgrimage was encouraged by church fathers like Saint Jerome. Pilgrimages also began to be made to Rome and other sites associated with the Apostles, Saints and Christian martyrs, as well as to places where there have been apparitions of the Virgin Mary. The crusades to the holy land are also considered to be mass armed pilgrimages.

The second largest single pilgrimage in the history of Christendom was to the Funeral of Pope John Paul II after his death on April 2, 2005. An estimated four million people travelled to Vatican City, in addition to the almost three million people already living in Rome, to see the body of Pope John Paul II lie in state. World Youth Day is a major Catholic Pilgrimage, specifically for people aged 16-35. It is held internationally every 2-3 years. In 2005, young Catholics visited Cologne, Germany. In 1995, the largest gathering of all time was to World Youth Day in Manila, Philippines, where four million people from all over the world attended.

The major Christian pilgrimages are to:

- Jerusalem. Site of the crucifixion and resurrection of Jesus.
- Rome on roads such as the Via Francigena. Site of the deaths of Saint Peter, Saint Paul and other early martyrs. Location of sacred relics of various saints, relics of the Passion, important churches and headquarters of the Catholic Church.
- Constantinople (today Istanbul, Turkey). Former capital of the Byzantine Empire and the see of one of the five ancient Patriarchates and spiritual see of the Eastern Orthodox Church. Hagia Sophia, former cathedral and burial place of many Ecumenical Patriarchs.
- Lourdes, France. Apparition of the Virgin Mary. The second most visited Christian pilgrimage site after Rome.
- Santiago de Compostela in Spain on the Way of St James (Spanish: El Camino de Santiago). This famous medieval pilgrimage to the shrine of Saint James is still popular today.

Other important Christian pilgrimage sites include:

- Assisi, Italy, St. Francis of Assisi and St Clare, relics
- Ávila, Spain, St Theresa of Avila, relics
- Bethlehem, in Israel, Birthplace of Jesus and King David.
- Canterbury Cathedral associated with Saint Thomas Becket.
- Cap-de-la-Madeleine, Quebec, Canada in honour of Our Lady of the Cape.
- Cathedral of Chartres, France.
- Miercurea Ciuc, Transylvania, Romania. Whit Sunday gathering of (mostly ethnic Hungarian) Catholics.

- Croagh Patrick, Ireland. Saint Patrick.
- Conques, France
- Cologne, Germany. Relics of the Three Magi.
- Czestochowa, Poland.Black Madonna of Czestochowa is housed pernamently in theJasna Góra Monastery
- Glastonbury, England. St Joseph of Arimathea.
- Goa, India. St. Francis Xavier
- Hill of Crosses, Lithuania
- House of the Virgin Mary, Turkey. Pope John-Paul II declared the Shrine of Virgin Mary as a pilgrimage place for Christians.
- Issoudun, France. Notre-Dame du Sacré-Coeur
- Kapel in 't Zand, Limburg
- Kevelaer, Germany
- Knock, Ireland
- Lichen, Sanctuary of Our Lady of Lichen
- Lisieux, France. Saint Therese of Lisieux, burial place.
- Lourdes, France. Apparition of the Virgin Mary. Place of healing.
- Mariazell, Austria. Marian Shrine to Austria and Hungary
- Medugorje, Bosnia-Herzegovina. Apparitions of the Virgin Mary at the present.
- Mount Athos, Greece. Orthodox monastic centre.
- Mount Nebo, Jordan. Traditional site of the death of Moses.
- Mount Sinai, Egypt, holy mountain to the ancient Hebrews, traditional site has been commemorated since time of Constantine
- Nazareth, Israel, hometown of Jesus
- Fatima, Portugal. Apparition of the Virgin Mary.
- Padua, Italy, St Anthony, relics
- Paris (Sacred-Heart Basilica Basilica of the Sacré Cœur; and Saint Catherine Labouré)
- Rosslyn Chapel, Scotland

- Sacri Monti, Italy. The Sacred Mountains of Piedmont and Lombardy.
- San Giovanni Rotondo, Italy, St Pio from Pietrelcina
- Guadalupe, Spain
- Sea of Galilee, Israel, site of Jesus' early ministry.
- Shrine of Our Lady of Guadalupe, Mexico City. Apparition of the Virgin Mary.
- St. Andrews, Scotland, it is said that Saint Andrew was given, by God, directions to the location of St Andrews
- St. Patrick's Purgatory, Donegal, Ireland
- St. Thomas Mount, India. Place where St. Thomas was martyed.
- Taizé Community, France, modern monastery that actively encourages pilgrimages to it
- Nidaros Cathedral, Norway
- Turin, Italy. Holy Shroud.
- Vailankanni, India. 16th-century Mary apparition site.
- Vierzehnheiligen, Germany.
- Walsingham, England. Virgin Mary apparition site.
- Wittenberg, Germany. Church of Martin Luther and centre of the Protestant Reformation.

Hinduism

Hindus are required to undertake pilgrimages during their lifetime. Most Hindus who can afford to go on such journeys travel to numerous sites including those below:

- Badrinath
- Kedarnath
- Gangotri
- Yamunotri
- Rishikesh
- Haridwar
- Benares
- Mandher Devi temple in Mandhradevi
- Vrindavan

- Mayapur
- Udupi
- Kateel
- Talapady
- Tirupati
- Palani
- Kukke Subramanya

The first four sites in the list above together comprise the Chardham, or four holy pilgrimage destinations. It is believed that travelling to these places leads to moksha, the release from samsara (cycle of rebirths). Vrindavan is most important place of pilgrimage for every Vaishnava, especially for the followers of Gaudiya Vaishnavism who regard Krishna as the original Personality of Godhead (God). Here one can attain love of God (prema).

Islam

Pilgrimage to Mecca-the Hajj-is one of the Five Pillars of Islam. It should be attempted at least once in the lifetime of all able-bodied Muslims who can afford to do so. It is the most important of all Muslim Pilgrimages. Many Muslims also undergo ziyarat, which is a pilgrimage to sites associated with the prophet Muhammad, his companions, or other venerated figures in Islamic history, such as Shi'a imams or Sufi saints. Sites of pilgrimage include mosques, graves, battlefields, mountains, and caves. Local Pilgrimage traditions-those undertaken as ziarah visits to local graves, are also found throughout Muslim countries.

In some countries, the grave sites of heroes have very strong ziyarah traditions as visiting the graves at auspicious times is a display of national and community identity. Some traditions within Islam have negative attitudes towards grave visiting.

The third religiously sanctioned pilgrimage for Muslims is to the Al Quds mount in Jerusalem which hosts Al-Aqsa Mosque and the Dome of the Rock.

Judaism

Within Judaism, the Temple in Jerusalem was the center of the Jewish religion, until its destruction in 70 AD, and all who were able were under obligation to visit and offer sacrifices known as the korbanot, particularly during the Jewish holidays in Jerusalem.

Following the destruction of the Second Temple and the onset of the diaspora, the centrality of pilgrimage to Jerusalem in Judaism was discontinued. In its place came prayers and rituals hoping for a return to Zion and the accompanying restoration of regular pilgrimages (see Jerusalem, Jews and Judaism).

Until recent centuries, pilgrimage has been a fairly difficult and arduous adventure. But now, Jews from many countries make periodic pilgrimages to the holy sites of their religion.

The western retaining wall of the original temple, known as the Wailing Wall, or Western Wall remains in the Old City of Jerusalem and this has been the most sacred site for Zionist Jews. Pilgrimage to this area was off-limits from 1948 to 1967, when East Jerusalem was controlled by Jordan. Some Reform and Conservative Jews who no longer consider themselves exiles, still enjoy visiting Israel even if it is not an official "pilgrimage."

SACRED TRAVEL

Sacred travel, or metaphysical tourism, is a growing niche of the travel market. It attracts New Age believers, primarily middle-aged women, and involves tours and travel to "spiritual hotspots" on the Earth.

Destinations are often ancient sites where there is a mystery concerning their origin or purpose, such as Machu Picchu in Peru, The Pyramids of Egypt, or Stonehenge in England. Some Christian sites such as the locations of the Black Madonnas and the Rosslyn Chapel in Scotland are also popular.

These travelers see the journey as more than just tourism and take the trips in order to heal themselves and the world. Part of this may involve rituals involving, (supposedly), leaving their bodies, possession by spirits (channelling), and recovery of past life memories.

SAFARI

A safari is an overland journey. It usually refers to a trip by tourists to Africa, traditionally for a big-game hunt and in more modern times to watch and photograph big game and other wildlife as a safari holiday. There is a certain theme or style associated with the word, which includes khaki clothing, pith helmets, and animal skins-like leopard's skin.

Etymology

Entering the English language in the late 19th century, the word safari means 'journey' in Swahili language. Originally from the Arabic (safara) meaning travel The verb for "to travel" in Swahili is "safiri", the noun for the journey is "safari". These words are used for any type of journey e.g. by bus from Nairobi to Mombasa.

Touristic Usage

Most people in the West still believe that a true safari can only be in East Africa, that is Kenya and Tanzania, and not in Africa as a whole. That is to say that if you were in South Africa doing some big game watching, you wouldn't be "on safari" even though the word is broadly used, because the word "safari" comes from the Swahili-speaking people who can be found along the Swahili Coast. Today the word is used generally to mean anything from big game viewing, photography, or even game hunting.

VIRTUAL TOURISM

Virtual tourism refers to pre-planning alternative touristic activity before your departure, by integrating multiple digital resources to explore regions of the world without having to physically travel. It helps focus attention onto people, places and exploring changes over time.

By using the internet, travel literature (travel guides and travelogues), Journals, Papers and television visual learning courseware graphically shows information necessary to make an informed decision about which places to visit and historic or scenic byways to explore.

It is an economical activity that employs people from several different specific areas, such as journalists and photographers, geographers, editors, cameras, writers, etc... and it is one activity related to promoting nature-based or people-powered outdoor recreation involving adventure-based tourism.

VOLUNTEER VACATION

Volunteer vacations are an opportunity for people to make a positive difference in the lives of others or to help improve or contribute to society, culture, or the environment while on vacation.

It is also a chance for people of nearly any age to immerse themselves in foreign or challenging circumstances, experience a different culture first-hand, and learn more about the world they live in.

According to the Travel Industry Association of America, more than 55 million Americans have participated in a volunteer vacation, and about 100 million more are considering taking one. Volunteer vacations attract people from all walks of life and all age groups-students on break or who take a year off between high school and college, singles, couples, families with young children, and older adults.

Despite obvious differences among these people, they typically share a desire to "do something good" while also experiencing new places and challenges in locales they might not otherwise visit.

Choosing a Volunteer Vacation

People choose to take a volunteer vacation for a variety of reasons, and often more than one applies. First and foremost is a desire to help-be it children, the elderly, the handicapped, animals, or the natural environment.

Some people have a specific cause in mind; say, protecting endangered gorillas or preserving the coral reefs off the coast of Australia, and they target organizations that offer such opportunities.

Other people have a more general idea of what they want to do; for example, help alleviate hunger or teach children to read.

Along with an altruistic reason for volunteering there are often others, such as a desire to see exotic or unusual places, an opportunity to experience new challenges, a chance to practice a foreign language, having an experience that will enhance their resume and/or job opportunities, and the fact that such trips usually provide a substantial tax deduction. When choosing a volunteer vacation opportunity, prospective travelers should consider several questions.

- Where to go?

  Volunteer vacation opportunities are available in every corner of the world, from the United States to Australia, China, Iceland, and the Amazon.

- How much does it cost?

  The program fees participants pay to take part in volunteer vacations typically (but not always) include room and board, project fees, travel medical insurance, and travel within the country in which the volunteer activity occurs. The fees usually do not include transportation to the country. Potential volunteers should check with the sponsoring organization to determine which costs are included in the program fee, and to learn how much of the fee is tax deductible.

- How challenging is it?

  Some volunteer vacations require a certain level of physical strength and stamina, especially those that involve working outdoors. Potential volunteers should always clearly understand the physical expectations and requirements and be sure they are medically capable of meeting them.

- What are the accommodations?

  Lodging options vary widely and may involve pitching a tent, living in unheated huts, staying with native families, sharing a dormitory-type residence, or checking into a comfortable hotel. Questions about food, water, linens, availability of power (including computer and cell phone access), medical care, and local transportation should be addressed during the evaluation process.

- How long?

  Most volunteer vacations last from one to four weeks; some can extend on for months. The vast variety of volunteer vacation opportunities usually means people can find more than one vacation that fits their needs.

- Any special skills needed?

People who have special skills-teachers, nurses, veterinarians, biologists, accountants, lawyers, photographers, farmers-are always welcome and in fact urgently needed in some locations. Most volunteer opportunities, however, only ask that people have a desire to help and a willingness to learn and follow directions.

- Is language a barrier?

  Since so many volunteer vacations are in remote, foreign locations, knowledge of another language in addition to English can be helpful and in some cases, strongly recommended. However, most potential volunteers do not need to know a second language.

- What about free time?

  The amount of time volunteers have to spend sightseeing or doing other activities away from their volunteer tasks varies with each assignment, as do the types of activities that are available. This information is usually provided by the sponsoring organization, and it can be helpful to talk or correspond with other people who have volunteered in the location previously.

- Who can participate?

  Volunteer vacations are available for singles, couples, students, families, and older adults. The age limitation is typically 16 to 18 years of age; a parent or guardian usually must accompany any person younger than 16. Volunteer vacations geared for families with younger children have their own special regulations.

HOW TO FIND A VOLUNTEER VACATION

Both for-profit and nonprofit organizations and companies offer volunteer vacations. Some organizations sponsor opportunities that focus on a specific issue, such as saving sea turtles or building homes for the needy, while others offer a broad spectrum of projects that center on areas such as education, poverty, public health, endangered species, and habitat preservation. While some organizations have projects in only a few countries, others offer options in dozens of locations on nearly every continent.

People interested in learning more about volunteer vacations in general or selecting one in particular can begin by exploring volunteer vacation directories or targeting organizations that offer specific opportunities.

Volunteer Vacation Directories

People who are uncertain about the type of volunteer vacation they want to take may find it best to start by checking a directory of opportunities by category. Charity Guide is a nonprofit that provides information on volunteer vacations in several different categories: environmental protection, children's issues, animal welfare, and health and safety. Travel with a Challenge provides a directory that caters to mature volunteers (age 45 years and older). Transitions Abroad is a portal for volunteer vacations involving social issues around the globe.

Organizations that Sponsor Volunteer Vacations

Potential volunteers can also scour the opportunities offered by organizations that sponsor volunteer vacations. Airline Ambassadors International distributes medical and other aid to children, families, and underprivileged communities around the world.

Global Service Corp. focuses its efforts in two countries, Tanzania and Thailand, and offers projects that last from two weeks up to six months. People interested in environmental and animal issues can choose from more than 130 projects in 47 countries offered by the nonprofit group Earthwatch. Cross Cultural Solutions has projects lasting from one to twelve weeks located in eleven countries.

One-week opportunities are the mainstay of Globe Aware, which sponsors projects in nine countries. Community development, conservation, and teaching are just a few of the types of projects offered by i-to-i in more than two dozen countries. One unique type of organization is Peace Villages Foundation, a Non-Profit Franchise run and paid for entirely by volunteers.

People who don't find what they're looking for with a sponsoring organization or who have a pet cause or favorite charity can contact the particular group or charity on their own and ask about volunteer vacation opportunities.

WINE TOURISM

Wine tourism refers to tourism whose purpose is or includes the tasting, consumption, or purchase of wine, often at or near the source. Wine tourism can consist of visits to wineries, vineyards, and restaurants known to offer unique vintages, as well as organized wine tours, wine festivals, or other special events.

Many wine regions around the world have found it financially beneficial to promote such tourism; accordingly, growers associations and others in the hospitality industry in wine regions have spent significant amounts of money over the years to promote such tourism.

The National Wine Centre of Australia is a tourism venue that showcases the entire Australian wine industry. It is an education hub for tourists, the general public and full time students.

The National Wine Centre is a teaching centre for wine-related academic programs of The University of Adelaide, Australia. The University of Adelaide, "the wine university", is one of the top two educators in the world for wine studies along with the University of California-Davis.

SUSTAINABLE TOURISM

There are many different definitions of sustainable tourism, or responsible tourism, that have been developed over the last decade. Most tend to assume that all tourists are responsible for respecting and conserving a location's economic, environmental, and socio-cultural balances.

Global economists forecast continuing international tourism growth, ranging between three and six percent annually, depending on the location.

As one of the world's largest and fastest growing industries, this continuous growth will place great stress on remaining biodiverse habitats, often used to support mass tourism.

Sustainable tourists are aware of these dangers and seek to protect their favorite destinations, and to protect tourism as an industry. Sustainable tourists face many responsibilities to reduce tourism's impact on communities, including:

- informing themselves of the culture, politics, and economy of the communities being visited.
- anticipating and respecting local cultures' expectations and assumptions.
- contributing to intercultural understanding and tolerance.
- supporting the integrity of local cultures by favoring businesses which conserve cultural heritage
- supporting local economies by purchasing local goods and participating with small, local businesses.
- conserving resources by seeking out businesses that are environmentally conscious, and by using the least possible amount of non-renewable resources.

The Multilateral Investment Fund MIF Focus on destinations where there is already a critical mass of

tourism businesses, MIF projects aim to boost the competitiveness of locally owned small and medium enterprises, helping them to organize themselves and work toward the shared goals of increasing income, employment and economic development.

See the Sustainable Tourism Action Plan and project proposal Guidelines.

Ecotourism

Ecotourism, according to Heather Robinson (2006), is a subset of sustainable tourism, differing by its focus on ecology.

Ecotourism is sustainable tourism that "contributes actively to the conservation of natural and cultural heritage; includes local and indigenous communities in its planning, development and operation, contributing to their well-being; interprets the natural and cultural heritage of the destination to visitors; and lends itself better to independent travellers, as well as to organized tours for small size groups. In simple words ecotourism means while practicing any kind of tourism one should not harm nature.

For today's fast changing world only the practice of ecotourism can save nature from ever growing human population. Ecotourism is the best way to practice any kind of tourism whether it is wildlife tourism, adventure tourism, or heritage tourism.

It is the duty of all mankind to preserve nature and different species, only then can they survive for a long time; mankind should respect nature and its rules.

Man should preserve nature for the upcoming generation, so they also feel the pleasure of being in nature as people of this and earlier generations felt.

Green Conventions, Meetings and Events

Large conventions, meetings and other major organized events drive the travel, tourism and hospitality industry.

Cities and convention centers compete to attract such commerce, commerce which has heavy impacts on resource use and the environment.

Major sporting events, such as the Olympic Games, present special problems regarding environmental burdens and degradation. But burdens imposed by the regular convention industry can be vastly more significant.

Green conventions and events are a new but growing sector and marketing point within the convention and hospitality industry.

More environmentally aware organizations, corporations and government agencies are now seeking more sustainable event practices, greener hotels, restaurants and convention venues, and more energy efficient or climate neutral travel and ground transportation.

Additionally, some convention centers have begun to take direct action in reducing the impact of the conventions they host.

One example is the Moscone Center in San Francisco, California, which has a very aggressive recycling program, a large solar power system, and other programs aimed at reducing impact and increasing efficiency.

With the advent of the internet, some traditional conventions are being replaced with virtual conventions, where the attendees remain in their home physical location and "attend" the convention by use of a web-based interface programmed for the task.

This sort of "virtual" meeting eliminates all of the impacts associated with travel, accommodation, food wastage, and other necessary impacts of traditional, physical conventions.

6

History and Growth of World Tourism

INTRODUCTION

The substantial growth of the tourism activity clearly marks tourism as one of the most remarkable economic and social phenomena of the past century. The number of international arrivals shows an evolution from a mere 25 million international arrivals in 1950 to an estimated 806 million in 2005, corresponding to an average annual growth rate of 6.5%

During this period, development was particularly strong in Asia and the Pacific (13% on average a year) and in the Middle East (10%) while the Americas (5%) and Europe (6%), grew at a slower pace and slightly below the world's average growth. New destinations are steadily increasing their market share while more mature regions such as Europe and the Americas tend to have less dynamic growth. Europe's world share declined by over 10 percentage points since 1950 whereas the Americas lost 13 percentage points. Though the Americas' performance has been most affected by the declines suffered in the past years, the fact is that its annual average growth rate for the period 1950-2000 was 5.8%, also bellow the average for the world (6.8%). Europe and the Americas were the main tourist-receiving regions between 1950 and 2000. Both regions represented a joint market share of over 95 per cent in 1950, 82% forty years later and 76% in 2000.

THIRD WORLD TOURISM CRITIQUE

Tourism has become one of the most prominent and influential global industries. It directly or indirectly employs one in every

10 employed people on earth, and maintains 3.6 trillion dollars worth of goods and services which is 10.6 percent of the gross global product. (Brown, 24.)

Tourism has become the mainstay of countless countries worldwide and is one of the greatest sources of entrepreneurial activity. Yet, despite these impressive statistics, and contrary to what most tourists, myself included, have been taught, tourism, especially in the third world, is far from the benign panacea of benefits for 'host' countries it is regularly portrayed to be.

Tourism bears a nearly direct lineage to perhaps the first arbiter of the first/third world dynamic globalization: colonialism. This is most obvious in that nearly all tourists come from the first world, notably Europe and the United States, and are also the primary owners of the tourist infrastructure. Professor McCall's observation that whites are "living it up" in South Africa is true, to a large extent, throughout the world, with tourism among the central modes of their enjoyment. Tourism, like colonialism, involves an occupation and domination of space, in this instance by the tourist structure and tourists themselves. It is also an industry that, like colonialism, is enabled by expansions of power.

Tourists, especially those going to the third world, venture forth to survey the lands and peoples over which they reign: to catalogue it, exploit it, revel in its submission, and leave it, both in body and mind.

Tourism, contrary to popular belief, generally benefits the tourist far more than it does the residents of the country they visit. The often vast government subsidies poured into enabling tourism in many countries come at the expense of those funds being used to directly help the majority of the country's usually destitute residents. While such funds do help many residents to some extent, usually in the form of creating mostly low-paying, unskilled jobs, the resources are essentially being shared with, if not outright given to, tourists.

Additionally, the funds spent by tourists while on their sojourns rarely help the average resident. The spending, if it stays in the country, largely benefits the owners of the tourist structure in the country. In South Africa's case, this constitutes the often already wealthy, disproportionately white upper-class. However, much, and in some cases nearly all, of the money spent by tourists does not stay in the country at all. This is primarily due to a large portion of tourist infrastructure being foreign owned. Examples of this ownership include tour services, hotels, travel agencies, and many of the stores placed in tourist centers. Furthermore, these owners often employ expatriates or international workers instead of locals.

For instance, while on the return flight from South Africa I sat next to, and nearby, several groups who had spent the entirety of their stay in private game parks. Each group had a series of pictures of their loved ones proudly bestriding the various animals they had so bravely slain during the course of their so-called 'expeditions'.

Upon inquiry, I learned that by dealing exclusively with foreign-based outfitters, suppliers, agencies and owners, as apparently "all" of their friends did as well, these groups had managed to stay in South Africa for nearly a month without directly contributing a cent to the local economy. When I asked one group member, a portly man named Bill from Texas, why he had decided to only use foreign companies he, at first, seemed somewhat surprised by the question, giving me a quizzical look as if to say "surprised you'd need to ask". Then he answered "our outfitters are pros, they know what they're doin, the South Africans don't." In Kenya, Thailand, Fiji, and many other countries, this 'leakage', as it is commonly referred to, of tourist spending approaches, and often exceeds, 60%. (Brown 58), However, to lesser extents it is present in nearly every tourism integrated economy, including South Africa's.

As more tourists and wealthy first-world vacationers frequent a country, inflation and a rise in land prices begin to occur as a result of the strength of first-world currencies and by the disproportionate wealth of the foreigners. This hurts local residents by creating a barrier between their lives and the artificially created world of tourists. Tourist areas become far too expensive for locals to enjoy. Subsequently, the only use of the areas most local residents will have comes from working as the maids, cleaners, and other basic-service providing employees needed to run the sites.

In South Africa, we stayed in the "Waterfront" one area that demonstrates this point well. Of all the South African residents I spoke to not a single person frequented this area, the reason always being the, what one person at SABC called, "exorbitant" prices. This same effect has manifested itself in South African property, amusement parks, aquariums, museums, shopping centers, and even such national heritage sites as Table Mountain and Robben Island. In my story for SABC I interviewed over 25 South African residents on the streets of Cape Town and not a single person had visited either Table Mountain or Robben Island. They unanimously cited, what one school teacher called, "insane" prices, while also stating that they would love to go if the pricing was not so high. Aside from this essentially financial separation, there are many instances where local residents have been physically removed from an area to make way for tourism. Often, this consists of the destitute who are perceived as a blight and/or crime threat, as in Times Square, and are forcibly removed in these instances are moved out of the areas as they are perceived to make the area less desirable for tourists. For those remaining destitute residents in the Cape Town, Waterfront area, many of whom seem to subsist largely from soliciting money from tourists, life is made incredibly difficult by the harsh treatment doled out by nearly everyone they come into contact with. In one instance, while I was eating with our group in a café in the area, one ragged local man came to the door and, in plain view of all the patrons, the manager opened the door and yelled at the man "go away and don't ever come here again!". The man was most likely there to ask the patrons for money, and, as it could potentially disrupt business, I am not entirely surprised by the manager's reaction. It is the structural dynamic the example demonstrates that is most appalling: with most residents already priced out of the area, the most common remaining residents I encountered lived in various stages of destitution and had to resort to humiliating acts to get by.

(Another cause of local resident displacement is the growing trend of ecotourism. Ecotourists want to see so-called 'unspoiled' nature. This, of course, does not include people. However, communities reside in many areas that might make excellent ecotourist havens. This conflict of interest is increasingly leading to confrontations between the developers who envision their own

Kruger Park (which itself, as Herman mentioned, displaced former inhabitants in its development) and the people, often indigenous, who reside on the land. Not surprisingly, with the all-powerful tourist lobby in their corner, the developers are not encountering much trouble.

Earlier this year, in an effort to clear the area for an ecotourism venture, 250 residents of the Ambulong shore village in the Philippines were evicted from their homes. As they had refused to leave earlier, the eviction was violent: police attacked the village, wounding many inhabitants and demolishing 24 houses. While the people have pledged to continue the fight for their homes, the outlook is clearly not good. In Bangladesh over 1000 families of the Khasi and Garoare indigenous groups face eviction from their tribal land for development of a park. In Brazil two villages near the resort town of Fortaleza have gone to court to show that a real estate agency that forced them off their lands to build an "ecological resort" broke the law. In Africa, more recent examples than Kruger include the Masai in East Africa and the Bushmen of Botswana. (Mail & Guardian June, 2002). Even when the indigenous peoples themselves propose to start ecotourism, as the Botswana Bushmen did, governments, as occurred in the Botswana case, often refuse to relinquish their potential earnings to the residents. (Mail & Guardian June, 2002)

Tourism also plays a significant role in the continuing economic subordination and dependency of the third world upon the core nations. The first world has a long tradition of forcing first world ideology and concepts upon drastically different third world countries, often their former colonies. One example if the first world (WTO/IMF)'s forcing of globalization and neo-liberal policies upon the third world instead of encouraging more third world appropriate concepts like localization. Another example is that by forcing third world economies to be based upon precarious and unpredictable exports (i.e. coffee and bananas) the first world effectively inhibits autonomous growth in the third world countries. Tourism is a similarly unpredictable and fluctuating business and is entirely dependent on, essentially, entertaining visitors from outside the country. Thus, tourist based third-world economies become both dependent on, and subordinate to, tourists. This comes at the expense of fostering more organic, autonomous and lasting growth. The result is the perpetuation of a structure in which strong, industrialized countries are able to impose terms of trade to their advantage upon weaker states. Within this broader perspective of relationships, the first world tourist visiting a third world tourist based economy is akin to a colonizer both visiting, and perpetuating the domination of, a colony.

This dependency in a tourist economy manifests itself in the subordination of the people, culture and structures of the society to tourist interests. If a third world country wants and IMF loan, it must demonstrate its compliance with the IMF's interests. The tourist/service relationship is, in some ways, a microcosm of this exchange. If a third world tourist economy wants tourist money, it must be sensitive to tourist interests. In this sense, tourism is a form of domination and of the master/servant dynamic tracing its lineage to the colonial era. I could sense this dynamic in many instances on our trip. Nearly everyone staying at the Breakwater Inn were white tourists.

However, the staff, especially the cleaning and maintenance crew, was composed almost entirely of local blacks who had to serve us everyday, clean up after us, and ultimately treat us as if we were somehow above them. The people who would transport our luggage were like our servants, as well as the unseen maids at all the hotels we stayed at. The hundreds of vendors we encountered on the trip were entirely dependent on tourists, and many of them utilized, either by choice or desperation, that same master/servant dynamic. Often they would say things to me like "oh please sir, please buy something, I will never forget you, and my family will always remember you." I heard variations of that pitch throughout our trip from vendors of all kinds.

It seems that many tourists either consciously or unconsciously fulfill their 'master' role. I often encountered tourists treating vendors, staff and other employees with shocking rudeness and almost scornful disregard. Professor McCall drew my attention to one tourist becoming enraged at the black cooking staff for giving him what he called ¾ of an egg, as opposed to the whole egg he expected. On the return flight a member of the safari groups sitting near me verbally assaulted a stewardess when she said that she would need to take his suitcase to a storage compartment on the plane as the overhead bins were overflowing.

The tourist, after arguing with her about why she had no right to move his suitcase anywhere, on the plane or off, then yelled, as if to accuse the entire staff of being inept and corrupt, that "If anything and I mean anything is missing from that suitcase, there will be hell to pay!". These examples add to the countless instances I can recall throughout my experience of encountering stereotypically "angry tourists". They seem to consistently be appealing to a sense that they deserve better than everyone else, and are entitled to utter subservience. To this end, I have come to accept that I, like all tourists in a third world country, could, and probably often do, symbolize arrogance, oppression and the subservience of much of the country's people. In South Africa I often did feel people holding variations of this view of me, and I understand why they did. Several people said that they resented me, and people like me, who came to their country. Others mentioned my arrogance, which I am sure I do have to some extent, as well as the collective arrogance of the first world.

With the spread and intervention of capitalism into Third World societies, tourism has also had the effect of turning Third World places, landscapes and people into commodities. Essentially tourists consume elements of a vacation in the same way as we consume other objects or commodities. This is perhaps most obviously evident in the packaging of African culture, history and imagery into convenient souvenirs sold by vendors throughout the tourist enclaves. Another example is the play we saw, entitled "African Footsteps" which commoditized African history into a sanitized, tourist-pleasing, and overly simplistic package to be bought and consumed by tourists eager to move onto the next item. Trips to the country are sold as a package, but it is more importantly the country itself that is being transformed, along with its uniqueness, people, and cultural heritage, to be sold as a commodity to the golden hordes of tourists.

In the vein of commoditizing is the 'otherness' that is fostered by the separateness of tourism interactions with the local peoples and surroundings. Tourists, like the first world they come from, have come to view the core and periphery nations as a situation of 'us' and 'them', 'them' being the societies outside the first world which are variably defined by ideas of simplicity, disease, barbarism, instability, poverty and as generally problematic. Much tourism entrenches this sense of 'otherness.' For instance, the township tours (link to chapter on township tours) we went on consisted of driving through people's communities in buses, stopping occasionally to look around while guarded by police, perhaps asking a few questions (if the people are lucky) and then gathering to get back on the bus from whence we came, never to be seen again. We were, however, preceding, and will be followed by, a never-ending string of the same buses unloading the same people. Only the faces will really change, but even they won't change too drastically. Eventually it will just blend into a blur of otherness. Now I imagine if that was my community, if that backyard our bus pulled up in was my backyard.

If I had busses stopping in front of my house to momentarily let out peering faces and cameras who would peruse my driveway before getting back onto their bus. Then, a day later, another bus, and then another, and another. I would feel on display, like a commodity being captured in the visitors' cameras and taken away. Above all, I would feel like I was 'other'.

The yearning of first-world tourists to venture to third-world locales is a kind of postmodern reaction to a certain meaninglessness and dissatisfaction with modern life. One backlash against the post-industrial complex is the desire to return to the purity of pre-modern life and to experience the supposed authenticity of 'unspoiled' land, people and environments. As the continuing existence of any people or environment entirely unaffected by humans is nearly impossible, fabrications are necessary to satiate this yearning. Professor Wittenberg, in his introduction to Kruger Park, spoke at length about the desire of those who created the park to maintain a place where, in this case white men, could go to reconnect with pure nature and experience what their forefathers lived in, re-creating such lost rites of passage as "the first hunt". Kruger, however, is not a real, natural habitat. It is an artificially maintained semblance of a time long past. This also holds true for the Zulu cultural village many of us went to see. It utilizes the desire to see pure indigenous cultures, but is in fact, no more than a reenactment of a lifestyle long since altered by the very societies of many who now come to gaze at the sights. These things are not real, they remain in a romanticized vision of "untouched" land and peoples that exists today only as a fantasy in the mind of tourists. It is a mentality that encourages the "disneyizing" of culture and of environments, creating some romanticized fantasy rather than grappling with the modern day reality and conflicts of the places. The vision of "untouched" "virgin" land and peoples has a long history in the collective Western thought, tracing back to the mythologized colonial voyages and stories of explorers pushing to the frontier. For instance, as we drove through the Kruger terrain I wanted to imagine going to the area for the first time, I even remarked to Herman "imagine what it would have been like for the first voyagers coming to this area....how incredible and desperately hard it must have been". He then noted about the high death rate for them, but I was already drifting off into imaging how breathtaking it must have been to see these lands for the first time, yearning to have that experience as well. I had not realized it, but the efficacy of that idealized story had firmly enraptured my mind as well. This seems due, in large part, to the historical education I received. I was taught far more about the Indians of the 1700's in American high school than about the Indians of today. Additionally, I was bombarded with the supposedly heroic tales of explorers like Columbus and Magellan who first witnessed untouched people and lands. Few seem to care about, or have any desire to face, the complex, often difficult realities facing modern indigenous peoples or the crises facing many remaining tracts of actual wilderness. They would rather see a reenactment of a lifestyle long passed, or an artificially idyllic, maintained nature preserve, and leave with their preconceptions intact than have to deal with the often ugly and difficult reality. Tourists, after all, are not there to feel conflicted and are not paying to feel guilt; they want it to be simple, romantic, and easy to deal with.

In spite of all these problems, it must be noted that in many instances, utilization of third world tourism comes at a cost of less than many alternatives. For some areas, such as small islands, tourism is often the most viable means by which to develop the economy. Furthermore, given the desperate economic state of many third world countries, with unemployment often in double digits, it must be considered that there may be little choice other than tourism. While the jobs in the tourism market are mostly low-paying and unskilled, any job is better than none. Clearly, this does not excuse the multiplicity of problems endemic to third world tourism. Yet, it is often this lack of better economic alternative that leads countries to accept them. Thus, the goal must be to ensure that no country is in a position to need tourism to survive.

Tourism is, by many metrics, the world's largest industry. It has become a permanent part of the modern global economy and is only becoming more widespread. However, the third world tourism industry is obligated to address the multitude of aforesaid problems before it can become an equitable form of development. This will require the creation of alternate forms of tourism that truly benefit the majority of a country's residents as much, if not more, than the incoming tourists. Until then, third world tourism will continue to serve as a perpetuation of the colonial legacy, providing enjoyable exploration for tourists and festering exploitation for locals.

CHEAP SIGHTSEEING TOUR

A cheap and easy sightseeing tour idea, explore your own neighbourhood like it were a new exotic location, introduction and tips.

Sightseeing in Your Own Neighbourhood

Whether we pay attention to it or not, we all belong to a neighbourhood of one sort or another. Some of us live in city neighbourhoods, some in suburban ones, others in rural neighbourhoods, such as the mountains or the high plains. What is your neighbourhood? Is it a place, a group of buildings, or a collection of people? Before you get into knowing your neighbourhood, look at the Almanac's neighbourhood map, drawn up by one who lived there. As he spotted items onto the map—which he got from the local town hall—he took notes on each item and keyed these notes to the map. You can do the same for your own neighbourhood.

Our sample neighbourhood is a suburb, about 1 1/2 hours from New York City. It contains 500 acres, about 200 houses, 275 apartments, and nearly 1,500 people. They are mostly young to middle-aged families with an average of slightly over 2 children per household. It can be described as a solidly middle-class neighbourhood. Listed below are its parts and a description of each:

1. *Shopping Center*. People from all over this town and surrounding towns come here to shop. The land was developed and owned by a national company and the stores are leased to large chains which are not oriented to the neighbourhood. Some smaller shops like the stationery and gift shops, however, are owned by neighbourhood people. They like the heavy traffic which the chains bring in. The neighbourhood on the whole, however, doesn't like it. Three years ago the shopping center was an orchard.
2. *Highway, U.S. Route* 1. Follows the old Boston Post Road. Four lanes of heavy traffic carry outsiders through this edge of the neighbourhood as well as neighbourhood residents to and from work and the many stores that line the highway strip. Two private companies have buses connecting the neighbourhood to the town and the nearest city. But the service is poor and is nonexistent on Sundays or in the evenings. The very young and the old who don't drive can't get out of the neighbourhood to do things. Take, for example, Mrs. Robin McKenna. You can meet her easily enough because, although she's 75 years old, you'll often find her hitchhiking along Shore Drive (4). Pick her up and she'll tell you that since the old trolley was abandoned 25 years ago, it's been harder and harder for oldsters like her to get into town. She doesn't drive, but all the large stores, doctors' offices, and meeting places are in the town or nearby city. She tells her friends to hitchhike but they're afraid. Mrs. McKenna admits that some strangers are weird, but most are friendly and all are interesting. Her regular rides get cookies from her at Christmas.
3. *Alps Road*. A feeder street for the neighbourhood it bounds. It is so narrow and winding over the small hills in the neighbourhood that the old farmers called it "Alps Road." Some of them live in older farmhouses along the road, but most have been squeezed out by single-family homes built over the last 10 years costing $30,000 to $40,000.

4. *Shore Drive.* Another feeder street and neighbourhood divider. It is also State Highway 142 and carries outsiders through the neighbourhood to the nearby shore and beaches which gave the road its name. Summer traffic is heavy and generally keeps people from crossing it to go to stores and schools in the next neighbourhood. The road has mostly older, single-family houses, lived in by older couples whose children have grown up.
5. *Echlin Company.* This factory makes automobile parts. It is owned by outsiders, employs a few people from the surrounding neighbourhood, and uses many inner-city blacks who commute by car from the nearby city because owning a house in the neighbourhood is expensive and nearby apartments are small and lived in only by whites. But according to realtors of the area, no discrimination takes place here. Bob Gillings thinks differently. He's black, lives in the nearby city, and hasn't found a place to live in this neighbourhood. "When the company moved from the city to this town, they promised the town fathers they'd bring good taxes but none of the workers. Too expensive for us to buy a house here. We can afford the rents here but we always get the 'no vacancy' sign when we ask. Heck, me and my wife are more comfortable in the city anyway."
6. *Old Colonial Farmhouse.* "For Sale." Although some of the town's famous families lived here, this home's place on the highway (2) makes its land more valuable for stores.
7. *Vacant Lot.* Owned by the owners of the shopping center next door (1), who want to build 152 apartments here. The neighbourhood opposes them because apartments would bring in more traffic, especially to Shore Drive (4), alter streams through the land (8), and possibly bring in low-income residents, such as the blacks who work nearby.
8. *Streams.* These collect water from the sloping land and carry it to the nearby river. These streams are relatively unpolluted since this part of the neighbourhood has been provided with sewer pipes beneath the streets to carry waste water to a plant which treats it before letting it

flow out to the river. During rains, the streams here often flood the lot (7), which temporarily holds the water before it goes downstream. Buildings around these streams would make the water overflow faster and flood downstream houses. This kind of flooding already happens at the nearby apartments, where one building has been situated in the path of a stream.

9. *Apartments.* Seven buildings have 55 apartments. Developed and sold as condominiums, only about half are owner-occupied. Nonresidents own the rest as rental investments. They provide little in the way of maintenance or play facilities for those who rent from them. The renters tend to have lower incomes than the owners, are younger, and have young children. Because the owners tend not to have children living at home, they don't want to spend money on building a play lot. So the children play in the parking lots.
10. *More Apartments.* All 150 are rented to older couples or young families. The neighbourhood used to be all single-family or lots. But a major developer bought the land, made a large contribution to the local political party in power, and got permission to build apartments here. Because the earth is too rocky to absorb so much sewage, the developer 1st had to put in a sewer line. The chairman of the Sewer Authority, who doesn't live in the neighbourhood, is a land developer himself as well as the boss of the political party which received the contribution. So Mr. Chairman was happy to extend the sewer lines. This made the entire neighbourhood suitable for apartments, and developers are madly rushing to buy up the open space.
11. *Open Space.* The play area for the apartments (10) was supposed to be here. But the developer forgot to build it. Instead he quickly sold the land and buildings to outside investors such as Dr. Robert Kelley. Dr. Kelley is a dentist who has his offices in the local town center and lives in a wealthier part of town. Many of his patients live in our sample neighbourhood but they don't know that their dentist owns these apartments. Dr. Kelley doesn't want them to know.

12. *Vacant Lot.* But not for long! Another developer wants to fill in the pond with rock and dirt from the nearby hill, which he'll tear away to build 150 apartments. Mark Robbins, who lives in the apartments (9) with his mother and 2 sisters, has spotted a muskrat family living in the pond. But the developer would rather have wealthier, childless families in condominium apartments living here instead of muskrats or little boys like Mark who befriend the local wildlife.
13. *Ballou Road.* A small, single-family housing tract owned and lived in by older, working-class families. Joe Ballou lives here. He built most of the houses and named the street that he put in for them. His youngest daughter, Lisa, is still in high school, but his other children are married and live in other suburbs. Joe doesn't build houses anymore. "The market isn't so good," he says. "And besides, my wife and I are getting old enough where we'd like to enjoy life." So he and his wife have spent the last 4 winters in Florida. During the rest of the year Joe occasionally remodels bathrooms and kitchens.
14. *Footpath.* Apartment dwellers shortcut to the shopping center or bus, rather than walk along the streets, which have no sidewalks in this part of the neighbourhood.
15. *Homes.* New, one-family houses worth $40,000 to $65,000. A typical owner is Bud Anderson. He is an accountant with a large firm in the city but he's planning to start his own firm soon. He and his wife Vicki send their 2 children to a private school on the other side of town rather than to the public one nearby (26) because "the quality of public schools here is poor." Streets in this section or tract have been named by the developer.
16. *Condominium Townhouses.* These townhouses have just been built on a lowland and marsh. The builder has installed a pond to collect the water that used to flow to the marsh, but this doesn't work and flooding now occurs. People who are buying the townhouses, according to the realtor, are very successful older couples. No one under the age of 18 is allowed to live here. "No burden on the schools," says the realtor. So far, families who have

moved here all have 2 cars, which has added significantly to the traffic on Alps Road. The designer of these townhouses, an architect by the name of George Boswell, has won an award for his scheme. He admits, however, that they should never have been built on this land: "It was really too wet for townhouses, but if it's going to be built it may as well be designed well." Whether the well-designed buildings survive on this soggy ground, only the future will tell.

17. *Streams.* Water on this side of the neighbourhood flows into a nearby tidal marsh and then into the bay.
18. *Farm.* This farmer presently raises corn for sale, vegetables for his family and friends. He also keeps some old horses and cows which graze on the fertile hillside. He has good, well-drained, upland soil which developers of nearby condominium townhouses covet. They've asked the farmer to sell, but he's holding out.
19. *Marsh.* Gradually being filled in by yet another developer, who plans 75 apartments here. His action has destroyed the marsh, forcing out ducks and other birdlife that once used the area. But, the developer argues, now that the area is filled in, how can the town deny me permission to build here? The neighbourhood wouldn't grant permission if it had its way, but it's the town's planning and zoning commission that will give permission. Its members don't live around here.
20. *Homes.* Large, newer homes on large lots. Mostly wealthy families live here with 2 to 4 children. Of course, they oppose the nearby apartments because they will reduce property values.
21. *Drain.* In this part of the neighbourhood, water flows directly into the bay either through a natural stream bed or storm drains beneath the built-up areas.
22. *Old Section.* Homes in this section of the neighbourhood were built on small lots and narrow streets over 50 years ago, as summer cottages for city people who wanted to be near the beach during the humid months. The houses are mostly wooden. Many have screen porches running around 3 sides. Since the soil here is quite rocky and

there are no sewers, waste often flows untreated and unabsorbed by the land, directly into the bay with its beaches. The area is no longer a desirable resort spot and over the years has become a year-round neighbourhood. Owners have winterized their cottages, closed in the porches, and either live here themselves or rent their places out to students during the winter.

23. *Baseball Diamond.* The only playground in the neighbourhood. Because the neighbourhood does not support the political party which has run the town for many years, the town doesn't build recreational facilities here. So Geno Pantani decided to take matters into his own hands. Geno moved here shortly after he married his wife Deborah. Ever since that time he's been a policeman for the local town. Now he's a sergeant. Having a lot of respect from his neighbours, he was able to get them to form a neighbourhood association. He was elected their 1st president and he took as his 1st task the building of a play lot. The association put up money for the land by taxing themselves. With their own hands they filled in the marsh, then bought benches and swings 2nd-hand from the city. Now they have a small play lot and baseball diamond, a facility that is well-used by kids and their parents alike.
24. *Vacant Land.* Held by a private local foundation that administers it for the benefit of town residents. Old evergreens line the pond on one side, steep cliffs line it on the other. Many hiking trails wind their way through the area, often alongside stone walls which mark the boundaries of old farms which were here in the last century. The pond is used by neighbours for swimming in summer and for ice skating in winter. It is called Altmansburger's Pond after the family who once owned and farmed the land. Their descendants live in houses at the end of the pond.
25. *Store.* At this corner is a local "mom-and-pop" grocery store owned by an older man and his wife who have lived next door for over 50 years. They know the neighbourhood—its residents and its history. Their son was not interested in continuing the business, however, so mom and pop

may close the store soon and the supermarket chain (1) will probably get their business.

26. *Public School*. Because it's on the edge of this neighbourhood, the school receives 1st through 4th graders from this neighbourhood and outside neighbourhoods. Older children attend the town-wide middle and high schools.
27. *Footpaths*. A narrow sidewalk along the road, trodden-down dirt paths through the woods. The town built the sidewalks so nearby children could walk safely to the school. The paths were made by children wearing down the shortest route home from school.
28. *Old Stone Wall*. An old property divider dating from the 18th century. Colonial farmers here cut the trees, and then dragged stones out of the fields and piled them along the edges. Crops no longer grow here and a 2nd generation of trees has sprung up—birch, pin oak, hickory, some maple and pine trees. According to the old-timers the elms were wiped out by the Dutch elm disease.

Now that you've examined the sample neighbourhood, you can start asking questions about your own neighbourhood: What makes it different? What makes it a neighbourhood? Is it part of a larger unit? You'll have to do a bit of legwork to answer some of these questions. But walking is the best way to get to know your neighbourhood. First, get an overview, maybe by car or bus. Whether you're new or old to your neighbourhood, you'll enjoy a special tour given by someone else. Many large cities offer such guided tours on foot or by bus. But if your area doesn't have one, be your own tour guide. Pretend you're a stranger and look around your neighbourhood through his eyes.

Determine the shape and boundaries of the neighbourhood by looking for physical obstacles. Our sample neighbourhood is shaped by the major streets that cut off foot traffic. Would you ever think of walking across a 4-lane highway to borrow a cup of sugar? There are natural boundaries, too, such as rivers and hills. These characteristics often give names to the neighbourhoods, such as "Riverside," "Valley Acres," or "Hollywood Hills." Next, notice the street and road system. Generally they are the 1st things built. Houses and shops come after the roads or trolley lines have been built to link the neighbourhood to the city and other neighbourhoods. What are the links in your neighbourhood? Some streets are laid in regular, straight lines while others, like those in the older section of our sample, follow the crooked foot and cow paths of another century. Go to the town clerk and ask how the streets were named. Some street names follow an alphabetical pattern such as Ash, Bay, Church streets. Or they may be named for States, such as Michigan Avenue in Chicago. Or they may be named for historical events or personalities. Most cities have a Madison Avenue or Washington Street. The avenues may run in one direction, the streets in another.

Traffic arteries, heavily traveled streets, are often called boulevards or highways. What happens along such arteries is different from what happens along smaller residential streets. Arteries often form commercial strips. Because they draw more traffic, stores, apartments, and factories are often located along arteries and major intersections.

Not only the homes, stores, and factories of your neighbourhood feed traffic to local roads. So do outside neighbourhoods. Ask yourself where your neighbourhood's roads and streets begin and end. Are they carrying your neighbours' cars or outsiders'? What about buses and heavy trucks? They may be carrying goods or people to and from or through your area. Since streets, roads, and parking lots can consume as much as 50% of your neighbourhood's land area, it's good to question who uses so much of your area's resources. By comparison, look to see how much of your area's land is given over to sidewalks, bicycle trails, parks, or pure open space. In our sample neighbourhood, one apartment area (9, 10) provides parking for cars but no play area for children. You might also note the noise level of major streets and compare it with that of smaller ones.

Walking or bicycling not only gives you more time to look closely at your neighbourhood, but also the occasional opportunity to talk to your neighbours. In addition, walking or bicycling will put your legs directly in touch with the land. In a car we tend to pay attention only to man-made features. On foot we know immediately if we're walking up the slightest hill.

The lay of the land is often hidden from us. Most neighbourhoods do not have mountains or rivers in or around them. But they may have been there at one time. Unknown to most residents are the natural and artificial streams flowing under the neighbourhoods. Fresh water is often obtained from these sources. Dirty water is put back. Do you know where water drains from your neighbourhood? Does it settle into the ground? What if the ground is too rocky? Perhaps the waste water is carried off to a nearby river or sewage plant. These natural and man-made watercourses follow the land downhill and sometimes carve it out. Find the low points and gulleys of your neighbourhood and you will find the spots where water is collecting either below or above the ground. Follow the streams. Find their sources and outflow.

If you need help, get a topographic map of the area from a local library or the U.S. Geological Survey. The map will show elevations, streams, roads, buildings, and other prominent physical features. Agricultural maps go further and tell the types of soil and vegetation. But even without the maps you can examine the earth directly: Is it sandy or rocky? Light or dark? Wet or dry? The soils of your area will often tell you its history. What was your neighbourhood before it was built up? An Indian burial ground? A farm? The Back Bay neighbourhood of Boston and the Marina neighbourhood of San Francisco were built upon dirt hauled in to fill what was once part of a bay. Perhaps your neighbourhood stands upon a sliced-off hill or a filled-in valley. If you can't find any old-timers to tell you, go to the nearest library and ask for some old maps.

A good place to go to find out about your neighbourhood's soils and vegetation is the nearby park. Look at the trees and shrubs that can be grown locally and talk with other strollers. The park caretaker can certainly tell you a lot about the trees and plantings. Ask him which trees were planted and which were standing before the park was built. Ask why certain kinds of trees are popular in the area. Perhaps the evergreens were planted in your neighbourhood to give privacy around the houses. Perhaps some trees have been planted to help retain sandy soil. Or still others, such as eucalyptus, might have been planted to shield crops from the wind when the neighbourhood was a farm.

You may find that the land in your neighbourhood once bore a forest. Was it cut for timber to build the neighbourhood's buildings? Or was the forest cut to clear the land for farming? Find out which crops grew successfully in your soil and test your answer by growing them in your own backyard.

Look also at the features of the park. Statues, monuments, markers, bandshells. They may reveal some local history. Find out what cultural events take place there. There are often important neighbourhood events such as parades or picnics. What was used to build the walkways or walls or fences in the park? These building materials will tell you a lot about the architecture and history of your neighbourhood. The same brick that was used to pave the walkway may have been used to build your house.

BUILDING STRUCTURE

What are most of the buildings in your neighbourhood built of? Wood? Stucco? Concrete blocks? Very often whole neighbourhoods or streets have been built at the same time and in the same style, sometimes by the same builder. Pay close attention to the shapes and styles of the buildings. Are the roofs flat or peaked? Do all houses have porches? Why?

What happens behind the building faces? How many families are in each building? Do the families who live in the buildings rent or own the property? If your neighbourhood has many apartments, most likely it is a rental neighbourhood, although apartments can also be owned as cooperatives or condominiums. Rental neighbourhoods differ from owner-occupied neighbourhoods. Renters stay for shorter periods of time than owners would. Who owns the apartments that are rented? Landlords may live in the building or they may live in a different neighbourhood altogether. If outsiders, they may or may not be concerned about the neighbourhood. Find out. Go to city hall, the tax office in particular, and compare the residential addresses of the property owners and the addresses of the properties they own.

How many of your neighbours work within the neighbourhood? How many outsiders come to your neighbourhood to work and make money? It may take some time before you're comfortable enough to ask such questions of your neighbours. If you prefer not to ask them directly, go to the main library and look up the census information for your area. The census will tell you the age of buildings, their condition, whether owned or rented. It will also tell you about the people: how many people live in the neighbourhood, where they work, and how long they've lived there.

But the best way to get to know the people of your neighbourhood is to get into friendly conversations with them. To do this, go to the local gathering spots and involve yourself in the activities which draw the people of the neighbourhood together. Such spots include the corner market, newsstands, the local bar or the drugstore. Store proprietors are a mine of information, especially if they're native to the neighbourhood. Supermarkets and chain stores, while their prices may be lower (you should find this out), are generally not as friendly. Moreover, find out if the larger stores draw shoppers from more than one neighbourhood. When you find the nearest small store, get to know the owner and ask him about his shoppers. He will probably tell you that they all come from the local neighbourhood and that he is devoted to them and the neighbourhood.

Activities which draw people together and tighten their sense of neighbourliness are such things as day-care centers, churches, schools, block parties, sports events, and politics. Canvassing for a political party or a legitimate charity provides a ready-made excuse to knock on doors and talk to your neighbours. You can find out what they think about their neighbourhood and where it's going, its needs, and their goals for it. Such activities not only will tell you about a neighbourhood, but they will make you a part of it.

7

Tourism Industry: A Business Approach

Businesses manage a world of information about sales, customers, inventory, demographic profiles, mailing lists, and so much more. At the very core of this information is a geographic location, an address, a service boundary, a sales territory, and a delivery route that can be illustrated and interactively managed on a map. GIS software is reshaping the business world. From multinational corporations to entrepreneurial start-ups, from hardware stores to hospitals, companies of every kind are introducing geographic analysis to solve business problems.

In the process, they're making better decisions, delivering better service, and finding new market opportunities. Businesses are using GIS technology to find solutions for marketing, site selection, asset management, risk analysis, regulatory compliance, delivery routing, customer service, demographic analysis, and much more. GIS enables businesses to better understand and evaluate their data by creating graphic displays using information stored in their databases. But a GIS does more than just display data; it enables users to interactively and dynamically analyze and manage the information linked to those locations. And by simply updating the information linked to a map, the map automatically reflects those changes. It is this analytical capability of the GIS which strongly supports the need for existence of such system for business planning. GIS allows the creation of map displays simply by pointing and clicking. GIS lets users visualize and analyze information in new ways, revealing previously hidden relationships, patterns, and trends. Business people in marketing, advertising, insurance, and retail are already using GIS to analyze markets, optimize media campaigns, pinpoint the best store locations, and model demographic spending patterns.

The present paper emphasis the power of GIS in support to the Tourism industry, wherein a customized package was developed in assisting a Tourister in selecting Hotels, to suit his requirements, and to suggest the tourister his needs such has nearest shopping center's to his hotel, or nearest place of Worship, or areas of interest closer to his hotel. The case study was made with respect to Chennai city, incorporating the spatial database of the city as point data, As Shape file (not to Scale), and associated attribute data pertaining to the spatial data was created on MS-Access. A easy interface for the user was customized where in the user can query on the datasets to retrieve tabular and spatial information. Provision was also made for hosting the information on the web, such that the Client can view the information and query using ArcExplorer 3.0 software, provided the spatial database should be hosted using Internet Map Server. The primary software used was ArcView3.2 GIS under windows environment.

TOURISM IN INDIA-ANOTHER CASE OF MISSED OPPORTUNITIES

Internationally, tourism occupies a very important place in the economies of several countries. Among the world's largest industry, it is forecasted to grow 4 per cent annually till 2010. It currently contributes about 11.6 per cent to the global GDP and employs about 9.4 per cent of the global labour force.

However, in India, the industry has largely remained ignored, performing well below its potential, despite the fact that India has a unique heritage and culture and a wide gamut of tourism attraction it has to offer to the world. Surprisingly, despite the winds of liberalization blowing across the country, tourism seems to have been the least affected. Even now, setting up a resort means getting as many as 72 clearances from different authorities! Will the tourism industry in this country be yet another victim of missed opportunities? Will the tremendous potential, and the resultant benefits to the economy that it has to offer, go unexplored? And just what is the potential like? According to figures put up by Confederation of Indian Industries (CII), an apex body representing Indian industry, by the year 2020 India could have

40 million tourist arrivals, constituting 4 per cent of the world travel. Currently, the country gets 2.4 million international arrivals or 0.4 per cent of the world travel. The report goes on to state that the industry could end up employing about 50 million people, as against 20 million now — 10 million directly and another 10 million indirectly. At today's prices the travel and tourism economy could grow as big as Rs.10 lakh crore or 7 per cent of the GDP, as against Rs 6 lakh crore now or 5.6 per cent of GDP. Foreign exchange earnings could grow ten times, from the current US $ 3 billion to about US $ 30 billion!

Speaking to domain-B, Mr. Ravi Bhoothalingam, president the Oberoi Group and head of the tourism committee at the CII said, "Looking at the tremendous potential the tourism industry offers, it is time the government pays some attention to the needs of the industry, lest it may turn out to be another case of "opportunity lost", which will be very sad." According to him, the travel and tourism economy in India accounts for 5.6 per cent of the GDP, supports 5.8 per cent of the total employment in the country and generates 10.8 per cent of the total exports from the country.

In spite of this, the capital investment that goes into the industry is a paltry 6.4 per cent of the GDP compared to the world average of 11.8 per cent. The government's support to the industry has fallen well short of expectations and budgetary and other allocations to the sector have been 1 per cent of public spending, as against global average of 6.8 per cent. Despite this partisan approach on the part of the government, tourism in the country has registered a fairly impressive growth rate over the last few years. Says Mr. Bhoothalingam, "We, at CII, have come out with a 17 point agenda, which needs to be incorporated into the new tourism policy on the anvil if the country wants to avail the benefits the sector offers."

One of the most vociferous demands is to declare tourism an "infrastructure industry", which will help it attract low cost funds, so important to keep any industry globally competitive. Despite being the largest net foreign exchange earner and the second largest gross foreign exchange earner, after the IT industry, tourism as a segment continues to find itself ignored by the government. Insufficient aviation seating capacity, pathetic road and airport conditions, poor rail infrastructure, inadequate economical hotel accommodation and relatively high level of taxation continue to be the bane of an average international traveller. According to the World Travel and Tourism Council, an international association of the tourism industry, "Tax paid by tourists in India, is the highest in the world. Indian hotels charge about 40 per cent tax compared to other Asian countries where the tax rate varies between 3 per cent and 6 per cent." It is not surprising therefore that repeat visits of international travellers to India are few and far in between. The Indian government however stays unmoved. Strange and very criminal considering that India, as a nation, remains starved of foreign exchange and an adequate support to tourism could go a long way in bolstering its forex reserves. Needless to say that forex "Earned" in this fashion is "India's own" and not borrowed!

Procedural hassles in getting visas and poor infrastructure (including roads which are pot-holed, dusty and narrow to say the least) are some of the major problems that need to be attended to. Against present requirement of about 130,000 hotel rooms, India offers just about 60,000. Says Mr. Bhoothalingam, "The biggest shortfall is in the three star category. Our archaic land laws, which make land acquisition a very cumbersome process, are doing precious little to solve this problem. They render the cost of putting up a hotel very high. There is a big gap between five star and lower categories of hotels. The government needs to create separate zones and then give liberal floor space index or FSIs for setting up two and three star hotels. This will dramatically and drastically change the economics of the hotel industry."

The industry is also worried about airline seat capacity. Against a demand of 10 million seats in the international segment the supply is just about 5.3 million and in the domestic segment against a demand of 19 million supply is just about 9.79 million. According to Mr. Bhoothalingam, the demand-supply gap will get compounded with the outbound traffic growing so fast. He adds, "Our airports are bursting at the seams. We not only need more airports, but also mush better roads. The Cochin airport is a fine example of private enterprise. Privatisation is the only answer and we have to move towards open skies. The government must accept that aviation is no longer a luxury — it is the basic need of a growing economy."

Visa facilitation is yet another process, which needs to be rationalized urgently. Stringent eligibility requirements and cumbersome procedure put off many visitors from visiting India. One of our major policy restrictive to the growth of tourism is "reciprocity", under which we give visas to citizens of only those countries which give to Indians. Countries like Bhutan, Nepal, Singapore, Seychelles, Maldives, Thailand, Turkey, Taiwan and Indonesia give visas on arrival without reciprocity as a condition. Thailand has a visa-on-arrival policy for over 140 countries and there is no reciprocity in every case. Suggests Mr. Bhoothalingam, "We should abolish visa requirements for main source markets such as USA, European Union and Japan. For other countries it should be visa-on-arrival. Finally we could have a third list of countries which could qualify for strict visa requirements." The government may however cite security concerns as prime reason for very strict visa requirements.

Advantages of tourism are plenty. It remains confined not just to urban agglomerations, but spreads its benefits deep and wide into the rural countryside providing significant gains for the economy. Further, by its very nature tourism is conducive to protecting the environment.

According to figures provided by the CII, an additional 1 million visitors can help generate revenues of Rs. 4,300 crore annually. For every Rs. 1 million of investment, tourism can help create 47.5 jobs, manufacturing 12.6 jobs and agriculture 44.7 jobs. With just 2.4 million arrivals (0.4 per cent of the world list of international arrivals) in fiscal 2000, India finds itself ranked a poor 43rd in the world list of international arrivals, despite the fact that it boasts of some of the most exquisite sites and locales, with some of the best monuments to see. Countries far smaller in size such as France (62 million arrivals — ranked 1st), Spain (41 million arrivals — ranked 3rd), Hungary (21 million arrivals — ranked 8th) and Poland (19 million arrivals— ranked 9th) are way ahead of India. Even a country as small as Sri Lanka, despite the ethnic conflicts plaguing it for the last 12 years, is ahead of India with about 4 million international arrivals.

It is time therefore that the government pulls up its socks and pushed tourism ahead. Else, it will be one more case of missed opportunities.

THE BOOMING TOURISM INDUSTRY

The year 2004-05 saw tourism emerging as one of the major sectors for growth of Indian economy, the foreign exchange earnings increased from Rs. 16,429 crore to 21,828 crore up to December. Similarly in the last year, tourism industry registered a growth rate of 17.3% in foreign tourist arrivals, which has been the highest in last 10 years. Foreign exchange earnings grew at an even higher rate 30.2%.

India's tourism industry is thriving due to an increase in foreign tourists arrivals and greater than before travel by Indians to domestic and abroad destinations. The visitors are pouring in from all over the world: Europe, Africa, Southeast Asia and Australia. At the same time, the number of Indians traveling has also increased. Some tourists come from Middle East countries to witness the drenching monsoon rains in India, a phenomenon never seen in desert climates. Domestic tourists are also fueling the industry's revival. Many of them escape from the summer heat on the plains to resorts in the Himalayan Mountains. One of the major beneficiaries this year is Kashmir, where a cease-fire between India and Pakistan has reduced violence, if not completely, at least enough to help revive the state's sagging tourism industry.

Among the most favoured tourist destinations in India, Kerala for its scenic beauty, Agra for Taj Mahal, Khujraho for its sculptures and temples, Goa for its beaches and some pilgrimages are the most important. Interesting feature of this growth is that it has come even as global tourism has dropped, due to the September 11 terrorist attacks in the United States, the outbreak of Severe Acute Respiratory Syndrome in East Asia, and the Iraq war. Even the disastrous tsunami didn't affect India's tourism industry, as tourist arrivals in India rose 23.5 percent in Dec 2004 and tourist arrivals crossed 3 million mark for the first time in 2004.. The disaster was expected to have a negative impact on India's tourism in terms of large-scale cancellations of tourists to India but nothing of that sort was seen.

Reasons for this Boom

There could be several reasons for the buoyancy in the Indian tourism industry. First, the upward trend observed in the growth rate of Indian economy has raised middle class incomes, prompting more people to spend money on vacations abroad or at home. Also, India is booming in the information technology industry and has become the IT center. Aggressive advertising campaign " Incredible India" by the government has also had contribution in changing India's image from that of a land of snake charmers, and sparking new interest among overseas travellers.

Tourism Contribution to the Indian Economy

It is not hidden that tourism is among India's important export industries. Even with comparatively low levels of international tourist traffic, tourism has already emerged as an important segment of the Indian economy. Tourism also contributed to the economy indirectly through its linkages with other sectors like horticulture, agriculture, poultry, handicrafts and construction. Foreign exchange earnings from tourism during 2003-04 were US $ 3,533 million (Rs 16,429 crore). Besides being an important foreign exchange earner, tourism industry also provides employment to millions of people in India both directly and indirectly (through its linkage with other sectors of the economy.) It is estimated that total direct employment in the tourism sector is around 20 million.

Measures Taken for Tourism Promotion

Recently, Indian government adopted a multi-pronged approach for promotion of tourism, which includes new mechanism for speedy implementation of tourism projects, development of integrated tourism circuits and rural destinations, special capacity building in the unorganized hospitality sector and new marketing strategy. A nation wide campaign, for creating awareness about the effects of tourism and preservation of our rich heritage & culture, cleanliness and warm hospitality through a process of training and orientation was launched during 2004-05. The aim was to rebuild that sense of responsibility towards tourists among Indians and re-enforces the confidence of foreign tourist towards India as a preferred holiday destination. More than 6500 taxi drivers, restaurant owners and guides trained under the programme.

Government also took several other initiatives to promote Indian tourism industry and increased the plan allocation for tourism i.e. from Rs 325 crore in 2003-04 to Rs. 500 crore in 2004-05. Road shows in key source markets of Europe, Incredible India campaign on prominent TV channels and in magazines across the world were among the few steps taken to advertise Indian tourism. In addition a task force was set up to promote India as prominent health tourism destination. However, in order to attract more visitors, India still needs to upgrade its airports, roads and other infrastructure to global standards. Even with the recent surge, tourist arrivals are just a mere percentage of those in such popular Asian destinations like Bangkok and Thailand.

Recent Development in Tourism Industry

India Tourism office at Tokyo won two International Awards in Tour Expo held at Daegu in Korea for excellent tourism promotion. Indian Pavilion won the Best Booth Design Award as well as Best Folklore Performance Award competing with major players in tourism such as China, Japan, Thailand, Malaysia and Canada. The theme of pavilion was the Buddhist pilgrimage in India. Multi promotional activities undertaken by Tokyo office drew a large crowd to India Pavilion, which added colours to the entire travel show. The Korea's leading newspapers published on the front page the Incredible India booth's photographs highlighting various aspects. The live Yoga performance and Indian traditional snacks at the pavilion were enjoyed very much by the visitors.

CURRENT STATUS AND FUTURE POTENTIAL

Tourism as an activity or as a phenomenon has been existing since the olden days. The quest travel often quoted as the "travel bug" is apart of human psyche. A result of this psyche is the birth and growth of the all encompassing "tourism industry". Goa has long been identified as a major tourism destination in India and the world over. The "flower children" of the 1960's ended up at the pristine and virgin beaches of Goa thus giving the first indications of what was to become of Goa as a tourist destination. Last year i.e., 2004-05 season witnessed a tourist inflow of the magnitude of 2.4 million (Tourism Statistics: Govt. Of Goa) which included more than 300,000 international tourists and 2,100,000 domestic tourists. These figures are being seen in the last few years with the growth in the immediate past three years being in the range of 9% to 27%. This kind of phenomenal growth in a short span is certainly not without its share of issues as far as tourism is concerned. Growth is an essential part of life and tourism industry is no exception. However planning for growth is a prudent activity if one desires to harness its full potential.

Many people have researched destination growth and Miossec(1976) identifies a five-stage pattern in the growth of a destination. The destination witnesses these stages slowly and each stage is indicative of the changes that occur both in the tourists' perception of the destination as well as in the nature of the reaction of the local community to tourism activities at the destination.

Britton (1982) has argued that the international tourism industry, due to the commercial power held by the foreign enterprises, imposes on peripheral destinations a development mode that reinforces dependency on and vulnerability to, developed nations. This would be seen in different intensities at different stages of the destination's growth path.

Pearce (1989) observes that tourism is encouraged as a means of increasing the inflow of foreign funds into the economy or pursued for political purposes and not as an end in itself. It is perhaps this focus on tourism as a means that is creating the myopia that destination development activity is suffering from.

Honey-pot Areas in Tourism in Goa

Tourists like to travel and explore different places, people, cultures, traditions etc., and experience them. This penchant for travel in fact is the backbone of tourism so much so that Smith (1995) calls it "geography in action". Given this nature of tourism it is but natural that most destinations try to showcase their products and product potentials for the tourists so that visitation can be increased. In most resource-intensive destinations where the natural resources of the destination are the most visited attractions, the development takes place rapidly in the early stages of destination development. In fact Butler (1980) identifies the stage as the stage of involvement wherein the local and outside investment is seen for the growth of the destination.

Further stage of development witnesses the loss of local control on investment n tourism as larger investment needs are felt by the destination to accommodate a larger inflow of tourists. In such a situation investments generally find their way to areas that have high resource interactive attractions, thus creating a honey-pot situation where the attraction is the main reason for which tourists come and related activities are planned around it.

Over a period of time this leads to either haphazard growth due to ad-hoc decision-making and ad-hoc development or saturation or both. In all the above cases destination resources get depleted in terms of quality as there is tremendous pressure on their capacity to service the tourists. In fact Jeffries (1971) indicates that resources by themselves are not products at a destination but need to be developed in quite different ways in answer to the needs of quite different markets. This shows that one needs to showcase the tourism resources at a destination in a manner that is conducive to tourists form a viewpoint of creating a good experience for them. This is possible only when there is an optimum utilization of the resource base. With honey-pot areas this rarely happens as the resource gets degenerated and results in a negative experience for the tourists. Though honey-pot areas at a tourism destination generate higher revenues the concomitant depletion of the natural resources around the area negate the economic benefits arising out of it.

Tourism Experience Development

Creating tourism experiences for tourists is the central theme of any tourism destination stakeholder. This has to be borne in mind when the developmental platform of tourism is debated. The need for proper planning as far as tourism product development or tourism attraction development could never have been more emphasized than in the process of creating experiences for tourists. One of the most desired experiences for tourists is to get the feel of being welcomed at a place, which she visits. If such experiences are designed then the tourist would certainly involve herself with the experience and create a better tourism experience for herself as well as for others around her. Currently Goa has seen a huge rise in the tourist inflows in the past three years and this is a good indication for the economic benefits to the industry in particular and to the general public at large. However one needs to look more deeply at this issue because there is more to economic benefits than meets the eye.

One needs to look as to who benefits and how the benefit percolates in society. Foster (1985) says that "the search for, and developing and launching of new products is essential for the long term survival in tourism. The slow rate of change in demand for tourism products disguises this necessity". This statement indicates that there is a dynamic activity that is necessary, which can look at the product development process effectively throughout the destination.

The Future

The increase in tourism arrivals heralds with it the imminent need for increased resource usage. This is evident from the requirement of increased beds per tourist in terms of hotels in all categories. At the current level of Tourist arrivals in Goa in 2004 of 24,48,959 the total bed requirement is 39,183 beds. If we fit a trend to the tourist arrivals then the tourist arrivals for the year 2016 are projected at 42,80,000, which needs a phenomenal increase in bed requirement of 69,400, which is almost twice the amount for 2004. This is only one area of resource development need and one can imagine what kind of resources are needed in terms of basic resources such as water, electricity, garbage disposal, land, roads etc.

Furthermore one needs to look at the kind of resources on the primary demand side of tourism such as increased demand on attractions, natural as well as man-made. Viewed from this point one is compelled to take a hard look at the honey-pot areas such as Calangute, Baga, Candolim, Palolem etc., and then incorporate the tourism attraction demand from tourists in future. This would certainly lead to the development of hinterland areas of Goa and most of this would be in the realms of Heritage and Culture. This is where the destination managers and stakeholders need to come together to create strong policies that are conducive to better tourism experience creation. Till recently tourism has been viewed as an economic activity that creates and distributes wealth at the destination. One needs to look deeply into this phenomenon and realize what impacts this has on the phenomenon of tourism itself. Most people call the traditional approach as the demand side approach in the sense that tourism is looked at from the benefits of demand for tourism. However the supply-side aspect is not taken with equal vigour. There are many organizations and stakeholders who are eager to market their product to the tourists but not many of them would get together and spend time, efforts and money in designing the tourism products that are offered to the tourists. The future of Tourism in Goa will certainly depend on how this is created. Economic benefit dispersion and resource generation, maintenance and dynamic evaluation alone will help Goa retain its pristine nature and benefit both the hosts as well as the guests.

Tourism dependent economies generally create products and services keeping in mind the tourists. However it would be prudent to view the local economy and population as the main demand sector and tourism as an add-on economy. The reason for this is the involvement of all sections of the local economy. Tourism products created and distributed to the tourists have a built in risk factor of competition, market backlash by way of tourism activities not occurring in the region due to exogenous factors. If the tourism products are a part of the local economy then there is lesser fluctuation as far as the demand is concerned and hence price stability is relatively ensured. This in itself is a great relief for investors who seek a stable business environment to enable them to take better investment decisions. This in turn would lead to a sense of stability for investors thus boosting their confidence in terms of bringing in new investments to bolster the supply side of a destination.

Robustness of a Tourism Destination

A tourism destination is as robust as its weakest link or weakest spot. As such creating a destination growth path that includes growth and stability of resource utilization is the need of the hour. At current levels of resource strength Goa will reach saturation point in terms of Carrying Capacity in the year 2018. This is indicative of how fast the tourism scenario is growing in comparison with the resource development process. Unless priority is given to the development of resources there is no hope for Goa to keep creating better tourism experiences for the tourists. The level of resources needed for tourism development is large and individual organizations may not be able to marshal them. Since most of the firms that are functioning at a tourism destination are small and medium enterprises it becomes all the more imperative that larger investments come in from the state itself or are outsourced through other means such as joint ventures, alliances, specifically created organizations that have access to larger funds, etc,.

In terms of creating an image for the destination and in terms of ensuring that the effects of tourism are spread throughout the destination strong cooperative environment needs to be created. Co-operation can exist in the form of alliances, joint ventures, Co-operatives for specific purposes etc,. Most resource specific activities could use these forms to foster the growth and development of tourism as well as that of the resource.

One such example is of the heritage tourism in Portugal, which is created out of a strong co-operative organization to rejuvenate the hinterland tourism. Rural tourism is fostered through this Co-operative organization caller TURIHAB and its success in restoring cultural and heritage tourism is quite astounding. One can safely say that the future of tourism in Goa will depend a lot on how the different stakeholders of the destination will co-operate and build a significantly strong Goa from the viewpoint of tourism.

CONCLUSION

Goa Undoubtedly is one of the most important destinations of India. International and domestic tourists have a special place for Goa in their hearts and it might be difficult for Goa to sustain that place in future unless it organizes itself for the delivering better tourism experiences to those visiting its wonderful locales. The forms of intervention to achieve this have to be designed by the stakeholders themselves and the future certainly is in the co-operative domain as well as in the development of tourism throughout the destination rather than at honey-pot areas.

8

World Tourist Industry and Travel Agencies

Tourism is the world's largest industry and so is of vital importance to the world economy. It's contribution has risen dramatically over recent decades: in 1950 an estimated 25.3 million international trips were made world-wide, by 1999, the estimated figure was some 26 times higher at over 660 million trips. Even since 1985, the number of trips has more than doubled.

The World Travel and Tourism Council (WTTC) estimate that in 1999 travel and tourism were directly and indirectly responsible for generating across the global economy:

11% of GDP;

200 million jobs;

8% of total employment; and

5.5 million new jobs per year until 2010.

The chart below shows the UK's percentage share of world tourism receipts and arrivals. The share of receipts has been generally declining for the past 20 years, although there has been some upturn over the last five years.

Worldwide, the number of international tourist trips rose by 8.7% per year on average between 1980 and 1997. Fastest growth was in the East Asia/Pacific region (which includes China, Hong Kong, Singapore and Thailand) and in the Americas. The latest 1999 preliminary figures from the World Tourism Organisation suggest the UK has fallen below China to sixth place and that the East Asia and the Pacific region as a whole continued to have strong growth rates and to have recovered from a slight downturn following the financial crisis. Arrivals in the region increased by 10.7% last year. Malaysia was particularly successful, with a growth rate of 43%.

OTHER ISSUES

National Minimum Wage

The profile of employment within the tourism industry (high proportions of female, young and part-time workers) meant that, after the retail sector, the hospitality sector is the sector with most workers affected by the national minimum wage (NMW) which came in to force on 1 April 1999.

The Low Pay Commission undertook some research in to the immediate affects of introducing the minimum wage. A survey of members of the British Hospitality Association found that the impact seemed to be limited to the hotel and catering sectors with nearly three-quarters reporting no effect on their business. The survey found that only 12% of businesses in London and the South East were affected, compared to between 27% and 38% of firms in other regions. The Commission said that introduction of the minimum wage was positively accepted in the sector. It quoted evidence from Tourism South and West Wales who said that a number of employers had expressed the view that "the introduction of the NMW has ensured that we can lay the low wage ghost which has haunted the careers in tourism and hospitality for so long".

The British Hospitality Association's main compliant about the NMW is the lack of regional variation.

VAT on Hotels

There is a general feeling in the tourism industry that one of the reasons that the UK is losing its market share of world tourism (see section VII) is because hotel prices are not competitive. The UK has one of the highest rates of VAT on accommodation in the EU; only Denmark levies a higher rate.

A study conducted on behalf of the BTA by Deloitte & Touche, The Economic Effects of Changing VAT Rates on the British Tourism and Leisure Industry, found the evidence of that international tourism receipts and expenditure are strongly influenced by the price of the UK's tourism services. The report highlighted the experiences of the Irish Republic whose government halved the VAT on visitor accommodation and restaurant meals in the mid 1980s. Following this reduction visitor numbers increased sharply, generating an increase in foreign exchange earnings of more than 50%. There was also a switch in behaviour of Irish residents who became more likely to holiday in Ireland. The report said that reducing the rate of VAT applying to visitor accommodation from 17.5% to 8%, would cost the Exchequer £400 million a year through the direct loss of VAT receipts. However against this are the gains from additional income and corporation tax receipts and savings in social security payments which would rise from £400 million a year to more than £700 million after ten years. It would also result in the creation of about 50,000 new jobs.

The British Hospitality Association (BHA) has lobbied hard on this matter, Martin Couchman, Deputy Chief Executive, BHA said: The imposition of VAT at such a high rate has an impact on the industry's prices, and this is holding this country back in the highly competitive international tourism market. We could be even more successful-and attract more visitors-if the level of VAT was reduced. The Government however has made it clear that they are not considering reducing the rate of VAT on accommodation: Mr. Hoyle: To ask the Chancellor of the Exchequer (1) what assessment he has made of the advantages and disadvantages of reducing VAT on hotel room charges; (2) what plans he has to use the taxation system to promote the UK tourism industry.

Dawn Primarolo: The Government currently have no such plans. UK tourism is enjoying record success and the tourism industry is about to benefit from the long term strategy "Tomorrow's Tourism: a growth industry for the new millennium" recently announced by my right hon. Friend the Secretary of State for Culture, Media and Sport.

This issue was debated at length in the Lords on 12 November 1998, when Lord Gordon of Strathblane argued for a cut in VAT on hotel accommodation to 12.5% or 8%. Speaking for the Government Lord McIntosh of Haringey said: [...] The noble Lord, Lord Rowallan, seems to believe that if one cuts the rate of VAT on hotel accommodation by 10 per cent. one is somehow cutting prices by the same percentage. Nothing could be further from the truth. Only 34 per cent. Of tourism spend in this country is on hotel accommodation. If VAT were cut to 8 per cent, that would be a reduction of 3 per cent. in total tourism spend. If it were reduced to the average of 12.5 per cent., to which my noble friend Lord Gordon of Strathblane referred, that would produce a cut of less than 2 per cent. in total spend. That is the absolute maximum because 12 per cent. of expenditure on hotels is by UK business visitors who can recoup the tax anyway.

Some £427 million is spent by overseas conference visitors to this country, many of whom can recover VAT. Also, 18 per cent. of hotel expenditure involves establishments that are below the VAT threshold. The effect on prices of cuts in VAT of the kind proposed would be only 1 per cent. or 2 per cent., to be generous. Noble Lords are right to say that tourism expenditure is price sensitive but the claim that matters can be improved by the sort of cut in VAT proposed is not proven. In fact, it is highly improbable. [...]

Licensing Laws

The Government has recently published a white paper containing their proposed changes to the licensing laws, Time for Reform: Proposals for the Modernisation of out Licensing Laws.

The proposals include:

A single integrated scheme for licensing premises which sell alcohol, provide public entertainment or provide refreshment at night.

A new system of personal licences which allow holders to sell or to serve alcohol for consumption on or off any premises possessing a premises licence. (Places providing public entertainment or refreshment at night which does not involve alcohol, would require a premises licence only.)

To minimise public disorder resulting form fixed closing time, flexible opening hours with the potential for up to 24 hour opening 7 days a week, subject to consideration of the impact on local residents.

The Government hopes that the changes will end the confusion of overseas visitors. The Tourism Minister, Janet Anderson said "Many visitors come form countries were liquor licensing laws are quite different. They find our regulations archaic and confusing. They are taken aback when time is called at 11pm in a public house, or told in a restaurant that they cannot order a bottle of wine because it is midnight"

The British Hospitality Association reacted favourably to the proposals:

> *The British Hospitality Association welcomes the White Paper on licensing reform as a major step towards freeing the hotel and restaurant industry from archaic restrictions and regulations concerning the service of drink.*
>
> *"The White Paper is most welcome," says Phil Phillips, the BHA's technical services manager. "It contains many of the amendments to the licensing legislation that we were seeking. For once, government has listened to the industry's reasoned arguments and introduced sensible proposals which treat members of the public as adults. "It will have the added benefit of helping tourism because it provides flexibility. It will enable businesses to tailor opening hours to meet local trade demands and allows visitors to Britain to have a drink whenever they want it-something which has been denied them in the past and which has always been an irritant to them."*

TOMORROW'S TOURISM ACTION POINTS

Tourism Summit

Progress on the 15 Action Points set out in Tomorrow's Tourism:

1. A blueprint for the sustainable development of tourism to safeguard our countryside, heritage and culture for future generations Leading role given to ETC, which has set up Task Force and will publish a strategy paper in Autumn 2000. Rural and Urban White Papers to be published later this year.
2. Initiatives to widen access to tourism for the 40% of people who do not take a long holiday ETC has conducted

research into holiday non-participation. Research results and outputs from working group sessions will help shape ETC policy. In March ETC will publish "Accessible Britain 2000", a practical travel guide for people with disabilities.

3. More money for a more focused and aggressive overseas promotion programme to bring in more overseas visitors The Government has granted the BTA an extra £5 million over the period 1999-2000 to 2001-2002. The BTA now has a target to increase from £27 to £30 its return on investment of each £1 of grant-in-aid.
4. New internet systems to deliver more world-wide tourist bookings for Britain and to provide information on attractions and travel options The BTA is on course to launch 36 new websites-one for each country where it is active or has an information service-by early 2000. 19 are already live. Some RTBs now have IT strategies and most regional websites now link to national product databases. Pilot project launched to integrate transport and accommodation data
5. New computerised booking and information systems to make it easier for people to book accommodation and travel The ETC is promoting Impact Through IT-guidelines for tourism organisations on the use of destination management systems. ETC is also working to secure compatibility of data between different systems. BTA's VisitBritain website now offers on line booking or e-mail enquiry facilities for some hotels and some local pilot schemes are underway
6. A major careers festival and image campaign to raise the profile and promote the image of careers in the hospitality industry Held successfully in June 1999. Reached over 100,000 potential emplo-yees. Second festival planned for October 2000
7. A hospitality industry programme to sign up 500 employers to work towards Investors in People standard to help raise the quality of training in the industry 800 have already signed up and 1000 more are going to be signed up. The Hospitality Training Foundation are leading this campaign

8. New strategic national body for England to provide leadership to the English tourism industry The English Tourism Council (ETC) was launched on 12 July with a new Framework for Action. Under the new Chairman, it has reconstituted the Tourism Forum; set up Task Forces to deal with key issues like: transport, sustainable tourism, resort regeneration and future trends; and made progress on other issues including these Action Points
9. A new grading scheme for all hotels and guest houses to give holiday makers and business travellers consistent quality they can rely on The ETC, together with the AA and the RAC, launched the new quality standards to consumers on 13 September. Participation in the new scheme has continued to grow (self-catering 10%, serviced 13%, from 98/99).
10. New targets for hotel development in London and a further £4.5 million for marketing to\ exploit its potential as a premier location for business travellers and holiday makers and as a gateway to Britain The Government has announced a further £4.5 million for the overseas promotion of London over the period 1999-2000 to 2001-02. Hotel targets are on schedule
11. More integrated promotion of our wonderful cultural, heritage and countryside attractions to enable visitors to enjoy the full range of what Britain has to offer More integration taking place in regional & local destination marketing, and new BTA promotions will help meet this objective. RTBs supporting work on regional & local cultural strategies. BTA co-ordinates UK Cultural and Tourism Group to share experiences and good practice in cultural tourism
12. The development of innovative niche markets, such as film tourism and sports tourism, to unlock the full potential of Britain's unique cultural and natural heritage ETC has completed research on potential niche markets, and will be working on market development strategies for the best markets identified. BTA Movie map was launched in July 1999. "Green Britain" map launched in September 1999. BTA launched the sports tourism strategy in January 2000.

13. Encouraging the regeneration of traditional resorts to allow leisure and business visitors to enjoy high-quality amenities and services The Government has reflected the needs of resort areas in the new maps proposed for the Objective 2 Structural Fund and Assisted Areas. The ETC is undertaking research, including on best practice. Its Resorts Task Force will consider ways in which resorts can develop sensible, effective regeneration plans and is due to report by the end of 2000.
14. More central government support for the regions to give each part of the country better resources to develop their own identity and strengths Creation of ETC has freed more money to go to RTBs. ETC decisions on RTB bids were announced on 9 February 2000 with allocations made on the merit of individual regional proposals and how they best fit with the national strategy; and lead RTBs identified in key areas.
15. A high profile annual Tourism Summit bringing together industry and government to monitor progress, plan future action and keep all sides working in partnership towards the same objectives Held on 1 March 2000.

NEWZEALAND'S TOURISM INDUSTRY

A key characteristic of New Zealand's tourism industry is its importance to our economy. Tourism has a substantial role in job-creation and export earnings. It is a demand-driven, service-oriented industry experien-cing rapid growth and innovation. The industry now faces the challenge of balancing economic, social and environmental dimensions to achieve sustainable growth.

Economic Driver

Tourism plays a key role in the growth of our economy through employment, foreign exchange earnings, investment and regional development. Tourism directly and indirectly contributes almost 10% of New Zealand's GDP.

Tourism is one of New Zealand's largest export industries, with international visitor expenditure in 2002 of $6.1 billion. The most recently available data for Domestic tourism is for the 2001 calendar year, which reports Domestic tourism generated $6.9 billion. See more information on visitor expenditure in the International Visitor Survey and Domestic Travel Study. Tourism is a vehicle for regional and community development. Many tourists look for unique, unspoilt or 'off the beaten track' locations, so are drawn to small towns and provincial regions that often most need economic development. Tourist interest in the Maori culture also fosters development of Maori communities and businesses.

Substantial Role in Job Creation

The New Zealand tourism industry is made up of 10 major public-listed companies and between 13,500 and 18,000 small to medium enterprises. Tourism supports nearly one job in ten in New Zealand, with around 90,000 full-time equivalent jobs provided directly through tourism and an estimated 60,000 indirectly. See the Tourism Satellite Account for more information about tourism's contribution to the economy.

Defined by Customer Demand

Tourism is defined by customer demand. When a tourist takes a taxi, for example, that taxi service becomes part of the tourism industry. In this respect, tourism cuts across a broad range of industries, including:

- transport,
- accommodation,
- retail,
- catering and
- financial services.

Many other sectors benefit through provision of goods and services that support tourism businesses, for example:

- construction,
- printing and publishing,
- manufacturing and
- insurance.

As a result, tourism policy issues involve a broad spectrum of areas and interests. Read more about the different policy issues in the Policy section.

Long-Haul Niche Destination

Whilst international tourist arrivals have been growing rapidly over the last two decades, New Zealand remains a niche destination. Our geographic location makes us a long-haul destination-it takes over 8 hours to get here from most countries. We have a different appeal than high volume tourist destinations like France, Spain, USA and the UK. Research indicates that New Zealand appeals to people seeking adventure, connection with nature, relaxation and revitalisation. Read more about New Zealand's appeal.

Draws on "Public Goods"

Tourism often draws on public facilities and goods such as oceans & rivers, beaches, parks and reserves. By drawing on these resources, tourism impacts on host communities. Careful planning and resource management is required to preserve the quality of these public goods for both tourists and host communities. Read about resource management and sustainable development in the New Zealand Tourism Strategy 2010.

Sold Overseas and Consumed Onshore

International tourism is a unique type of export-products & services are sold to customers overseas but consumed in New Zealand. This presents the challenge of ensuring that the total tourism experience is consistent with visitor expectations when they purchase their trips to NZ. Read more about consumer needs and motivations and perceptions of New Zealand.

Intangible and Perishable Experiences

Tourism largely involves intangible experiences that customers cannot keep, except in photos, videos and memories. Tourism products and services tend to be perishable in nature-for example-excess hotel rooms, airline seats or bungy jumps on one day cannot be accumulated for use at a later date.

Support Networks

There are many tourism associations to support different aspects of the tourism sector. The lead industry body is the Tourism Industry Association New Zealand-a membership based organisation representing the interests of over 3,500 businesses from throughout the tourism industry. Their purpose is to provide leadership, guidance and appropriate services for the benefit of its members in order to contribute to a viable and sustainable tourism industry.

Sector-specific organisations include the Inbound Tour Operators Council (ITOC), Holiday Accommo-dation Parks Association of New Zealand (HAPNZ) and the Adventure Tourism Council.

CSR IN THE TOURISM INDUSTRY?

For the past 20 or more years, sustainable development has been at the forefront of many government agendas. This debate has concluded that sustainability should be adopted as the way forward to preserve ecosystems and biodiversity, limit growth and improve the quality of life of host populations. Tourism has been put forth as a way to gain income and provide access to market opportunities for small and medium size enterprises, especially in low income countries.

There has also been no shortage of research supporting the need to keep tourism pressures in check, address existing impacts and extend the planning horizon to create more sustainable development in the longer term. The past few years have seen a steady growth in the adoption and endorsement of the principles of sustainable tourism as a development approach which has led to the creation of many initiatives to address concerns such as environmental conservation and protection.

Social issues were brought to the forefront more recently, particularly since Kofi Annans' 10-point Millennium Challenge, and include fair trade, poverty reduction, local and community economic development. Initiatives include codes of conduct, specific guidelines and certification schemes and accreditation. This study is a follow-up to earlier reports commissioned by the World Bank Group which have assessed Company Codes of Conduct and International Standards, Implemen-tation Mechanisms for Codes of Conducts as well as various Foreign Investment Advisory Service (FIAS) reports.

The objective of this study was to assess whether the development of national certification schemes may help countries to :

(a) address expectations of tourists, investors and supply chain actors such as tour operators and travel agencies,

(b) ensure the sustainable development of their tourism industry,

(c) ensure a localisation of the corporate social responsibility (CSR) agenda by guaranteeing that certification standards are developed in accordance with national criteria, and

(d) whether certification schemes have contributed to spreading sustainable tourism practices or would align with international criteria or standards.

This report finds a number of limitations as well as opportunities. For a variety of reasons, sustainable tourism has gained increased recognition among industry and governments. However, according to travel trade interviewees, only a small percentage of consumers pay attention to these standards and for all intents and purposes, none are willing to pay extra for adherence to environmental and/or social standards. In spite of this, industry has increasingly focused on sustainable/responsible tourism measures and practices, particularly in Europe. Industry associations, Non Governmental Organisations (NGO's) and governments have been effective in developing guidelines and policies relating to sustainable tourism, but there is a need to focus on the implementation of these guidelines to move the agenda forward.

Through secondary research as well as interviews with over thirty large and specialty tour operators, certification programs and tourism experts, this report found that certification schemes, although increasing in their number and scope over the past ten years, have not enabled Small and Medium Sized Enterprises (SME's) greater access to market opportunities, nor have they moved the tourism industry significantly forward towards sustainability.

Guidelines within the industry are becoming more common, however, implementation and evaluation is still weak. What has been positive is that the efforts of certification programs have enabled companies to reduce costs, mainly related to the environment (water, waste, and energy savings). This cost saving advantage or training aid has helped improve management practices and processes, however there is little incentive to continue being part of a certification label as there is no proven marketing benefit. Certification programs are costly to run and most are subsidised by governments or international funding agencies. They are also costly to join for the individual operations, and so far have not delivered on promised marketing benefits and consumer awareness. Overall, industry awareness of such schemes is negligible. On the other hand, certification in eastern Europe has helped increase awareness of some niche products, such as non-tourism related companies (organic farms), by bringing them into the tourism fold, through agritourism-type packages. This is only marginal and countries are still very much dependant on larger tour operators and travel companies to promote their product.

To date, CSR is largely driven by publicly traded European companies who see it as a way to reduce any potential risks that might negatively impact on the value of their stocks. Thus, they will work with their supply-chain partners to ensure that these, too, will be more environmentally-and increasingly, socially-, responsible in their operations. For transparency purposes, they expect annual reports from their partners that document improvements made, and will usually provide technical/structural assistance (ensure local participation, community involvement and stakeholder dialogue) and expertise to help them tackle improvements year over year. If certification is to continue and be successful, a number of criteria are needed. First, there is a need for one global body to set and monitor the adoption of industry wide criteria. Second, there should be more business to business marketing rather than business to consumer, as consumer awareness and interest are extremely low. Third, demand needs to be created among consumers through increased industry responsibility reporting and educational campaigns. Fourth, if certification is to be successful, there is a need to achieve critical mass.

Currently there are fewer than 1% of companies worldwide that have achieved certification and therefore even those tour companies interviewed that would be willing to support such initiatives do not have enough product to choose from which will not alter their cost base, as tour operators are still driven primarily by price. In the Americas as well as Europe, there have been efforts to amalgamate certification schemes, however the complexity of programs and politics in different countries has not permitted much success. Fifth, quality must be linked with environmental and social management so that certified products can guarantee that a level of quality has been achieved and the 'experience' of the product is still elevated. As this report called for the evaluation of using CSR in the tourism industry, there are a number of recommen-dations put forward. CSR calls for consistent sets of policies, practices and programmes that steer business operations. For this agenda to be promoted, each stakeholder group must play a critical part. Certification, although fundamentally a positive approach, is not having a significant effect on spreading sustainable tourism practices overall. Initiatives focusing on the larger players will have more impact as the majority of tour operators and hotel groups have operations in developing countries and are key buyers in the industry.

The focus on CSR initiatives, educational and training campaigns for the industry as well as education of the consumer, could have higher initial impacts than attempting to move certification forward to become more mainstream. Overall there is a need to:

- Agree on international standards that can be addressed step-by-step and seen as appropriate by local and international operators
- Build on the work done to date by organisations such as FTO & VISIT (Tourlink), ISO and the European Union Flower
- Link quality with environmental and social criteria in guidelines, reporting and accreditation efforts
- Pressure associations to integrate and implement guidelines
- Consolidate guidelines and charters to be wide reaching and industry specific (tour operators, hotels, etc.)
- Utilise the existing certification framework; however create a brand around local community action and CSR focused initiatives for businesses to see it as a viable business proposition
- Link development monies with CSR criteria so that developers and managers focus on a longer term framework for product life cycles Industry to:

- Adopt and implement sustainable supply-chain initiatives (this will aid SME's in low income countries through a trickle-down and multiplier effect)
- Report on corporate social responsibility initiatives
- Focus on business to business marketing rather than business to consumer marketing (as consumer awareness is currently low)
- Continue to raise awareness to consumers through philanthropy and marketing efforts
- Adopt certification or use certified products through supply chain partners Governments to:
- Develop holistic and comprehensive tourism development strategies in partnership with community and industry stakeholders (including major foreign tour operators or industry associations, where appropriate), that include realistic expectations for the social, cultural and environmental benefits to be reaped from tourism
- Create positive investment structures to support and encourage sustainable development of tourism destinations
- Pressure industry associations to report on how they are achieving more sustainable tourism (e.g. industry associations are asking their members to sign up to guidelines and charters but few are enforcing this as a criteria for membership)
- Legislate for corporate social reporting
- Facilitate arenas to share best practices between sectors (hotels, tour operators, airlines and cruise lines) so that they can learn from one another
- Ensure sustainable tourism measures are seen as a core value in wider development plans and policies rather than solely focusing on economic benefits
- Legislate or provide incentives to businesses who adopt internationally recognised certification schemes or standards within their country.

Previous reports have pointed out disagreements with how far down the supply chain companies should monitor, that there is little standardisation in the monitoring or reporting of companies, and that there is a need to focus on why standards are not being implemented. This report acknowledges these issues and also recognises that CSR within the tourism industry is behind other industries in all aspects. However, as tourism affects so many other sectors and is a critical economic driver in low income countries, it is believed that great strides can be made to address concerns of poverty alleviation, local economic development and conservation by pushing for greater adoption of CSR. This study highlights current issues for sustainable tourism, certification and codes of conduct, identifies key challenges that tourism will continue to face, and proposes some recommendations for CSR implementation.

OVERVIEW

The worldwide tourism industry currently accounts for 760 million people and accounts for roughly a tenth of global employment and capital formation. In most countries, especially low income countries, tourism is seen as a viable option for economic growth, but current unsustainable tourism practices can impact the health and well-being of the environment and community as well as tourism itself. In many low-income countries tourism is significant to the economy or is growing, and long-haul travel is growing at the fastest rate doubled from 1997-2001)

In most industries, CSR standards and practices have been developed by the private sector to respond to external pressure. In tourism, however, the use of codes of conduct and certification is not widespread and is not based as yet upon agreed international standards. It is difficult to make generalisations about CSR without first examining the context in which sustainable tourism operates, its demand and also assessing the numerous certification schemes, codes of conduct and best practices within the industry.

The purpose of this report is to inform FIAS advisory work on CSR and certification with regards to the feasibility and desirability for low income countries to use certification and accreditation as tools for sustainable development.

BACKGROUND AND METHODOLOGY

This study is in response to the World Bank's research on CSR codes of conduct and social and environmental guidelines. The World Bank's CSR Practice Investment Climate Department commissioned research to determine whether adopting national certification schemes built on private sector standards and whether these initiatives can be used to enhance both the country and visitor experiences.

It is assumed that enhancement would result in better promotion and marketing, which would lead to increased market opportunities through better linkages into the supply chain.

This report is based on both extensive secondary research and a large number of key informant interviews. First, a review of existing research on codes of conduct and certification schemes was undertaken, followed by a review of research on the demand for sustainable tourism. Supplementary interviews with key stakeholders, experts, scheme directors, tour operators and travel providers were then carried out to assess demand for sustainable tourism, the success of certification schemes and consumers' willingness to pay. Companies approached to be interviewed included the largest tour operators, specialty operators in both Europe and North America, certification programs and industry experts (see Appendix A for the full list of organisations interviewed).

It should be recognised that this report is not exhaustive in its nature as not all codes of conduct or certification schemes were analysed. In addition, some potential interviewees could not be contacted, and therefore some opinions may have been omitted. Once codes and certification schemes were identified, they were assessed with regard to broad CSR categories, such as their human rights, labour rights, environmental standards and social and community impact.

The tourism sector's codes of conduct and certification schemes were analysed to gauge their effectiveness and market potential. Interviews with certification players as well as large and eco/adventure tourism operators and travel providers were also undertaken to evaluate the benefits of certification schemes and to determine demand for sustainable tourism.

In the interest of obtaining as much information as possible from interviewees, assurances were given that no direct quotes would be used to identify them or their company. Therefore, all statements are those of the authors' and should not be attributed to any particular interviewee.

COMPONENTS OF SUSTAINABLE TOURISM

Sustainable development has been defined as development that meets the needs of present and host regions while protecting and enhancing opportunities for the future.

Sustainable tourism, in addition to the criteria of sustainable development requires a holistic, integrated perspective that takes into account all the industries and resources upon which tourism relies. The set of criteria or principles that define the conditions for its achievement comprises:

Protect and conserve sustainable resources

Be a multi-stakeholder approach

Be environmentally responsible

Maintain the well-being and involvement of the local population or host

Provide meaningful and fairly remunerated employment for the host population

Have economic benefit

Have a long-term view

Have a triple-bottom line approach (environmental, social and economic)

Be equitable

Government must play a leadership role (e.g., impose a 'greater good' approach)

Obtain optimum guest satisfaction and educate tourists about environmental and social concerns

The definition of corporate social responsibility (CSR) has many similar elements to sustainable tourism in that both focus on how stakeholders should be identified and engaged and that initiatives should be measured to determine their impact on others. Whereas CSR relates to a company's obligation to be accountable to all of its stakeholders in all its operations and activities with the aim of achieving sustainable development not only in the economical dimension but also in the social and environmental dimensions, sustainable tourism was first seen mainly from an environmental perspective and has only recently incorporated social and community aspects. Today, it is commonly recognised that sustainable tourism is more than just environmental conservation of a natural area, but that is must also address the quality of life of those visiting it and those being visited.

Sustainable tourism development is about making all tourism more compatible with the needs and resources of a destination area. Tourism needs to take into account a holistic and comprehensive approach that balances tourism development with other activities yet tourism is made up of many sectors and is very fragmented, therefore effects and monitoring processes through one company or mechanism has been difficult. The supply chain of product to end user is not often controlled by solely one party or individual and different elements are often operated by multiple stakeholders. This therefore has led to difficulties in controlling elements of corporate social responsibility.

At Kotu Beach in The Gambia, staff at the Bungalow Beach and Kombo Beach hotels have helped to make a big difference to the earnings of local people and create a more relaxed environment for their guests. Until recently guests at the hotels were constantly approached on the beach by various local vendors offering them goods such as fruit and fruit juices. The hotel guests so disliked being harassed they were discouraged from using the beach and both the hotels and tour operators viewed it as a major issue. In an innovative project completed in 2002, the juice pressers, fruit sellers and the craft sellers in the local market worked with the local hoteliers to understand and find ways to overcome the problem. It used a multi-stakeholder approach to bring together the informal guides, fruit sellers, juice pressers and craft sellers with the tour operators and hoteliers to discuss how things could be improved. The juice pressers and fruit sellers were keen to reduce the level of hassle on the beach. Each adopted codes of conduct which they now enforce as a group. The hotels also assist the women's' marketing efforts by putting up 'What's On' boards in the hotels to advertise the stall. The women have higher earnings and the hotel guests can use the beach again without being disturbed. Incomes at the craft market increased three-fold between the two seasons-the tourists spend more when they are not pestered in the market and some new products and better merchandising have also helped. A number of rural communities in Asia have been engaged to make cushions and tapestries for the guestrooms of Banyan Tree resorts. These initiatives complement ongoing efforts by Banyan Tree Gallery to showcase cottage crafts and the work of indigenous artisans at its lifestyle galleries, as well as the Museum Shops, a collection of outlets in Singapore museums from which visitors can purchase a piece of ancient Asian art recreated as contemporary ornaments, accessories and stationery. This arrangement has the two-fold benefit of keeping traditional arts and crafts alive while providing Asian communities with a means of earning a living.

Labour Standards as Part of Sustainable Tourism

Environmental aspects have been the priority of official certification programmes and voluntary initiatives since the early 1980's and only recently have social or community issues been added. Human rights and labour issues have been more focused upon in developing countries rather than in Europe and North America, partially because social legislation has been more comprehensive in Western countries. Additionally, more advanced concepts such as "the triple bottom line" (environmental, social and economic) are just now being incorporated into definitions and initiatives.

There are a number of labour issues which affect the tourism industry. These include women's rights, fair wages, long working hours, qualification and skills requirements for employees, inability to join trade unions, importing of labour and displacement of traditional employment to benefit from tourism dollars. Tourism workers often do not earn a living wage and are dependent on tips and service charges. Many workers have temporary contracts or none at all, work long hours and are employed in low skilled areas such as waitressing and/or house cleaning.

According to the ILO, tourism workers and managers are often "imported" by the large international hotel and leisure chains (six of the seven leading multinationals of the sector are North American), which pick up the major part of the profits. By contrast, local populations benefit only from low or semi-skilled, poorly paid jobs (cooks, maintenance workers, chambermaids, barmen, gardeners, bus drivers, etc.).

According to a report recently submitted to a tripartite meeting of the ILO, this sector is known for low pay (for example, in the European Union, it is less than 20 per cent of the average salary), difficult working conditions (irregular schedules, Sunday/holiday work, unpaid overtime), and many clandestine jobs. Women make up 70 percent of the labour force in tourism and there are numerous cases of youth or child workers (half the workers in the sector are up to 25 years old).

Although few tourism codes of conduct, industry policies or schemes (see appendix B, C, D & E) so far have specifically addressed labour or human rights concerns, child labour and prostitution have been widely addressed in the Caribbean, Thailand and parts of Africa through initiatives such as ECPAT (End Child Prostitution, Child Pornography and Trafficking of Children for Sexual Purposes). Awareness of exploitative labour has also increased due to campaigns such as the recent initiative by Tourism Concern: Sand, sea and sweatshops.

Since 2002, major hotel groups, airlines and tour operators have signed up to the code which involves

- establishing an ethical policy regarding commercial exploitation of children
- training staff
- providing information to officials about abuse at various destinations
- and providing information to travellers (in-flight videos and flyers)

Some programs which have developed out of ECPAT include The Youth Career Development Program which has expanded to be the Youth Career Initiative (YCI). YCI contributes towards the eradication of the commercial sexual exploitation of children by giving girls aged 17 to 20 employment training for the hotel and travel industry. The program targets youths from poor communities and the program uses hotel expertise in human resources development to provide disadvantaged youths with the skills to work in the hotel and travel industry. The program started in Thailand in 1995 and has grown from 9 graduates and one hotel in 1995 to 550 graduates and 23 hotels in 2003. The program is now being extended to the Philippines, Romania and South Africa. Governments, NGO's and the industry are only now starting to address these issues, and although environmental elements and biodiversity issues are a crucial underpinning to achieving wider sustainable tourism development goals, it is now being recognised that labour and community equality/participation issues do affect the success of the tourism product and experience.

DEMAND FOR SUSTAINABLE TOURISM

Within the tourism industry it is generally agreed that there are increasing overall societal and environmental concerns, and that this will increase the demand for more sustainable destinations and travel preferences. These, in turn, will increase the pressure for destination management policies and tour operator responsibility. The destination developments of the 1960/70s, which were the result of overbuilding, are expected to face severe decline as consumers look for more attractive destinations that feature a clean environment and well preserved natural and cultural attractions. Another trend affecting sustainable tourism is health and wellness.

Active or adventure holidays, wellness and spa products and sun destinations are likely to increase in popularity. Authenticity or 'experiential tourism' is another trend. Artificial type destinations (e.g., theme parks), which do not meet higher consumer quality standards, will decrease as the consumer searches for the greater authenticity. Furthermore, there has also been an increase in tourists seeking meaning from their vacation experiences with a resultant noticeable increase in the number of organisations that offer volunteer based travel or educational travel, notably from non-traditional NGO's such as Volunteer Services Overseas (VSO), etc.

The market share of sustainable tourism is difficult to assess as many consumers do not just purchase one type of holiday. During the same year, they may choose a typical package sun and sand holiday as well as one that specifically caters to nature and adventure. Sustainable tourists are approximately 50% free and independent travellers (FIT) and 50% package tour travellers (those travelling with a tour operator)

The majority of tourists seeking nature or adventure type holidays typically travel with niche or small scale operators as mass operators tend to accommodate sun, sea and sand packages. The number of operators offering more nature or adventure tours has increased in Europe over the past few years, whereas in North America, specialty travel operators have existed for over a decade. Overall, the percentage of consumers who consciously look for sustainable travel packages or ecotourism has been estimated to be as high as 5% of the overall market for travel, although up to 30% feel that it would be 'nice to have' but without an accompanying willingness to pay (World Tourism Organisation-WTO). With increased awareness of general societal issues regarding sustainability, this number is expected to increase somewhat.

Sustainable tourism demand is difficult to assess as most figures are anecdotal evidence of market share. A number of surveys have been completed over recent years which have assessed demand for more sustainable forms of travel. A report by the WTO in 1997 presented information to indicate that ecotourism (not sustainable tourism) accounts for 20% of the world tourism market. The International Ecotourism Society Report, whose statistics were cited worldwide in other reports, indicated that ecotourism contributed US$154 billion in receipts for 2000 and was growing at a rate of 20% per year compared with 7% for tourism overall. This number has not been substantiated in any recent reports.

According to National Geographic, there are 55 million 'geo-travellers' in the United States who are environmentally and socially responsible and have ceaseless expectations for unique and culturally authentic travel experiences that protect and preserve the ecological and cultural environment. 38% of these travellers would be willing to pay a premium to patronise travel companies that use sustainable environmental practices (although it should be noted that only 1% of US travellers take holidays overseas). In Europe, 95 % of Swiss tourists consider respect for local culture to be highly important when choosing a holiday and approximately 87% of respondents in a responsibletravel.com survey suggested they were also interested in locally produced food, local culture and using local guides when on holiday.

The Association of British Travel Agents (ABTA) survey said that it was very important that their holiday did not damage the environment (45%) and that it benefited the people of the destination they were travelling to (for example, through jobs and business opportunities (30%). None of the tour operators interviewed have found that their clientele was willing to pay a premium for these criteria to any substantial degree.

Although consumers may indicate that they expect environmental and social issues to be taken into consideration on their holidays, they do not take it upon themselves to ensure these criteria are being met. Responsibility for ensuring more sustainable tourism falls in the hands of the operator. In the UK, over 80% say tour operators should have responsibility for preserving the local environment and culture and ensuring that local people benefit from tourism.

The same percentage of people are more likely to book a holiday with a company with a 'responsible' travel policy-a 28% increase since 2001. A report in 2000 declared that 55% of consumers believed that travel agents have a responsibility to provide the information, while 48% think tour operators should provide it. Social or environmental considerations, although they may be expected to be addressed in the brochure or on the website of an operator or travel provider, are not demanded when booking travel packages. From interviews with large and specialty operators it was found that no specific consumer requests for specific environmental or social criteria were requested or enquired about when booking their holidays. The only customer issues or questions were regarding stray animals or if there was an animal protection group to look after stray dogs or donkeys clients had encountered. Additionally, environmental and social criteria do not affect most tour operators' choice when selecting their package components as their primary focus is on price and second on quality. In a study done in 2003, almost 70% of tour operator clients expressed no concern or interest in eco-social issues when selecting their products and only 8% expressed a specific interest when selecting their tour Overall, less than 10% of the market booking ecotours in the US is requesting information from their operators on eco-social standards.

Examining eco-tourism, a WTO report in 2002 prepared for the International Year of Ecotourism (IYE) found that ecotourism was closer to 5% of the market compared to 20% as reported in

2000 and although awareness had increased, there was little evidence that ecotourism had been growing, let alone rapidly. Furthermore, although a 2003 survey of successful ecolodge owners and regional ecotourism experts worldwide found that the U.S. market was cited to be the largest and most significant ecotourism market in the world the GeoTourism study found that less than 10% of the 55 million that were classified as geotourists preferred to travel outside of the United States therefore hardly contributing to tourism revenues in low income countries.

Consumer Motivations

Consumer surveys indicate that there is a willingness to pay for more sustainable types of tourism. In the STI survey (2004) 75.4% of self-declared environmentally oriented consumers declared they were willing to pay $1-20 extra per ticket to mitigate the green house gas effects of their travel. Seventy-seven declared they would switch online travel sites to one that made contributions on their behalf to offset the portion of their emissions. The National Geographic geotourism survey suggested that 61% of those interested in environmentally and socially sensitive travel would pay 5-10% more to use such companies. The Mori (2002) study suggests that package holiday makers would pay more if money went towards preservation of the local environment and reversing some negative environmental effects of tourism (47%), workers in the destination are guaranteed good wages and working conditions (49%), hotels serve food produced locally (36%) or money went to support a local charity (22%).

These consumers said they would be willing to pay up to 10% more for a holiday (1-2% more = 36% of holiday makers, 5% more-39%, 10% more = 18%). In practice, however, there was no evidence that this research led to actual purchase behaviour. From interviews conducted, there was no indication that consumers were willing to pay more for sustainable tourism products even though they may indicate it in research. As one industry leader noted, "In several surveys done in the last years, a considerable number of people always affirm they would be ready to pay for it. But unfortunately the reality shows that the customer's decisions are often dominated by other criteria, and mostly by price. There is obviously a contradiction between intention and behaviour. It is what we call a cognitive dissonance.

However, in many destinations, it is common practice that tourists on an excursion in wildlife reserves pay an extra fee for nature protection activities and this is well accepted". For example, TUI offered a program for ski holiday tourists to purchase a tree to reduce carbon emissions (£10 purchased a tree and a map of where it was planted). Only 1 in 20 bookings subscribed to the program even though it was listed on a full page of the holiday brochure. Specialty operators also did not have much participation, either.

Explore, the UK's largest adventure operator, offered clients to offset their emissions through Climate Care. There has only been a 3% participation rate. By contrast, niche operators see environmental and social issues as part of their core business and often have programs to support such initiatives (see appendix C). These operators are more likely to search for accommodations or areas which are seen as 'green', however, due to a lack of critical mass and awareness by operators, there are few examples of companies using certified accommodations. Sustainability issues are also not perceived to be a key factor in the tourist decision-making process. A report in 2000 notes that surveys have been unable to conclude that environmental, social or sustainability criteria are a key concern in holiday decision-making by tourists-even so-called ecotourists are not often motivated to travel because of interest in being 'responsible' or 'environmentally concerned. It is clear that marketers need to connect consumer motivations with actual purchasing. As one expert noted, "consumers are willing to make a greener choice if the product comes from a company [or destination] they already know and trust, it doesn't require (m)any behavioural changes to use, and it's at least as good as what they're already buying in terms of aesthetics, style, taste, etc.".

The majority of travel globally is still mass tourism which consists mainly of sun, sea and sand tourism package holidays provided by large operators (TUI, First Choice, Mytravel). Price, accommodation quality and personal security rank as the most important considerations of booking holidays. Consumers are susceptible to health and safety issues, however, with cleanliness and quality being major factors in their destination choice. From existing research and interviews with tour operators and other experts, it can be concluded that consumers would change their destination choice as a result of bad press about health (e.g. dirty beaches) or safety issues, but not for lack of environmental or social responsibility on the part of suppliers. If evidence suggests that consumers are looking for more sustainable product in tourism yet are driven mainly by price or health issues, there is a need to rethink a strategy to shift product and packaging so that product offered to the consumer integrates wider issues of sustainability.

OVERVIEW OF CERTIFICATION SCHEMES

Certification can be described as the process of assuring consumers and industry that the company being assessed has met a set of minimum standards. Within the tourism industry, certification started in the early 1990's. Since 1992, a number of schemes have been developed.

The purpose of certification has been to achieve voluntary standards of performance which meet or exceed baseline standards or legislation. The process starts with a body that sets credible certification standards (through standards which are industry relevant, measurable and obtainable). The certification body must be without conflict of interest and the indicators should be recognised by an accreditation body. The applicant or business then is assessed according to the indicators and, if successful, receives recognition, usually through the form of a logo, to inform the consumer that they have met minimum criteria. The aim of certification is to foster responsible environmental, social and cultural behaviour and provide a quality product to consumers. To be considered reliable, certification programs need to have a 3 rd party audit and effective assessment as well as clearly defined accreditation criteria. According to Toth (2002), elements of a credible certification system include:

Adequate, appropriate standards developed/accepted by all affected interests-interpretation of standards;

Trained, qualified assessors-standard defining training and qualifications;

Professional/ethical operations at all levels with no biases or conflicts of interest;

Qualified, financially stable certifying body-if there are multiple certifiers, an accreditation mechanism is needed;

Even-handed certification and accreditation;

Transparency;

Defined procedures;

Appeals mechanism;

Recognition by relevant agencies and/or customers-compliance with accepted criteria (e.g. ISO/IEC Guides) facilitates recognition; and

Acceptance in the marketplace or by regulators-marketing and promotion.

It should be noted that the above definition defines elements of a credible certification system, not necessarily one that incorporates all elements of sustainable tourism. As many schemes do not address social or labour issues in detail, these issues have not been addressed to date.

DEVELOPMENT OF SCHEMES

There are many certification schemes regarding tourism that relate to sustainability. The best known NGO or country initiatives include Voluntary Initiatives for Sustainable Tourism VISIT (Europe-wide), the Costa Rican standard Certification for Sustainable Tourism (CST), Green Deal Guatemala), and Scotland's Green Tourism Business Scheme (GTBS). The best known industry certification programmes are Green Globe and Blue Flag. Green Globe offers product as well as destination certification, while Blue Flag certifies beaches. There are two industry based standards which do not solely address tourism: ISO 14001 which addresses environmental impacts and ISO 9001 which addresses quality assurance (both mainly used by larger hotels rather than small operators or accommodations). The majority of funding and attention towards certification has addressed tourism-only schemes. These are the 'eco' schemes that focus mainly upon SME's. A number of eco certification projects are in the pilot or development phase such as Mexico, The Caribbean, Sub-Saharan Africa and Peru and countries such as Kenya and Botswana are considering them.

The majority of European ecolabels have related to environmental criteria, however, developing countries such as the Americas and South Africa have included social and cultural aspects as major components. Development of certification and eco-labels has been irregular and although there are benefits of putting forth such programs to set baseline standards, programs are not world-wide, nor is there a critical mass of certified products. There are few programs in low income countries as 2/3 of the approximately 7,000 certified tourism products are in Europe. Approximately 40% of programs started before 1996 with an additional 40% between 1996-2000 and a number of new initiatives developed since 2000 (European Centre for Ecological and Agricultural Tourism (ECEAT), eastern European programs and Central and South America).

Programs and practices vary region to region. Most schemes are national in scope, such as the CST, Guatemalan Green Deal and South Africa's Fair Trade Tourism label. The model for certification in Latin America is the CST and this is now being expanded to become the Network of the Americas to include Guatemala, Brazil, Ecuador and other newly proposed schemes. Most countries in this region have implemented (or plan to such as Mexico & Peru) a national program using the CST as a model 'although the costs of starting and operating a certification program have meant there has been little progress'. Although publicised as a model for tourism certification, the CST program has few certified products and the Network of the Americas does not have many in total (e.g., only 21 products have been certified in Guatemala).

In Europe, the VISIT program has created an inclusive system to raise standards and cooperation among current European programs, and markets approximately 4,000 certified products through ethical trade fairs (green travel market) and to tour operators. The most successful certification program, Blue Flag, has extended its program outside Europe to the Caribbean, North America and Africa although this program only applies to the certification of beaches.

Green Globe is an industry standard which currently operates out of Australia but has certified properties worldwide. Destination certification has been gaining momentum in recent years due to issues of sustainable destination management and Green Globe's program offers a comprehensive approach for multiple players. Measurability and implementation of this scheme, however, has been questioned. Green Globe is one scheme that does offer certification of more than just ecotourism or small scale products as they offer services for tour operators, hotels, destinations, etc. Some larger scale companies have obtained certification (all-inclusive resorts such as Sandals, Casuarina Beach, Almond Beach and some Hilton and Marriott properties). In 2002, a project called the Sustainable Tourism Stewardship Council (STSC) was set up with the aim of harmonising and providing mutual recognition of schemes, and to set up an international accreditation agency-but little progress has been made since its inception. Reasons include the lack of an over-riding body to adopt international certification, confusion of existing criteria and competition between existing schemes (who did not want to merge their labels).

The majority of certification schemes accredit accommodations (approximately 63%), whereas only 7% address tour operators, mainly ground operators specifically dealing with ecotourism. Approximately 40% of the criteria or indicators in standards relate to management issues and the remaining 60% relate to specific actions such as environmental benchmarking (34%), economic indicators (8%) or socio-cultural criteria (12%). The majority of programs to date (with the exception of Green Globe, Blue Flag and ISO) have targeted small operations or ecolodges rather than larger scale tourism accommodations.

Standards can be divided into product standards (reflecting the appropriate characteristics a product is expected to have) or process standards (reflecting the appropriate characteristics from products to final distribution).

Larger tourism operators, mainly hotels, have few connections with smaller certification schemes and opt instead for international standards such as ISO 9001 which provides a quality assurance accreditation or ISO 14001 which provides environmental accreditation. These schemes are not widely adopted, however, due to a lack of awareness and marketing and many larger chains having their own internal monitoring or benchmarking systems.

Benefits and Issues

The benefits of certification are seen to be wide-spread although the majority of programs uphold marketing and training as their primary benefits. With the designation of a logo, certification is thought to give companies a competitive advantage and increased linkages into the distribution chain and to consumers through marketing (inclusions on web sites, travel fairs, brochure recognition), all of which would be assumed to give businesses competitiveness. Additional benefits perceived from certification include:

The ability to distinguish sustainable tourism from 'greenwashing'

The encouragement of voluntary improvements

Showcasing best practices

The use of the standard as a blueprint for future development

Training of management procedures

Cost savings

Peer recognition

Achievement beyond legislation compliance

Determinants of success of schemes have been linked to marketing which to date, has been largely unsatisfactory with the exception of some ECEAT schemes due to the small number of certified products and therefore reduced appeal to large operators to use them in their product choice. Also, the sheer number of schemes and labels makes it difficult for tour operators to incorporate them as they would have to educate the consumer about the standards behind each one and differences among them. This is beyond what tour operators deem practical for hard copy brochures. Larger certified operators (through organisations such as Green Globe or ISO) have seen cost savings and overall improved management structures. Some benefits to the community are improved environmental conditions of facilities or infrastructure improvements such as new access roads (although often larger hotel chains build water or sewage plants only for the hotel complex rather than the community or village at large). As most certification schemes do not include labour or social/community issues, the local community has not greatly benefited. In addition, companies have not generally seen marketing benefits, and therefore have participated in schemes largely for cost savings or reporting purposes.

Ecolabels in Eastern Europe were developed to promote organic farms and rural accommodation and promote them to the increasing number of tourists visiting these regions. The Czech Republic's scheme has seen 135 accommodations certified which have been promoted through publications of the Countryside Holiday Guidebook and or the Heritage Trails. As many visitors to Eastern European countries have been VFR (visiting friends and relatives) or independent tourists, farm stays and rural accommodation was a unique and relatively new type of tourism which has since led to the growth of agro-tourism in Europe. The newest initiative is the new "national ecolabel for tourist services" which has been accepted by the Czech Government three weeks ago and will be used as a tool for the new governmental "Tourism Policy" since 2007 (because of the EU programming period 2007-2013).

Failures of certification schemes

Issues around certification are widespread and varied. As Font (2003) suggests, the majority of certification schemes for tour operators address ecotourism operations rather than large mass market operators who supply the majority of the world's tourism and have the main access to the market. Therefore it has not helped respond to industry pressure as most operators have not heard of the numerous schemes or choose their product based on price. Additionally, there is a lack of critical mass as less than 1% of tourism businesses are certified. Thus, tour operators do not have enough products to choose from and often schemes do not ensure quality standards in their accreditation. Issues include:

Lack of critical mass (too few certified products, certification is not wide-spread)

Too many certification programs and other industry awards have led to confusion Lack of awareness by industry, consumers and government

Lack of unified brand (too many programs compete against each other, duplicate efforts, yet vary in their criteria)

Low consumer demand and a general tiredness with labels of all kinds

Lack of credibility (local certification schemes with no international recognition)

Lack of proven marketing benefits (and lack of marketing by certification bodies)

Lack of incentives for hotels or businesses to join

Lack of readiness to disclose information (Businesses do not wish to disclose information to obtain certification)

Cost of adherence (e.g., Green Globe, ISO) and perception that recognition/label can be 'bought'

Types of and Participation in Schemes

The most successful certification program to date has been Blue Flag, an internationally recognised program for measuring the health of beaches. Over 2,700 beaches have been certified. Success can be linked to health and safety as tourists do not want to bathe on polluted beaches. As noted earlier, beach health and cleanliness is a motivating factor in choosing a holiday therefore, having an internationally known system that assures beach health is an economic incentive for a hotel owner near a beach. The Blue Flag program greatly reduces the cost of evaluation by using existing infrastructure to take measurements of the environment. Overall, certification within the tourism industry has been difficult to achieve because tourism is multifaceted and includes a mix of services and products. Most certification and supplier development is voluntary (between 10-25% of suppliers have met the voluntary sustainability related standards), but there is little consensus that certification is actually viable. There are also few accommodations or organisations that have been certified. In Europe, where the most ecolabel or certification programs exist, less than 0.5% of accommodations have been certified. The four best known certification programs for ecotourism and SMEs (ECOTEL, CST, NEAP and Green Globe) have less than 2000 members in total. In Costa Rica only 5% of hotels have been certified, with only 46% of them advertising their certification.

It has been suggested by the new InterAmerican Bank MIF project for a Sustainable Tourism Certification System that certification for sustainability of tourism will increase competitiveness and market access of small and medium sized enterprises in Latin America. The EU has funded the VISIT scheme and the Green Travel Market to promote certified products and the Cooperative Research Centre for Sustainable Tourism (CRC) in Australia has partnered with Green Globe. However, a thorough review of existing reports on this topic shows that there are no market demand studies available to support this assumption.

Many programs also focus specifically on eco-lodges or other small scale accommodation, such as agro-tourism accommodations. Although this form of tourism can bring positive benefits to the areas in which it operates, its very nature does not make it suitable for mass tourism operators who control the vast majority of travel. There is also a lack of awareness among businesses, although the GTBS in Scotland affirmed that they had good take-up over the first three years, and that their membership is now increasing by about 30% per annum. In Costa Rica, initial participation in the program was also high, however, to date there are few hotels that have achieved a full five star rating. The CST stated that the department was receiving approximately 300 requests for certification per year before the 'oath of legality' (must be notorized by a Public Notary) was put into place. Now they are only receiving 10 requests per year.

There is also a lack of awareness among consumers. In Christchurch, New Zealand, interviews with 295 visitors found that only one-fifth recalled any place with ecolabels, and only 13% had ever heard of any tourism ecolabel. In a survey of 100 tourists in Australia, not one of them chose his or her hotel based on Eco-Australia certification. It is estimated that less than 1% of consumers were aware of the existence or criteria of any tourism certification program (for consistency). Some certification programs assessed did not claim to attract increased business but focused instead on improving management procedures and reduce cost savings. The GTBS said applicants have higher occupancy rates than average for Scotland. This, however, must be accepted with caution as these applicants tend to be well managed companies who would likely achieve these results even without certification. In Guatemala, companies gain more through management techniques to reduce costs and improve efficiency than they do through marketing.

There are also problems with transparency as some businesses in Guatemala do not want to disclose their practices in order to obtain an ecolabel. Certification cannot be seen to counter the problem of 'greenwashing' as schemes are mainly small scale and there is not enough industry pressure to make a difference. There is no world-wide method of monitoring certification and therefore overall compliance and improvement is hard to gauge.

Roles and Costs

Approximately 60% of certification programs are led by private tourism organisations or NGO's; the remainder are government led. The investment for the development of eco-labels differs from the maintenance of the programs. Development of programs is almost evenly split between NGO's, public and private sector (1/3 each, respectively), whereas almost 2/3 of programs are engaged in a multi-stakeholder collaborative approach regarding decision-making and advice giving. The costs of developing certification programs are often put upon governments, however, large governance structures are pricey and programs may need a further layer of organisations to help industry implement the standards. There is a high cost for SME's to apply for certification unless it is subsidised by government (application procedure and operation of program), and it is often not the priority of the government to run these schemes. Past studies showed that examples from Fiji, Dominican Republic and Venezuela failed in their early attempts to set up programs. NGO's are not able to afford the start-up costs of wide-scale certification projects and are therefore either government subsidised or address specific areas (e.g. Ecuador's Smart Voyager program in the Galapagos, PAN Parks in Europe, Kenya lodge accreditation). Unless subsidised, not all firms will have the same potential access to become certified.

Most programs have addressed these issues through scaled fee structures which are linked to overall company turnover or number of staff. In Costa Rica, the government has successfully subsidised first time applications to the CST. In Australia, costs are kept low but this then impacts the amount of marketing possible. Green Globe, as an industry run program, has higher costs and is linked to the stage of certification. While some certification programs can provide sufficient benefits, cost is an issue for both the company (who may find it costly to implement criteria to become certified) and the program itself as it needs to run its operations and audit the companies applying.

Some companies find ways to repay the fees as they find that meeting some of the criteria make them more eco-efficient and therefore they can justify further certification costs based on the savings realised. For smaller companies, certification programs might need to consider encouraging applications from co-operatives of small firms or under a destination umbrella. Costs are seen by many businesses as high due to the time needed for site visits and filling out forms and questionnaires. Certification can help reduce operating and management costs, although it should be noted that not all adherences to social criteria reduce cost.

Research has shown that substantial energy, waste and water savings can be realised by implementing sustainability criteria into operating processes and procedures. Credible environmental tourism certification programs, with respected standards and rigorous criteria, should be careful in considering broadening their approach to include social issues. 'A tokenist introduction of social issues might instead lead to criticisms for being environmental programs under a sustainability label' and could also raise costs and expertise needed to administer them. It is generally quite difficult to measure social/community impacts through certification.

If certification is to continue to move forward, sustainability criteria need to be assessed alongside health and safety standards as quality assurance is critical to selling a better product. Although eco-certification claims to address environmental and sometimes social criteria, basic health and safety factors are not always considered and some certified ecolodges in Central America have been found to lack basic hygiene and safety. Although ISO 9000 addresses quality assurance, it is not linked to other schemes and has only been adopted by some hotels rather than entire chains or others in the tourism sector.

The main selection criteria for customers to choose their travel packages remain price, safety and quality. Environmental and social criteria will only be considered when these primary criteria are satisfied.

STAKEHOLDER ROLES AND GOVERNMENT INVOLVEMENT

Government roles have mainly involved providing an institutional framework as well as grants or loans. An advantage of government led schemes is that they are usually longer term in focus. Promotion of best practices has also taken place and there is an expectation that governments will take a more active role. Through the assessment of schemes, however, there is no evidence to support that governments are effective at marketing such schemes and often there is a lack of willingness to share information or cooperate with other schemes. There are few motivations for governments to be involved in certification.

There is no market potential as the number of consumers actively supportive is minimal, and most often governments have adopted schemes as part of their wider development strategy (e.g., Costa Rica's Chamber of Commerce (CANATUR) was instrumental in setting up the scheme but has had no part in marketing it). From previous research on the subject and discussions with existing certification programs, it has been suggested that international governmental bodies need to play a more active role. One is a cooperative arrangement with the WTO, and the other a more integrated relationship. An International Sustainable Tourism Commission (ISTC)-an autonomous body functioning as an executing agency of the WTO-has been proposed. There is no evidence, however, to suggest that there would be an increase in certification if this were to be the case as many countries who already offer programs do not want to give up their brand and there is currently a lack of global criteria used in certification.

NGOs

NGO's have also been responsible for running some certification programs, however the high costs of operations questions the feasibility and long term sustainability of this option. The role of NGO's has been to raise awareness and apply legislative pressure. As certification schemes need large upfront and ongoing investments, subsidies are required, and often NGOs partner with industry associations to implement programs. Politically active NGOs are also exerting pressure, particularly on public companies, to take more of a leadership role with respect to CSR.

Industry

There are some industry schemes such as Green Globe, ECOTEL, ISO and CERES. Industry also plays a role in operating schemes such as Guatemala's Alianza Verde (Green Deal). Positive aspects of independent certification are that programs are self-sufficient and would not be relying upon government support. Industry-led schemes are also more willing to share information and partner with other certification schemes to move towards a wider brand and reduce costs for themselves and operators.

Future Involvement

Certification incentives could help build industry buy-in. Interviews with tour operators and existing research suggests that tax write-offs, preferential access to areas (e.g., beach property or remote parks) and preferential marketing for supporting schemes would be beneficial, however, the majority of businesses use certification as a means of cost savings, improving management practices and to comply with the requirements for corporate reporting. The main weakness of certification is the overall lack of reporting and monitoring. Certification has been seen to positively affect resource management but does not necessarily deal with labour or social issues and therefore most companies who promote their certification also provide additional forms of reporting.

Certification also has mainly addressed small companies rather than larger operators, accommodation providers and other service providers who make up the majority of the market.

The Spier estate comprises a 155-room hotel, conference facilities, golf course and winery. Their triple bottom line approach to sustainability has the vision to create a sustainable "micro-ecology" which enhances heritage and culture, generates wealth for all stakeholders, helps meet social and economic needs, and provides the infrastructure to encourage new community lifestyles compatible with the vision for the Winelands. Over 150 indicators measure aspects from compliance with employee regulations, energy and water usage, to the impact of the HIV/AIDS prevention and treatment initiatives. Some of the ways that Spier has contributed to CSR initiatives include:

- Procurement of natural gas from local, black owned business
- The establishment of a crafts market on the estate where individuals sell their craftwork
- obtaining the S.A. Fair Trademark (FTSSA)
- reduced wastewater by 20%
- created 19% new employment abiding by laws of equal opportunity
- given 65 hectares of land and water to 16 small farmers from historically disadvantaged backgrounds (as part of a wider land-reform program)

To advance certification schemes a number of options have been put forward by NGO's, industry and government. The WTO guidelines call for higher government intervention to move sustainable tourism forward. National and regional certification schemes declare there is a need for higher government intervention through the establishment of a global set of criteria, promotion and monitoring. They have also noted that a joined-up government approaches to policy development in destinations (participation from both government and industry associations) is needed to help promote certification and that the overall supply chain needs to be focused upon. Interviewees have been suggesting that overall awareness and one overarching standard is needed if certification is to continue but that financial incentives, verification procedures and mandatory reporting are the most effective means to ensure participation and compliance. Since larger brands and companies dominate the sector, they can have more influence than small scale, bottom-up, locally based initiatives in the adoption of sustainability criteria and reporting.

Currently it is the NGOs, politicians and the financial market which are pushing for sustainability measures to be incorporated. Publicly traded companies, in particular, are being forced into compliance since financial analysts want to avoid risks at all costs; these companies are benchmarked against other global players such as Cendant, Marriott, Hilton, Carnival Cruises, etc., and CSR is therefore seen as key for their investor relations. However, the majority of the certification initiatives within the tourism sector to date have focused on the small scale voluntary initiatives that are not facing pressure to conform.

Operators within the supply chain that report their compliance are in many ways better monitored than if they were certified. TUI, in particular is very strong about tracking and demonstrating continual improvement, and assisting their suppliers through expertise in achieving these improvements. Accor, an international hotel chain also monitors through its purchasing organisations in each country.

In 2002, Accor's Purchasing Department Developed a Sustainable Development

Purchasing Charter which aimed to promote and monitor good labour and environmental practices in the 15 countries where it has a purchasing organisation. In 2003 the charter was sent to Accor's 2,000 preferred suppliers (the group's total spend is more than 1 billion Euros) who were asked to complete a questionnaire in order for the company to monitor supplier compliance. In 2003, Accor also set out a new Subcontracting Charter that clearly defines working conditions for outside cleaning personnel in hotels managed directly by Accor, covering areas from work schedules to training programs and the calculation of hours paid.

CODES OF CONDUCT AND ROLES OF REPORTING

Codes of conduct were first developed in the 1970/80's and were predominantly focused on visitor management and environmental management. Their aim was to raise awareness in industry. There are a number of these codes within the tourism industry, put out by international bodies (WTO, UN, TOI, TIES, etc.), however, there is not industry wide awareness nor is there any monitoring of compliance. The tourism industry is fragmented and difficult to monitor due to the complexity of stakeholders in the value-chain. Codes of conduct tend to be voluntary or informal and vary considerably from sector to sector (hotel, cruise, airline, and operator) and in what they cover (labour, environment, social, economic). There are two types of codes of conduct. One is put out by organisations such as the WTO or industry associations and the latter are self-imposed guideline of what the corporation deems ethical business behaviour and it's done to reassure investors and consumers.

This research supports a recent World Bank Group report that there is virtually no effective monitoring or implementation mechanism yet in place for CSR practices, and that even defining sustainable tourism can be difficult as criteria are interpreted differently by different stakeholders. There are, however, a growing number of guidelines and charters on sustainable tourism which have been put forth by both government and industry.

CODES OF CONDUCT-ROLES AND PARTICIPATION GOVERNMENT

Governments have endorsed the concept of sustainable tourism and signed on to multiple charters, such as the Lanzarote Charter for Sustainable Tourism in 1995 or the EU's 'Working Together for the Future of European Tourism'. However, few charters or country codes actually outline specific measurable targets, as most tourism policies have been driven by economics and divorced from environmental and social costs. There has been raised awareness by destinations in mature stages of development that conservation and social issues could be a challenge as many communities were economically dependant on tourism. There has also been an increase in the adoption of Local Agenda 21 principles for destination management in the past few years. Currently no government body has regulated the need for reporting in the tourism sector.

NGO's

NGO roles have been mainly to put pressure on development agencies and governments to address issues of sustainability, to put pressure on supply chain and distribution channels to change methods of procurement and to develop codes of conduct such as Conservation International's Marine Recreation Guidelines for water sport supplier procurement or the International Tourism Partnership's Siting and Design Guidelines for new hotel construction. Tourism Concern has been a leader in the pressure applied for the inclusion of human rights and labour issues to improve working conditions in tourism destinations. Over recent years, NGO's have called for businesses and governments to report on their environmental and social practices to ensure transparency of operations but currently these are only in the form of advocacy.

Industry

Many individual operators are working toward incorporating sustainability into their products and almost ¾ of tour operators or travel industry associations interviewed (and niche adventure/ nature specialty tour operators) had a responsible or sustainable tourism code or policy, although not all evaluated or monitored compliance. Currently, a number of large scale tour operators are developing sustainable supply-chain policies. European tour operators tend to be most active in this regard, possibly due to the initiatives by the Federation of Tour Operators (FTO) and the Association of Independent Tour Operators (AITO) and the fact that most of the larger ones are publicly traded companies. Although becoming popular, there is a lack of uniformity of codes in spite of the growing number of associations that are making charters or codes mandatory. Elsewhere in the world awareness is much lower.

The Netherlands Association of ANVR tour operators implemented a Product Oriented Environmental Management System as part of their Responsible Tourism Program. The program is obligatory for all of its 200 members. It includes an action package with steps tour operators need to take: internal management and involvement of staff, purchasing, and contract management for the provision of transport, accommodation excursions and entertainment in the destination. The association believes that success factors for travel organisers depend on intact nature, clean beaches and authenticity of destinations. The ANVR, a federation of 3 membership associations: Association Air and Business Travel Agents (VLZ), Association Travel Agents (VRA), Association Travel Organisers (VRO), is focused on outbound tourism. Committed tour operations showed interest in working with certified products even though this cannot always be communicated effectively to clients. Most companies have set their own standards rather than use certification labels as these do not exist in all destinations where tour operators work and there is not enough product that is certified to choose from. Tour operators also feel that the number and variety of different schemes makes it very difficult to educate their customers or their staff. The most successful initiatives which have helped spread more sustainable practices are those for supply chain management. Through the development of association charters or standards such as TUI or the Accor Group, many SMEs worldwide could improve their access to market if they abide by these criteria and offer their services to these buyers (who will need to replace suppliers who are non-compliant if they are to uphold their commitment to their initiatives).

Hilton has adopted a new Standard for Business Partners and Suppliers which includes standards on child or forced labour, employee representation, health, safety and environmental management, discrimination, disciplinary practices and employee compensation and working hours.

Hotel chains have been addressing their environmental concerns for some years. A number of them set up the International Hotel Environmental Initiative in 1992 which focused on environmental improvements and is now starting to address social and community issues. Most of the larger hotel chains comply with environmental standards and have environmental policies and standards ranging from in-house benchmarking systems (Accor, Hilton Group, etc.) to environmental standards manuals (Rezidor, Starwood, Fairmont, etc.). Although not widespread in adoption, some hotels are now promoting when they achieve international certification such as ISO 9001 and 14001 (some Taj, TUI, ITC Hotels, Sol Melia, Baja Inn Hotels). Some hotels have subscribed to local certification systems (such as Rezidor hotels in Scotland attaining the Green Tourism Business Scheme or Rezidor and Scandic hotels in Scandinavia receiving the Nordic Swan ecolabel), however they are few in numbers. There are growing examples of hotel companies who have helped sustainability through backward linkages in lower income countries (see box 9), but to date hotels and large tour companies are not pressured into having to receive a social and/or environmental license to operate as most communities and developing destinations do not have awareness of tourism, let alone the negative issues which may surround it.

Orient-Express inherited a large plot of land as part of the staff accommodation complex in Aguas Calientes, Peru. Orient Express employees who live within the hotel complex and local church workers have started growing their own vegetables which they sell back to the hotel, the Machu Picchu Sanctuary Lodge. In this area of Peru, the hotel had problems finding quality food items, especially vegetables, and now purchases these from their employees.

Reporting

Industry has historically suggested that it will respond to consumer demand for sustainable tourism and that this is where the demand must come from, however, there is evidence that increased CSR is the result of the increased pressure by NGOs, politicians and the financial market to monitor or evaluate codes of conduct or tourism policies which address sustainable or responsible tourism. Reporting comes from constant need for ongoing-communication with suppliers. A notable organisation that is driving progress in this area is the Global Reporting Initiative (GRI), which aims to 'raise the level of sustainability reporting to that of financial reporting'. The Tour Operators' Initiative, in cooperation with the GRI, developed a Sector Supplement to the GRI 2002 Sustainability Reporting Guidelines providing Tour Operators' performance indicators. Forty-seven indicators were developed to measure tour operators' performance in addressing the environmental, economic and social impacts of their business operations. The tour operators' supplement adds to, but does not replace, the 2002 GRI Sustainability Reporting Guidelines' section on performance indicators. The supplement was not designed to capture sector-specific aspects of the various service industries associated with a package, such as transport, accommodation, and other tourism services.

Many companies produce reports that are aimed at their own employees, in order to help explain and support the roll-out of a company's new sustainability policy. Some companies also report for reasons of reputation; such companies are keen to capture their leadership work and/or combat negative perceptions that may have arisen about their sector or brand. A social report can also be a useful communication tool to highlight responsible business practice across a company's worldwide operations. Publicly traded companies need to report on CSR initiatives as part of their investor relations and to demonstrate that they are proactive in reducing potential risks. Thus, larger hotel chains, for instance, have moved significantly towards CSR reporting and have been included in the Dow Jones Sustainability Indicator and FTSE4GOOD index (Accor, Hilton and Intercontinental).

Industry association-led initiatives include the Tour Operators Initiative (TOI) and the IHEI. Both these organisations do not have a specific code of conduct but rather coordinate efforts of tour operators or hotels, respectively, to harmonise performance indicators, monitoring, reporting and tools to assist supply chain partners. The three-year programme aims to standardise sustainability checklists with those of certification programs. The project's goal is to merge/assimilate criteria of the FTO with VISIT (VISIT covers mostly environmental criteria, whereas the FTO includes social and labour issues). The aim is to achieve transparency, a cost-effective distribution system, and to link different supply chain initiatives to provide a common toolkit for travel providers.

CSR AND LOW INCOME COUNTRIES-RECOMMENDATIONS

It must be recognised that without political stability, security and basic infrastructure, tourism will not be fostered by any of the larger international companies, as risks to customers would be deemed too large, and therefore CSR cannot be considered in largely non-democratic countries.

Certification Conclusions

Certification has resulted from confusion over terms in tourism such as 'sensitive, green, and eco', and the desire to legitimise them has led to multiple schemes being developed worldwide. While certification schemes may be described as ways for SMEs in lower income countries to obtain access to market, interviews with both major and specialist tour operators, travel providers and certification programs do not support this view. Most of the certification schemes have only certified small numbers of attractions or businesses and have not linked into the wider distribution channels due to low awareness and lack of critical mass. In addition, the majority of certification schemes address ecotourism operations rather than large mass market operators who supply the majority of the world's tourism and have the main access to the market. There also remains considerable variety in standards, criteria and indicators in certification usage. From this study it can be ascertained that although Costa Rica and other countries have widely known and recognised schemes, they are not able to keep up due to lack of staff and finances for operation. Voluntary standards have not been found to increase access to trade unless governments have assisted with mandatory legislation or trade access structures. Industry is cynical about government taking responsibility for the implementation of sustainable tourism practices and also that investment into better social and environmental performance will increase access to market.

There are a lack of internationally accepted principles for certification criteria (although programs such as VISIT and the Network of the Americas are a partial attempt to overcome this) and there is currently a lack of critical mass of products. Certification was also found to be unsuccessful in allowing greater access to new market segments with the exception of some Eastern European countries who noted that organic farms and rural based accommodations gained an increasing number of tourists (providing they were in accessible locations with other amenities/attractions nearby). The lack of awareness about certification programs and the low incentive for international operators or larger players to take part are largely to blame. Certification schemes at their very best will only allow access to niche market segments, unless they become more widespread and focus on more than just ecotourism and small scale ventures. Operators and certification programmes and research studies have suggested that a global brand is needed if certification is to be pursued more seriously. One brand would help certification to be internationally recognised and also comply with generally accepted international criteria, and thus have a stronger chance of brand recognition in industry. However, no single approach has so far been put forward successfully due to the varying degrees of infrastructure in countries and the lack of sufficient markets to attract certifiable product. If certification is to be moved forward, there is a need to link certification with quality.

"Case after case has demonstrated that consumer demand develops long after a certification program is well established," according to Amos Bien of The International Ecotourism Society (TIES). The recent report on ecotourism certification suggests that consumer demand takes between 8-15 years (sometimes as long as 20) to develop and that quality, safety and price must be satisfied before the consumer will consider other factors. There is also a need to create demand for sustainable tourism among the travelling public through the linkage with existing quality standards. One example where quality has been linked to certification programs is Green Globe, which has partnered with Australia's AAA to award green stars to products, thereby using an existing quality standard to promote eco friendliness. Their advertising notes research that suggest 62% of travellers say that endorsement will encourage them to consider one accommodation over the other.

Although ISO 9001 is a quality standard it is not linked with other certification standards. In addition, the education of governments about the benefits of long-term planning to ensure sustainability of the destination will also provide them with the skills to understand that long-term planning can ensure a more quality rather than quantity focused approach. Most industry players noted they would be willing to abide by a national level certification scheme as long as it was transparent, did not raise costs of product and achieved a critical mass of certified products. In order to achieve effective certification schemes or guidelines in low income countries, a multi-stakeholder participatory approach was suggested that included international organisations, such as tour operators or industry associations, to represent individual companies and contribute to the development/adoption of schemes. Recommendations also included that there needs to be an assurance that Government engages with effective systems and builds proper partnerships and that there is a long-term commitment to the process. Industry is not willing to increase its costs unless it can be translated into increased profits or the cost can be transferred to the consumer. Incentives for gaining participation into schemes by larger operators who could push certification through their supply-chain were suggested, particular tax incentives, preferential access into natural areas and marketing incentives. It should be noted, however, that there are a number of issues within certification schemes themselves which need to be addressed before governments propose this on a wide scale to industry. For certification to advance it needs to be credible, demand driven, open and transparent, self supporting, accessible and link into a consensus of international standards.

Recommendations

This report advocates that countries with more developed infrastructure are better placed to reduce negative effects of tourism than the development of certification schemes, and that adopting CSR and measures of reporting will have a greater positive effect on industry overall. In many low income countries there are problems of lack of tourism planning, established tourism ministries as well as clear roles and objectives. Therefore focusing on public-private partnership to forward the CSR agenda should have a greater overall positive impact and advance sustainable tourism in the industry. However, if certification is to continue, recommendations include:

Rather than develop new certification schemes in each country, have governments endorse existing and internationally known standards, such as ISO 14001 and 9001 and ILO standards.

Continue with efforts to merge certification systems and provide for recognition or convergence of schemes to ensure wider participation and the inclusion of labour and community elements within certification and evaluation initiatives Create a more homogenous market and avoid overregulation in service sectors For elements which are not covered by international agencies (ISO etc.) develop or adopt one internationally recognised brand with baseline criteria to cut down on confusion and multiple criteria Focus on larger tourism companies and international brands operating in developing countries in addition to ecolodges and SMEs to promote wider scale adoption Promote existing industry codes of conduct or guidelines to ensure they are widely disseminated, implemented and monitored/evaluated.

Move towards mandatory certification and reporting (for national recognition of sustainable tourism, a critical mass must be achieved) Integrate quality assurance and health & safety standards into schemes or link with other programs (e.g. GTBS links to a quality assurance accreditation scheme)

Focus on capacity building and awareness campaigns primarily to engage business-to-business marketing and government-to-business marketing and awareness.

Ensure that local certification is implemented through a credible local or regional association to ensure participation and ease of access (but still linked to the overall global brand)

Award achievement rather than commitment (to ensure confidence). Encourage individual business reporting which would improve awareness and obtain confidence in the credibility of certification initiatives.

Recommendations for Achieving Sustainable Tourism and Access to Market for Low Income Countries Supply Chain Initiatives.

In order to enhance sustainable tourism development in low income countries, there is a need to focus on elements of the tourism industry which can affect a greater number of products and businesses and contribute environmentally, socially and economically to lower income countries. SMEs as well as larger businesses in developing countries need to align themselves with European and North American buyers through abiding by CSR and sustainable tourism initiatives that are widely adopted (for example, TUI has made clear that they will not rely upon external auditors for checking accommodations in their programs; therefore businesses reporting on achievements will help link them to buyers who are looking for conformance). Restrictions or initiatives for more sustainable tourism may not come from low income countries as they are more than ever dependant on the free market economy. Restrictions must come from buyers in Northern Asia, Europe and North America and there need to be incentives for industry to apply supply chain CSR/sustainable tourism standards. Supply chain initiatives can aid in creating more sustainable forms of tourism through:

- Employment: commitments from tourism companies to employ local people at fair wages and provide job training
- Local economic linkages: local procurement of food, supplies and services
- Minimising negative cultural and environmental impacts: through sustainable charters and codes adopted by large industries (such as abiding by international environmental and social regulations which may be ignored or not monitored in local destinations). Also through corporate reporting, education to consumers and businesses on traditional cultures and behaviour will be promoted
- Participation in planning and decision-making processes: through the procurement of local operators and services,

community and local views will be fed back through the supply chain

- Linking quality assurance and certification: if buyers adopt criteria for their suppliers, suppliers may use certification programs to obtain the necessary training and knowledge to attain baseline or minimum standards

Recommendations: Encourage SMEs to focus their criteria to match those of international buyers so that they can align themselves with buyers who demand CSR criteria.

Governments should increase pressure on industry associations to ensure supply-chain practices are publicly accessible Provide standards for reporting, including common terminology, disclosure of information, methods of evaluating performance, quality management systems and assessment of evaluation bodies .

Provide incentives for both small and larger tourism businesses to adopt supply chain sustainable tourism/CSR criteria. Incentives suggested include:

* Rewarding good practice or suppliers that meet minimum standards set
* Facilitating more business to business marketing-through distribution channels; instead of business to consumer marketing as this is not yet strong enough to influence the consumer
* Promoting best practices that showcase that success needs to include Profit and Returns on Investment in order to build the business case for the industry

Ensure low income countries incorporate tourism into their development policies and provide incentives for larger international companies to adopt certification measures and supply chain guidelines which will benefit SMEs and the local community.

Reporting

Business reporting on social and environmental issues has potentially helped increase loyalty and a sense of distinctiveness. Some businesses ascertain that promoting their responsible/ sustainable business practices can give them a better market position by distinguishing and differentiating their approach.

Initiatives must be industry led as labour standards and other elements of sustainability are not visible to the consumer but crucial nonetheless to the long-term wellbeing of the destination. CSR reporting means a company is more transparent and accountable to external stakeholders, enabling investors to avoid risk and consumers to support more sustainable businesses, therefore having a multiplier effect. Reporting was deemed essential by the corporate interviewees to ensure that efforts are maintained, and initiatives continued. It also makes it possible for others in the supply chain and at destinations to duplicate successful practices. Currently there is low brand loyalty as consumers make decisions primarily based on price; CSR initiatives could potentially lead to increased brand loyalty and product differentiation. As there is currently little consumer support or awareness, information databases need to be linked so that environmental and social criteria can be provided to the client when they are booking their holiday.

Recommendations: Governments should focus their capacity-building efforts on suppliers, using such methods as legislated compliance (e.g., environmental, reputation and business probity), ensuring that resources are available for training and learning by suppliers and, where needed, fill resource gaps Increase public-private partnerships of training for environmental and social awareness and mitigation strategies Offer incentives and reporting guidelines to the tourism sector distributed through industry associations. Support training and sharing of best practices Encourage industry associations to make adherence to sustainable or responsible tourism policies a condition of membership and to report on progress Encourage CSR reporting from tour operators, airlines, cruises, hotels and destinations themselves so that they can understand the impact they themselves are having. Reporting will also provide measurable criteria by which companies and destinations can be compared.

Providing for a Sustainable Industry

To ensure that a more sustainable form of tourism is pursued, there is a need for stricter legislation coupled with joined-up government. Both industry and certification bodies interviewed noted that a such an approach adopts a concerted effort using all the arms of government-central, regional and local government and public agencies, as well as the private and voluntary sectors to form private/public partnerships. Integration into wider sustainable development plans as well as destination management plans is imperative, and a bottom-up as well as a top-down policy approach is needed. Pressure on governments to incorporate tourism into their wider development policies may help raise awareness about the need for sustainable tourism and the benefits of long-term planning approaches, however there is a strong need for training of employees and industry players at the local level. Stricter legislation in low income and developing countries is often fraught with issues of corruption, lack of monitoring and lack of governance, as there are often neither tourism master plans that incorporate sustainable tourism practices or measures nor incentives for industry to adopt them on their own initiative. To date, few developing countries have imposed social or environmental criteria to foreign investors, seeing only short term economic gains instead of long-term, holistic, sustainable tourism development.

Recommendations: Ensure transparency through a multi-stakeholder process Include sustainable tourism in all levels of policy formulation from national tourism policy to local destination management plans Recognise the difference between local vs. international stakeholders and the incentives or encouragement they need to adopt more sustainable forms of tourism practices Ensure that tourism is seen as a core or pillar in countries' wider development plans and policies

Ensure that development of tourism in low income countries includes education and training of local communities Provide for sustainability experts to be included in new tourism developments to ensure social and environmental criteria are considered in proposals and funding Ensure stakeholders are identified and consulted throughout the tourism development process and play an active role in decision-making Promote positive investment structures for integrated tourism master planning-focusing on risk mitigation through sustainable development and planning of tourism.

CONCLUSION

Sustainable tourism can help overcome many of the negative impacts associated with tourism development. Based on the interviews conducted, it is clear that guidelines alone are not strong enough to overcome the short-term profit motive of many operators, governments and destinations. At the same time, national certification programs are too numerous, with too many varying criteria, and not enough accredited product to be effective at this point in time. The analysis indicated that there are emerging trends and recommendations to be gained from this examination, however, it is not suggested that these codes or schemes are standardised within the tourism sector, nor is there a convergence of themes within them with the exception of the International Labour Organisation (ILO) and environmental criteria which often addresses similar issues of waste, water and energy management.

In summary, the conclusions of this report are fourfold. First, there is little overt demand for sustainable tourism therefore more research is needed to determine how product can be shifted to include sustainability. If the consumer and the industry are driven by price then there is a need to re-think the strategy of how to include sustainability within current cost structures. Second, there is low awareness and success of certification programs to date. There is a need to further develop the concept of an international certification label for the travel and tourism industry that is inclusive (environmental, social, cultural etc.), affordable, monitored, and reported. As there are already a number of recognised and internationally accepted schemes, these should be promoted to extend their reach rather than developing new schemes which add to the confusion of both the industry and the consumer.

Third, in order to achieve more sustainable forms of tourism, it needs to move away from voluntary measures towards reporting where progress can be measured and buyers and suppliers held accountable for their actions. Fourth, CSR could help with a number of issues facing tourism with regard to promoting sustainable tourism practices, however, industry must see government involvement and support if they are to increase their own involvements in CSR. There is a need for governments to step up to the challenge of ensuring more sustainable forms of tourism will be supported and to reassure investors and players in the tourism sector that government will support and encourage sustainable tourism management and development.

Sustainable Tourism Diagnostic Checklist

The purpose of this checklist is to attempt to align CSR practices within the tourism industry and public sector development of tourism. It contains a series of criteria that strive for optimal roles for good business practices and development. It should be noted that different criteria will be different for each sector of the industry (for example airlines would not be operating tours or tour operators would not be gaining acquiring land).

In addition, due to the nature of the tourism industry, many businesses within this sector may be too small to fulfil all criteria and this tool should be used as a guideline only. A number of elements of this checklist are critical to ensure the development of a sustainable tourism industry. This does not mean that other elements are not important, however, the elements marked with an * are the minimum standards for which broad enforcement/compliance is desirable and realistic. It should be noted that different countries will have different laws and regulations, and that basic international standards as set out by ILO and other such organizations should be followed in due process.

Economic

General Policies and Planning

- Policies to accommodate cultural customs, traditions and practices of staff throughout the organisation*
- Disclosure of loans, monies and taxes from third parties*
- Policy to support voluntary eco-labels and certification where possible
- Public disclosure of health and safety policy for operations, staff, end-user and management in accordance with national and international laws*
- Annual environmental, social and economic report available in public domain*
- Policy and compliance of anti-corruption measures*

Management Systems

- Governance structure*
- Management systems*
- Corporate accountability and risk assurance committee
- Compliance with local laws and regulations*

Employee/HR Principles

- Clear policy and guidelines on labour standards in accordance with local labour law *
- Established working hours and terms of overtime, sick leave*
- Abolishment of child labour, sexual discrimina-tion, forced, bonded or compulsory labour*
- No tolerance of physical, psychological violence or verbal abuse*
- Recognition of right of employee to be represented by trade unions or other associations and recogni-tion for negotiations on behalf of associations*
- Recognition and access for employee feedback and established mechanisms for grievances, redress, appeal
- Respect for human rights (including indigenous and tribal people)*
- Compliance with ILO conventions on child and forced labour*
- Recognise freedom of association; non-discrimination; programmes to combat sexual exploitation of children and to combat and mitigate the social impacts of HIV/ AIDS; citizen participation in planning process*
- Provide evidence of recruiting local residents (including destination nationals) for destination posts including management positions (in accordance with local and international law)
- Preference to local employment (within legal constraints)
- Established wages consistent with national standard*
- Honoured reasonable employee benefits-Access to health care, dental, vacation pay, maternity rights, meals or food allowance, transportation allowance, travel, performance bonuses*
- On-the job training for skills and upgrading of skills
- Training for environmental and cultural sensitivity-both within community, corporate culture and to tourists*
- Fair redundancy, compensation and termination terms*

Note: Many labour standards should reflect compliance with ILO standards Supply chain /procurement procedures:

- Provision of purchasing of local food and equipment from local community
- Creation of networks of environmentally/socially responsible businesses within the destination area
- Use of locally sourced and produced materials, foods, etc. (within legal constraints)
- Describe processes through which suppliers, by type, are consulted during development and implementation of the supply chain management policy,
- Description and disclosure of supply chain policy and targets for social, environmental and economic measures
- Description of suppliers who have sustainability policies and implemented a sustainability management system and/or have a staff person with management responsibility for corporate sustainability.
- Adoption of fair competitive practices for procurement and service contracts*
- Provision of information on quality of products and quality standards
- Fair payment of contracts and service agreements within national legal standards*
- Applied health and safety practices in accordance with national and international laws for suppliers and purchasers*
- Promotion and public encouragement of environmentally and social practices within supply chain
- Published supply chain practices code
- Promotion of labour standards through supply chain

Environmental Reporting/Management Systems

- Established policy and compliance with local and international environmental management, transport and hazardous waste principles*
- Established formal Environmental Management System (EMS) (performance based)
- Disclosure of improved EMS management, operations and organizational structures (attempt to integrate EIA into standard EMS)

- Annual environmental report
- Policy and timely disclosure of environmental reporting to shareholders and public stakeholders including:
- Assessment of significant risk of products, services and/ or operations*
- Incorporation of risk assessment and mitigation*
- Conducted and application of environmental impact assessment (EIA) in all new building or construction in accordance to international and local laws*
- Conducted independent EIA to assess and avoid conflict for both environmental implications as well as social/ community implications-obtain clear permission/license to progress from both environmental and social community*

Environmental Management

- Incorporation of published standards for new siting and design for new construction, refurbishment and renovation of property
- Consultation with affected stakeholders regarding risk mitigation
- Disclosure of environmental risks to affected stakeholders within reasonable timeframe*
- Established effective procedures to address environmental damage to resources and risk mitigation plan to overcome hazards or deterioration*
- Environmental impact assessment checklist or guideline to assess adverse social impacts
- Support of conservation efforts
- Standard training of risk management, environmental awareness of products and services*
- Established tour size (tours or excursions group sizes for tours are kept to minimum size (under 16 passengers)
- Established tourist/resident ratio on peak days or season*
- Established standards for impacts for specialized tourism products/services (golf, diving, beaches, hiking, heritage sites, etc.) *

- Use of sustainable forms of tourism for touring or use of low emission gasoline
- Established measures to increase public access, visual and landscape impacts
- Assessment and measures for protection of local Flora y Fauna, wildlife, open spaces and forest, biodiversity, marine/eco/terrestrial habitats, water, air and noise*
- Establishment of Green areas and gardens
- Mitigation of visual and landscape impacts
- Established appropriate scale for design and building of tourist facilities/accommodation
- Use of appropriate building materials (aestheti-cally sensitive to area and renewable where possible)
- Environmental education to staff, management and consumers of risks and possible reduction of energy, water and waste

Water

- Efficient use of water*
- Reporting on usage of potable water
- Re-use of grey water

Energy

- Use of renewal energy sources*
- Reduced use where possible of energy intensive practices*
- Reporting on fuel usage cost, CO_2 emissions Usage of alternate and other energy sources, including solar, wind, geothermal, biomass, small-scale hydro energy, and methane based composting systems
- Waste
- Compliance with national and international regulations of hazardous waste*
- Provision of consumption of annual waste
- Optimal use of Non-corrosive biodegradable chemicals / cleaning products*
- Recycled / eco-friendly products, Post-consumer recycled paper and products

- Established recycling program
- Reduction of non renewable resources where possible *

Pollution

- Assessment and mitigation of noise and air pollution
- Assessment and mitigation of air quality

Social

Guests

- Encouraging responsible use of alcohol
- Evidence of environmentally friendly materials for guest/ client promotional materials
- Education to consumers about local traditions/cultures*
- Education of ecological and biodiversity to guests*
- Assurance that guests do not purchase products made from endangered species*
- Responsible advertising customer satisfaction and feedback
- Encourage customer engagement through
- feedback systems
- awareness and education means surrounding environmental and social issues and protection Community engagement and benefit
- Training programs extended to local community
- Planning gains-infrastructure or public building (e.g. hospitals) that are donated through development
- Appropriate land acquisition *
- Accessibility for public and local community to beaches and attractions and special consideration given regarding local rates and membership*
- Established and accessible community feedback system for feedback and participation in new development*
- Disclosure to employees and community of health and safety risk as well as occupational hazards/diseases/health risks
- Established policy or guidelines for community engagement and non-commercial stakeholders

(community groups, NGOs, non-shareholding government authorities, universities etc.)*

- Recognition and protection of the integrity of the community social structure*
- Recognition and respect for local tribal and indigenous groups*

Health and Safety

- Accident and insurance prevention*
- Senior management accountability
- Regular training*
- Systems to respond to and prevent threats
- Clean bathroom, potable water and food storage
- Established house keeping standards
- Clear policies and guidelines established for health and safety measures including accidents and disease*
- Clear policies and guidelines developed for fair and equitable hiring/termination
- Clear policies and guidelines developed to address social issues (e.g. aids/HIV, etc in accordance with national standards) *
- Established effective management system for promoting health and safety*

Accessibility

- Accessibility measures for the handicapped
- Consideration of environmentally sound mean and modes of transport

Contribution to Local Development

- Evidence of changes in tour package or hotel operations to minimise negative environmental and social effects on local community
- Charitable donations to socio-cultural projects
- Charitable donations to environmental or conservation projects
- Contributions of annual hours of in kind / volunteer to local communities

- Describe measures taken to identify and offer commercial opportunities and assistance to non-contracted suppliers that support community development*
- Indicate total funds (in cash and estimated value of in-kind contributions) for conservation and social development projects.
- Describe programmes for philanthropic and charitable donations in relation to conservation and community development projects.
- Deployment of market research, distribution networks and retail channels to support community-based enterprises
- Provision of emergency assistance (e.g. for natural disasters)
- Rescue and protection of Historic-Cultural Patrimony.

Bibliography

Abram, Simone: *Tourists and Tourism: Identifying with People and Places*, New York, Berg, 1997.

Andrew Holden: *Tourism: A New Perspective*, London, Prentice Hall, 1995.

Andronicou, Antonios: *Tourism in Cyprus*, New York, Oxford University Press, 1979.

Apostolopulos, Y., S. Lewadi: *The Sociology of Tourism*, New York, Routledge, 1996.

Ashworth, Gregory J.: *Marketing Tourism Places*, London, Routledge, 1990.

Baldacchino, G.: *'Global Tourism and Informal Labour Relations: The Small-scale Syndrome at Work'*, Mansell, UK, 1997.

Baum, T.: *'Human Resource Issues in International Tourism'*, Butterworth Heinemann, UK, 1993.

Bennett, O.: *Financing for Tourism Projects in Developing Countries*, England, Wiley, 1994.

Bevan, D. L., and D. W. Soskice: *Appraising Tourist Development in a Small Economy*, London, Heinemann, 1976.

Boissevain, Jeremy: *Coping with Tourists: European Reactions to Mass Tourism*, England, Berghahn, 1996.

Boniface, B.G. and Cooper, C.: *Geography of Travel and Tourism*, Butterworth Heinemann, UK, 1994.

Brogan, E.: *Human Resource Development in Tourism: The Scottish Perspective*, England, Wiley, 1994.

Bruce, David : *Tourism Strategies for Rural Development*, Sackville, New Brunswick, 1993.

Bruner, Edward M.: *In International Tourism: Identity and Change*, London, Sage, 1995.

Brunt, P.: *Market Research in Travel & Tourism*, Butterworth Heinemann, UK, 1997.

Burns, Peter: *Tourism: A New Perspective*, London, Prentice Hall, 1995.

Butler, R., Hall, R. and Jenkins, M.: *Tourism and Recreation in Rural Areas*, Wiley, UK, 1998.

Butler, Richard W.: *Tourism and Recreation in Rural Areas*, Chichester, U.K., 1998.

Chambers, Erve: *Tourism and Culture: An Applied Perspective*, Albany, State University of New York Press, 1997.

Clough, Richard: *Construction Project Management*, New York, John Wiley & Son, 2000.

Conlin, M. and Baum, T.: *Island Tourism: Management Principles and Practice*, Wiley, UK, 1995.

Cooper, C.: *Tourism: Principles and Practice*, London, Pitman, 1993.

Cooper, C.P.: *Progress in Tourism, Recreation and Hospitality Management*, Belhaven Press, UK, 1990.

Creque, Darwin: *A Study of the Tourist Industry in the U.S. Virgin Islands*, North Carolina, Amalie, 1964.

Curtis, Mary E.: *A Heritage Tourism Tool: National Register of Historic Places*, Radnor, Pennsylvania, 1993.

Daniel, R.: *Recent Advances in Tourism Marketing Research*, New York, Hawthorne Press, 1996.

David Taylor: *Cost-Benefit Analysis of Local Tourism Development*, Corvallis, Oregon, 1994.

David W.: *Tourism Planning*, Chicago, Council of Planning Librarians, 1995.

David, L.: *International Tourism Policy*, New York, Van Nostrand Reinhold, 1990.

David, W.: *Tourism Planning*, Chicago, Council of Planning Librarians, 1995.

Davidson, R.: *European Business Travel and Tourism*, England, Wiley, 1994.

Deegan, J. and Dineen, D.A.: *Tourism Policy and Performance: The Irish Experience*, ITBP, UK, 1997.

Douglas C.: *Heritage Tourism is in the Future of Many Alabama Communities*, Auburn Univ., Auburn, 1991.

Douglas, Pearce: *Change in Tourism: People, Places, Processes*, New York, Routledge, 1995.

Edgell, David L.: *International Tourism Policy*, New York, Van Nostrand Reinhold, 1990.

Edward, M.: *In International Tourism: Identity and Change*, London, Sage, 1995.

Fesenmaier, Daniel R.: *Recent Advances in Tourism Marketing Research*, New York, Hawthorne Press, 1996.

Foley, M.: *In Tourism: The State of the Art*, England, Wiley, 1994.

Forbes, A. H.: *Tourism and Transport Policy in the European Union*, England, Wiley, 1994.

Fowler, Peter: *Heritage and Tourism*, New York, Routledge, 1993.

France, Lesley: *The Earthscan Reader in Sustainable Tourism*, California, Island, 1997.

Frew, E.: *International Charter Travel—a New Opportunity for Australian Tourism*, England, Wiley, 1994.

Garfield, Donald: *Partners in Tourism: Culture and Commerce*, Washington, DC, American Association of Museums, 1997.

Gimblett, Barbara: *Destination Culture: Tourism, Museums, and Heritage*, California, University of California, 1998.

Glenn Kreag, and John Sem: *A Training Guide for Rural Tourism Development*, Minnesota: Rural Tourism Center, 1995.

Gorman, Michael: *Design for Tourism: An ICSID Interdesign Report*, New York, Oxford University Press, 1972.

Gunn, Clare A.: *Tourism Planning*, New York, Crane Russak, 1979.

Harrison, David: *Tourism and the Less Developed Countries*, London, Belhaven, 1992.

Haylock, R.: *Timeshare—the New Force in Tourism*, England, Wiley, 1994.

Heise, Dorothy: *Promoting Tourism in Rural American*, Maryland, National Agriculture Library, 1991.

Hitchcock, Michael: *Tourism in South-East Asia*, London, Routledge, 1993.

Holden, Andrew: *Tourism: A Commodity of Opportunity for Change?* Chichester, England, 1994.

Howard Green: *Tourism and the Environment: A Sustainable Relationship*, New York, Routledge, 1995.

Hudman, Lloyd E.: *Tourism: A Shrinking World*, Columbus, Grid, 1980.

Huit, Groupe: *The Sociocultural Effects of Tourism in Tunisia: A Case Study of Sousse*. New York, Oxford University Press, 1979.

Hunter, Colin, and Howard Green: *Tourism and the Environment: A Sustainable Relationship*, New York, Routledge, 1995.

Inskeep, E.: *Training for Tourism in Developing Countries*, Chichester, England, 1994.

Ireland, Lewis: *Quality Management for Projects and Programs*, Upper Darby, PMI, 1991.

James Makens: *Marketing for Hospitality and Tourism*: New Jersey, Prentice-Hall, 1998.

James, Valentine Udoh: *Tourism Development: A Research Note on Africa*, Connecticut, Praeger, 1996.

Jenkins, C. L.: *Tourism in Developing Countries: The Privatisation Issue*, Chichester, England, 1994.

Jenkins, J.: *Tourism and Recreation in Rural Areas*, Chichester, U.K., 1998.

Jeremy, B.: *Coping with Tourists: European Reactions to Mass Tourism*, England, Berghahn, 1996.

Jett, Stephen C.: *Tourism in the Navajo Country: Resources and Planning*, Winslow Rock, Navajo Tribe, 1967.

John Bowen, and James Makens: *Marketing for Hospitality and Tourism*: New Jersey, Prentice-Hall, 1998.

John Sem: *A Training Guide for Rural Tourism Development*, Minnesota: Rural Tourism Center, 1995.

Joseph T. O'Leary, and Muzaffer Uysal: *Recent Advances in Tourism Marketing Research*, New York, Hawthorne Press, 1996.

Julia, Sharpley: *Rural Tourism: An Introduction*, London, International Thomson Business Press, 1997.

Kirshenblatt-Gimblett, Barbara: *Destination Culture: Tourism, Museums, and Heritage*, California, University of California, 1998.

Klar, Lawrence R.: *Rural Tourist and Non-Tourist Communities in Massachusetts: Quality of Life Patterns*, 1980-1990, Pennsylvania, Northeastern Forest Experiment Station, 1993.

Knox, J.: *Tourism Research Priorities in Hawaii and the Pacific*, Honolulu, University of Hawaii, 1979.

Knox, J.: *Tourism Research Priorities in Hawaii and the Pacific*, Honolulu, University of Hawaii, 1979.

Komilis, P.: *Tourism and Sustainable Regional Development*, Chichester, England, 1994.

Kosters, Martinus J.: *Tourism by Train: Its Role in Alternative Tourism*, Philadelphia, University of Pennsylvania Press, 1992.

Koth, Barbara: *A Training Guide for Rural Tourism Development*, Minnesota: Rural Tourism Center, 1995.

Kotler, Philip: *Marketing for Hospitality and Tourism*: New Jersey, Prentice-Hall, 1998.

Laufer, Alexander & Hoffman, Edward: *Project Management Success Stories: Lessons of Project Leaders*, New York, John Wiley & Son, 2000.

Lawrence, R.: *Rural Tourist and Non-Tourist Communities in Massachusetts: Quality of Life Patterns*, 1980-1990, Pennsylvania, Northeastern Forest Experiment Station, 1993.

Leonard J.: *An Introduction to Tourism*, New York, Butterworth-Heinemann, 1997.

Lloyd, E.: *Tourism: A Shrinking World*, Columbus, Grid, 1980.

Marcouiller, David W.: *Tourism Planning*, Chicago, Council of Planning Librarians, 1995.

Margaret Whitla: *Tourism Strategies for Rural Development*, Sackville, New Brunswick, 1993.

Martinus J.: *Tourism by Train: Its Role in Alternative Tourism*, Philadelphia, University of Pennsylvania Press, 1992.

Mary, E.: *A Heritage Tourism Tool: National Register of Historic Places*, Radnor, Pennsylvania, 1993.

McConnell II, D. W.: *Nature-Based Tourism and Rural Coastal Development: Observations, Options, and Trends*, South Carolina, Clemson University, 1990.

McCool, Stephen F.: *Linking Tourism, the Environment, and Sustainability*, Ogden, Utah, 1995.

Middleton, Victor T. C.: *Sustainable Tourism: A Marketing Perspective*, Woburn, Massachusetts: Butterworth-Heinemann, 1998.

Mieczkowski, Zbigniew: *Environmental Issues of Tourism and Recreation*, Lanham, University Press of America, 1995.

Muzaffer Uysal: *Recent Advances in Tourism Marketing Research*, New York, Hawthorne Press, 1996.

Nelson, Bob and Economy, Peter: *Managing for Dummies*, Foster City, IDG Books, 1996.

Potts, Thomas D., and Allan P. C. Marsinko: *Developing Naturally: An Exploratory Process for Nature-Based Community Tourism*, South Carolina, Clemson University, 1998.

Purcell, Douglas C.: *Heritage Tourism is in the Future of Many Alabama Communities*, Auburn Univ., Auburn, 1991.

Richard, W.: *Tourism and Recreation in Rural Areas*, Chichester, U.K., 1998.

Ryan, Chris: *Recreational Tourism: A Social Science Perspective*, London, Routledge, 1991.

Sharpley, Richard: *Rural Tourism: An Introduction*, London, International Thomson Business Press, 1997.

Soskice, D.W.: *Appraising Tourist Development in a Small Economy*, London, Heinemann, 1976.

Stabler, Michael J.: *Tourism and Sustainability: Principles to Practice*, New York, CAB International, 1997.

Stephen F.: *Linking Tourism, the Environment, and Sustainability*, Ogden, Utah, 1995.

Stephen, C.: *Tourism in the Navajo Country: Resources and Planning*, Winslow Rock, Navajo Tribe, 1967.

Suggs, C.: *Tourism Research Priorities in Hawaii and the Pacific*, Honolulu, University of Hawaii, 1979.

Valentine, Udoh: *Tourism Development: A Research Note on Africa*, Connecticut, Praeger, 1996.

Victor T. C.: *Sustainable Tourism: A Marketing Perspective*, Woburn, Massachusetts: Butterworth-Heinemann, 1998.

William W. Swart: *Planning for Tourism Development: Quantitative Approaches*, New York, Praeger, 1976.

Index

A

B

C